Adam Eve and Louth Carpets

and the story of Eve & Ranshaw Ltd

Adam Eve

Adam Eve and Louth Carpets

and the story of Eve & Ranshaw Ltd

also The Lincolnshire Stuff Ball

David Robinson OBE

Published to mark the
Centenary of Louth Museum
1910 – 2010

ACCREDITED MUSEUM
MLA
MUSEUMS LIBRARIES ARCHIVES COUNCIL

E&R LOUTH

THE TEXTILE SOCIETY

Published by

Louth Naturalists', Antiquarian and Literary Society

Louth Museum, 4 Broadbank, Louth, Lincs LN11 0EQ
Tel: 01507 601211 Email: louthmuseum@btconnect.com

Registered Charity No. 504370

2010

ISBN 978-0-9539533-6-3

Book design by David Robinson

Endpapers
Actual size pattern of the replica of an early
Louth ingrain flat weave double ply carpet
– topside (front) and underside (back).
See page 85.

Printed by Cupit Print, The Ropewalk, 23 Louth Road, Horncastle, Lincolnshire LN9 5ED

Contents

Introduction

IT HAD been thought that with the name Adam Eve he must have been a foundling. Not so. Among the Eves of Lincolnshire there were at least five named Adam. In fact it was our Adam's father James who was a foundling. Adam, the eldest child born in 1755, was not interested in following his father as a farmer and sheep grazier, but went into business (1781) in Louth as a mercer and grocer, a common combination then.

He quickly established himself as an 'eminent mercer'. He was also an entrepreneur and risk taker, seeing the possibilities in buying out the subscribers to the water-powered wool spinning mill (1786) on the River Lud. He also perceived the potential of the mill for making flat weave carpets to meet the growing demand for floor coverings among the expanding population of Lincolnshire – a niche market. More than that, he developed an export trade to Europe and America with his quality products.

The initial finance for this enterprise was the dowry his wife Sarah brought when they married in 1786. Sarah is somewhat shrouded in mystery; we know virtually nothing about her except that she was an 'amiable and much accomplished' lady. However, it could be said that without Sarah and her dowry there might never have been any Louth carpets. Nonetheless, in the fluctuating economics of the Napoleonic Wars Adam found it necessary to borrow from his family and others, but when he died he was a wealthy man.

Sarah was unable to bear children, so Adam made an 'arrangement' with widow Eleanor Paddison. Three illegitimate sons were adopted by Adam and were left substantial legacies in the hope that they would continue to run the carpetmaking business, which in different ways they did.

The carpet, the wall to wall broadloom floor covering of today, we take as a normal part of the home. The project to research Louth flat weave carpets and the names of the weavers who made them started in 2006 with the aid of a grant from The Textile Society. The more information that was found, the more questions there were requiring answers. One result was the emergence of a detailed story of the shop business from foundation by Adam to the Department Store of Eve & Ranshaw. And this publication is generously sponsored by Eve & Ranshaw Ltd.

The core of the book is about Adam Eve's contribution to the history of carpeting the home. It tells the life story of Adam Eve, his social and sporting activities and his carpetmaking enterprise (the only one in Lincolnshire) against the background of local wool production, the export of which was prohibited – the long staple coarse fleece of the Lincoln Longwool sheep, ideal for carpets. The factory workforce were largely skilled weavers who migrated to Louth from Kidderminster, Market Harborough, South Yorkshire and Durham. Louth carpets were highly commended at the 1867 Paris Exhibition, but demand declined in the 1870s as the wider market looked to pile carpets, and the factory closed in 1883.

Adam passed the shop in Louth Market Place to his younger brother William who went into partnership with John Campbell, a former teenage apprentice from Howden, who played a key role in the growth of the shop. To follow were three other Eves and three Ranshaws and the business has been Eve & Ranshaw since 1880. David Sandwith is the owner today. The story of the shop includes a record of apprentices and assistants, the early ones living on the premises. The final chapter is about the Lincolnshire Stuff Ball, started in 1785 to promote the use of local wool. To gain admittance to the Ball the gentry and their ladies had to wear clothing made of wool – the Lincolnshire Stuff – available in Adam's shop.

John Campbell

Fundamental to the writing of this book has been access to the extraordinary collection of documents in the Eve & Ranshaw archive, now deposited in Louth Museum. It includes leases and agreements for management of properties, transfer of spinning mill subscriptions, shop stocktaking records, and even the IOU slips of paper recording Adam's borrowing. Census records from 1841 to 1901 were scoured for names of factory workers and shop assistants. And there were fortuitous connections with descendants of some key figures – Henry Paddison (one of Adam's adopted sons), and two families of carpet weavers – the Spiveys and Burdetts. Plus the serendipity of coming across pamphlets about the controversies relating to the prohibition of the export of wool in an antiquarian bookseller's catalogue and of finding in an auction sale a book about the parish registers of St Giles, Scartho which recorded the true story of Adam's origin.

David Sandwith

Putting together all the pieces of information involved being a history detective (magnifying glass essential for some old documents), constructing family trees, large and small, researching the method of making ingrain flat weave carpets, one clue leading to another, and refraining from going down fascinating but not directly relevant side trails. And discovering, almost at the end, that Eric Hickman, the son of one of today's Non-executive Directors of Eve & Ranshaw Ltd, Charles Hickman and his wife Sara, is in the business of the design and supply of carpets. Circle closed.

Acknowledgements

Jill Belcham for permission to use pictures of Eleanor Paddison (p26) and Henry Paddison (p29); Ruth Burdett for family history about the Burdetts; Norman Cawkwell for picture p139; Gill Chatfield for help checking census returns; Andy Cooper for use of picture p42; Richard and Chris D'Arcy for photographing Louth carpets; Eve & Ranshaw Ltd for sponsoring this book; Ruth Gatenby for checking census returns; Clare Harrison for picture p98; Charles and Sara (nee Vamplew) Hickman for Vamplew family history; Geoff Hill for miscellaneous searches; Jean Howard for newspaper searches, cataloguing carpets, proof reading and indexing; Susan Ison for Paddison family history research (particularly Henry), transcripts of Wills of Adam Eve and Charles Paddison, and related information; Michael and Jean Kerrigan for information on Ivy House; Lincoln Longwool Sheep Breeders' Association for images on pages 50, 53 and 59; Louth Town Council for grant aid and permission to use images on pages 32, 53, 66 and 81; David Luckham Carpet Consultant for guidance and advice and arranging manufacture of replica carpet; Mo Mant for pictures of replica carpet in Danson House (p85); Mark Oliver for picture of winding gear in former wool warehouse (p56); Anna Peacock for condition research on one carpet in Louth Museum (p100); Margaret Pinchbeck for search of Carpet Design Register (PRO, Kew); Clive Rhodes for advice on surviving examples of Louth carpets; David Sandwith (Eve & Ranshaw Ltd) for donation of archives to Louth Museum and use of pictures on pages 174, 180, 184 and 185; John Sass for technical information on waterwheels; Stuart Sizer for photography and help with census returns; Christopher Spivey for family history about the Spiveys; Janet Stevenson for permission to quote from her memoirs about working in Eve & Ranshaw; The Textile Society for the initial research grant; Ruth Tinley for miscellaneous archive searches; George Upson for photographing Louth carpets; Claire Weaver for Eve family history information; Brian Williams for use of shop inventory of mercer Judith Hardy (p139). All other illustrations – Louth Museum and author's collection.

A Lincoln Longwool ready for shearing

The Old Lincoln Breed

Chapter 1

Wealth from Wool

THE PRODUCTION of sheep's wool was for long the staple of Lincolnshire's wealth. In medieval times the Cistercian monks of Louth Park Abbey (founded 1139) just east of the town, were well organised sheep farmers, with an annual production of some 6,000 fleeces. Sheep were bred on the Wolds at Lambcroft Grange (on the northern edge of Kelstern parish) and Binbrook, and on the Middle Marsh, and then grazed on the 'rich fatting marshes [the Outmarsh, the flat siltlands between the Middle Marsh and the dune-fringed coast] best adapted for the growing and forcing of heavy wool'. Most of the fleeces were for export through the nearby ports of Suine (in Grainthorpe parish and now some two miles from the sea), Saltfleet and Wilgrip (Crook Bank in Theddlethorpe St Helen parish) to the worsted manufacturers of Flanders and northern Italy who required long staple wool.

The monastery also created employment and wealth for the town in spinning, weaving, fulling, dyeing and tailoring. Fullers were also known as walkers as they walked on cloth in running water from Aswell Spring to full or felt the cloth to give it a smooth finish. Hence the name Walkergate, now Queen Street, where the fulling and dyeing parts of the woollen industry were centred. Louth merchants acted as middlemen in the wool trade, including exporting through Boston to the Continent, the wealth so generated being devoted to the building and enlarging of the parish church of St James.

Replica of an early Louth carpet

After the dissolution of the abbey in 1536, its lands passed into private hands, sheep graziers following the same pattern of raising on the sheepwalks of the Wolds, where there are still farm names such as Sixhills Walk, Hainton Walk, Benniworth Walk and Binbrook Walk, and fatting them on marsh pastures. The Will of Christopher Marshall of Theddlethorpe in 1679 lists his Lincoln Longwools – 75 ewes and lambs, 79 sheep hogs, 58 wethers and 4 tups. For the next two centuries Lincolnshire was regarded as the 'mother-county' for long-woolled sheep, the Lincoln Longwool, the 'largest sheep in Europe'. Its strong white lustrous fleece was described in the 1720s by Daniel Defoe as 'wondrously heavy, sending down long unctuous wool in pendulous masses almost to the ground'. Another description, in 1756, said that the sheep are 'large, tall, heavily loaded with strong limbs and a stout gait in walking. They carry a great deal of wool but it is coarse. They were first bred in Lincolnshire ... and are fond of living on salt marshes'.

In fact the sheep were so heavy with wool, particularly in the weeks prior to clipping, that they could fall over on their backs – the Lincolnshire term is farweltered – and shepherds needed to visit flocks more than once a day, and dogs were also trained to right or turn them. Wool was weighed by the tod (28 lbs) and longwool fleeces made as few as two or three to a tod. The staple – the length of the strands of wool – was also important: on the longwool it ranged from 10 ins to 18 ins and could be as long as 21 inches. The staple also had a good number of crimps which meant that when combed and spun it made a strong thread.

Lincoln Longwool shearling ewe

In the early 18th century Lincolnshire's rural economy was dependent on supplying long or combing wool for the worsted manufacturers in East Anglia and the West Riding of Yorkshire. The whiteness of the wool took dye well, and its strength appealed to manufacturers supplying the coarse, stiff cloth that fashion then demanded. Middlemen or staplers visited farmers after the clipping in July, the farmer relying on the stapler to negotiate a reasonable price. However prices could be influenced by external factors, such as the drought in 1723, and the American War of Independence 1775-1783 when the price of a tod fell 50% from 17s (85p, or £54 today) to 8s 9d. Another reason for general decline was the competition from cotton which had a serious effect on producers of coarse long wool. At the same time the agricultural revolution of enclosure of the old open fields and 'wastes' and the application of four-course rotation of crops led to more mixed farming.

The attempts to bolster wool growing in east Lincolnshire by stimulating local spinning and weaving and promoting the wearing of locally made woollen garments will be described in a later chapter, but first we need to trace the development of the Improved Lincoln breed. Although the wool may have been good for worsteds, and later carpets, the white faced Lincoln breed was regarded as ugly and ungainly, with a heavy boned carcass long in proportion to width, and long legs, and the mutton was poor and coarse-grained. When a North Somercotes sheep farmer invited a Methodist preacher to Sunday dinner he asked his foreman to say grace:

'O Lord above send down thy love on us poor creatures 'ere below;
Send us some meat that's fit to eat, and tek away this danged owd yow.'

Landowner Charles Chaplin of Tathwell firmly believed that the Lincoln Longwool could be improved by selective in-breeding, (although he did experiment crossing with Teeswater) while Robert Bakewell of Dishley (Leics) in the 1790s believed in cross-breeding Lincolns with Leicesters, and there were fierce debates about which was best. Sir Joseph Banks of Revesby, who took a keen interest in producing a fine clothing wool, bought two Lincoln ewes from Mr Fowler of Ketsby to put to a Spanish Merino ram at his experimental farm at Spring Grove in Middlesex. The eventual outcome was to cross New Leicester rams, or tups, with ewes of the old Lincoln breed to produce the New Improved Lincoln – with a heavy somewhat finer fleece and good meat. Tups were hired for the season from specialist ram breeders, the 'tup men', to improve flocks. About 1810 a large ceramic Willow-pattern punchbowl with the legend 'Success to the Lincolnshire Breed' and images of sheep was made by Chetham of Longton (Stoke on Trent), now on display in Louth Museum. Might it have been commissioned by the Chaplins of Tathwell?

A pattern from a Louth carpet
(see pages 106-107)

The Lincoln Longwool punchbowl
Sponsored by the Lincoln Longwool Sheep Breeders' Association

Apart from aesthetic qualities of the New Improved Lincolns, they were also a response to low wool prices. Production costs on the other hand remained relatively constant: 12s (60p, or £21 today) a week plus cottage and perquisites for a shepherd, and 2d a head for shearers who could clip up to twenty in a day. By the beginning of the 19th century, the pure Old Lincoln breed was confined to the Outmarsh.

Part of the painting *The Ford near Louth* by Peter DeWint, early 1820s

When artist Peter DeWint made one of his trips into the Wolds from Lincoln in the early 1820s, one of his watercolours near Louth shows a flock of black-faced sheep being droved by men on horseback. Could they be Blackface, very suitable for carpet making? Was the flock on the way to Louth sheep fair, or more likely being moved from the Wolds to the 'fatting pastures' of the Outmarsh? Those pasture lands were rented by Wold farmer-graziers. For example, Adam Eve of Haugham, nephew of Adam Eve who is the central character of this book, rented fields in Theddlethorpe with such names as Great Harp, Lea Bratts, Little Dog Close, Big Spout Close and Crook Bank Skittle Close.

It is against this background of sheep grazing and wool production in east Lincolnshire that Adam Eve, the future shop owner, seller of worsted and carpet maker in Louth, grew up as a farmer/grazier's son at Scartho. So we must first look at his character and place in the Eve dynasty.

Louth Sheep Fair 29 April 1911

St Giles church, Scartho, 1796. *Drawn by J. C. Nattes*

Chapter 2

The Eve Dynasty

"On the eve of S James, in or about 1725, a farmer was crossing the churchyard of Scarthoe, when he was startled by hearing the crying of a child, and on looking about discovered a beautiful child, richly dressed, and by its side a bundle of clothes, on some of which was embroidered a coronet. The farmer carried the little one home to his wife, and having no children of their own they soon became fond of the boy and brought him up as their own, calling him James Eve, from the fact of his being found on the eve of S James. These worthy people lived at one time at Hambleton Hill, near Market Rasen. The boy was never enquired after, though his clothes were kept for years hoping they might lead to his identity.
One day there drove down Walesby Hill a nobleman's carriage; servants and horses and all the appointments betokened wealth. The boy, it seems, was near, for a gentleman stepped out of the carriage, and calling the boy up to him, gave him a golden guinea, saying, 'You are nearer related to me, my lad, than you think'; he then drove away.
This James Eve was the father of Adam Eve the carpet manufacturer of Louth".

A. J. Eve (in 1907) who recorded the story of the foundling

THIS INFORMATION, as handed down in the family, was sent by A J Eve of Sausthorpe to the rector of Scarthoe, Revd Ernest E Crake, in 1926 and included in his little book *The Parish Registers of St Giles Church Scarthoe 1562-1837.* Allan James Eve (1861-1927), who farmed at Sausthorpe from the late 1880s, was the great great nephew of Adam Eve (1755-1831) the carpet manufacturer. That story is the only written record of the oral history of the origin of the man who was in fact the third Adam in one branch of the Eve tree, a Christian name which had been passed down the generations.

There were other Eves in north Lincolnshire, stemming from Alexander (1675), at Beelsby, Barnoldby le Beck, Saxby All Saints and Kelsey, but we are concerned with the stem from the farmer who found the baby boy. He was Adam Eve, born 1700 at Beelsby. James is recorded as baptised at All Saints, Waltham on 19 February 1725. Adam [1] married Ann Bold (1700-1758) and they went on to have eight children of their own – Ann (1730), Mary (1731) and Martha (1733), all born at Waltham, Adam [2] (1734), Elizabeth (1736, died in infancy), Edward (1739), Elizabeth (1740) and Margaret (1742), the last four at Scartho, where their father was Churchwarden of St Giles 1741-42. It is highly likely that Adam [1] was a sheep grazier. When he died in 1744, his widow married Thomas Kew of Scartho (1718-1758) and they had one son, Thomas (1747-1752).

James the foundling married Mary Thompson of Irby on Humber and they had seven children – Adam [3], baptised 18 May 1755 at St Helen's, North Ormsby, and the others were born at Scartho: John (1757), Alexander (1761-63), Ann (1763), Mary (1769, died in infancy), William (1776) and James (1779). The thatched mud and stud farmhouse where they lived was near the centre of the village (based on evidence from the Enclosure Award). On the site today are shops on the road to Louth opposite the entrance to Church Lane. The life of Adam [3] who became the carpet manufacturer will emerge later, but it is convenient here to introduce the rest of the extended family of nephews and nieces as some of their marriages were to have a significant impact on the history of the Eve & Ranshaw shop which Adam founded.

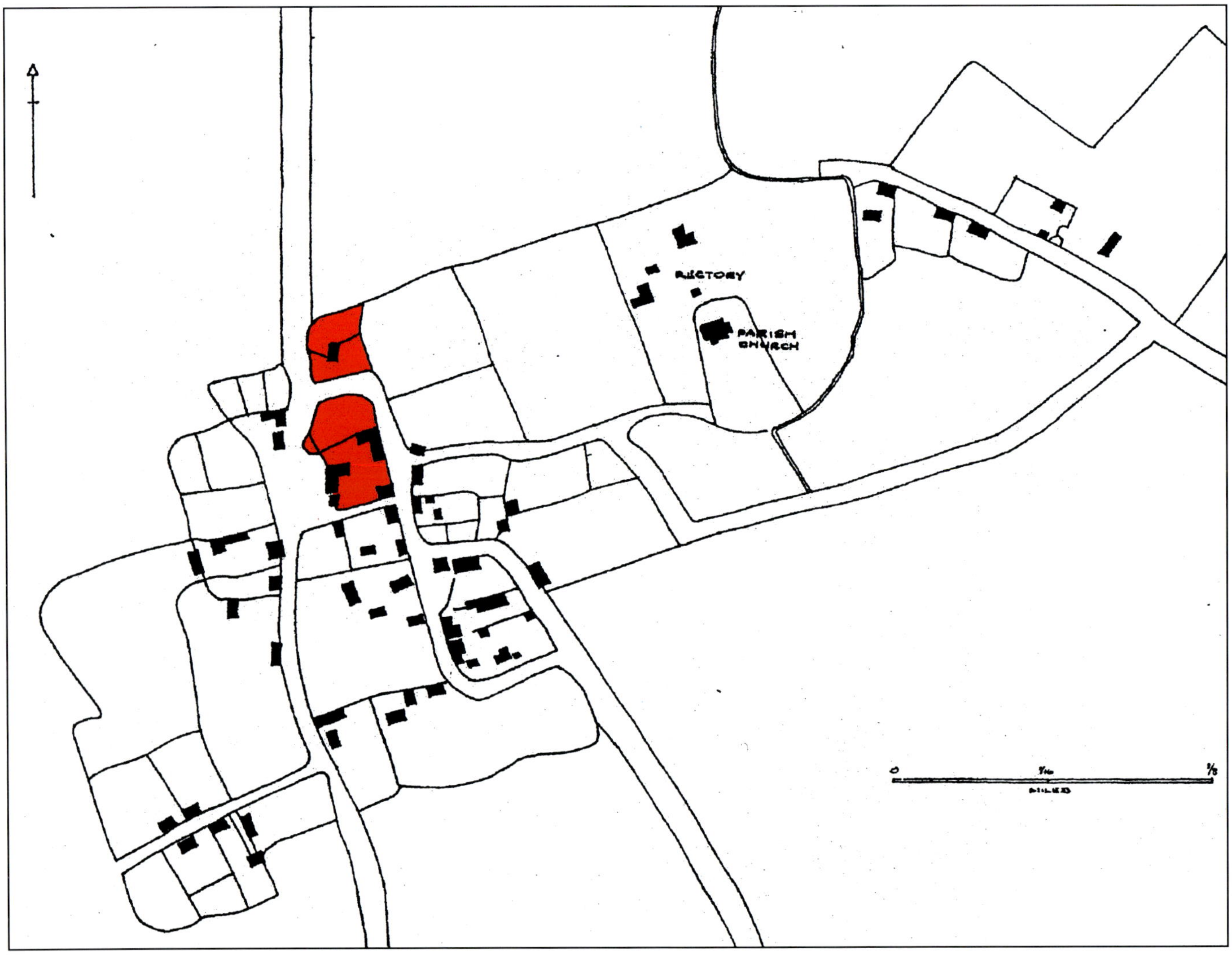

Scartho village towards the end of the 18th century.
The Eve farmstead is shown in red

James, like his father, was a sheep grazier, and when he died in 1788 the property and rights of common passed to his second son John. There is a bit of a mystery about John's status as a landowner at the time of the enclosure of Scartho parish in 1795-98. He was rated at £87 10s (£2,500 today), the sixth highest in the parish, and claimed 81 acres on the basis of a farmstead and three cottages and rights to pasture 90 sheep, 24 cattle, 13 geese and five horses. However, at least one claim was disallowed, he sold 1½ acres to George Tennyson, and was not allotted any land in the open fields – but he did own 2½ acres with the farmstead and cottages in the village. It seems that his sizeable flock of sheep and other livestock were on land tenanted from Lord Yarborough or George Tennyson.

John had married Elizabeth Welldale (1753-1828) of South Elkington and they had two children: Adam [4] (1788-1863) and Ann (1790). Ann married Thomas Grant, gentleman, of Nichol Hill, Louth, while in January 1815 Adam, by then 26 and a successful grazier at Sixhills, married by special licence 19-year old Anne Bowmar, daughter of grazier Joseph Bowmar of Goltho (near Wragby). This was a significant marriage, with fourteen children, the marriages of two of whom influenced the future of the Eve and Ranshaw shop.

St George, Goltho
(photographed 1972)

The wedding at the little brick-built 16th century church of St George at Goltho would have been attended by the groom's uncle Adam the carpet-maker, and very likely by William Espin of Bullington, then 18 and a contemporary and near neighbour of the bride. Perhaps his much older half-brothers Thomas (48) and John (42) were also present. As all three Espins played some part in the story of Adam [3] and his carpet factory, it will be useful at this point to sketch in the Espin family.

Thomas Espin (1767-1822) and brother John (1773-1822), and their elder sister Elizabeth (1765, who married William Hardwick of Goltho), were born at Holton Beckering. When their mother died their father, Thomas, a farmer, moved to Bullington (the next parish to Goltho), remarried and had four children including William (1787-1865). Sons Thomas and John, both topographical artists, draughtsmen and surveyors, came to Louth in 1790 when Thomas was appointed master at Dr Mapletoft's School (on the corner of Northgate and Broadbank now the site of flats). In 1818 Thomas built Priory Cottage on Eastgate as a Mathematical, Nautical, Architectural and Commercial Academy. At the time of the wedding at Goltho of Adam [4] and Anne Bowmar, John was a partner with Adam [3] in managing the Louth carpet factory. William became a schoolmaster at Mansfield, moved to Priory Cottage to teach when Thomas died in 1822, and then ran the carpet factory for four years when Adam [3] died in 1831.

Adam [4] and Anne had their first two children, Ann (1815) and Elizabeth (1816), at Sixhills, the next three at Langton by Wragby – Mary (1817), Adam [5] (1818) and Ellen (1819, died in infancy), and the other nine at Ivy House Farm, Haugham (470 acres): John Bowmar (1821), James (1822-24), Ellen (1823), Thomas (1824), James (1826), Emma (1827), Eve (1829), Matilda (1833) and Charles (1834). The influential marriages were Ann Eve to William Bowmar, son of Leicester dyer Thomas (her mother's brother, originally from Goltho) in 1846 and John Bowmar Eve to Elizabeth Cortis Ranshaw of Missenden in 1860. The latter had eight children including John Frederic (1862-1902) who would manage the shop, and Frank Bowmar (1866-1925) who became a successful veterinary surgeon and lived in Ivy House, James Street, Louth which had been built for Adam the carpet maker and his wife in 1794.

Natural dyes on the bound edge of a Louth carpet

Other marriages were Adam [5] to Elizabeth Bowmar (William's sister) who went on to farm 360 acres at the Manor House, Theddlethorpe All Saints, James who married Leonora Rainey in 1856 – he served as a journeyman draper in the Louth shop and then set up as a draper, silk mercer and milliner in Spilsby: they had three children, one of whom was Allan James Eve who wrote the historical note for the rector of Scartho; and Eve who in 1860, married Edward Rainey (Leonora's brother), pharmaceutical chemist, auctioneer and estate agent, of Spilsby. If you feel confused by all these inter-marriages – refer to the Eve family tree.

Going back to James the foundling's family, Ann married Richard Clarke, draper of Market Rasen: his youngest son Adam would be an executor in the first Will of Adam the carpet maker, and of their four girls and two boys, Elizabeth married John Campbell (1782-1852) from Howden, Yorks, who went on to manage the Louth shop, become a leading citizen of the town and have his portrait painted by Bennett Hubbard, and be an executor for Adam. Mary died in infancy, and William (1776-1829), who would enter into a partnership for ten years with his elder brother Adam to run the Louth shop (and then as senior partner with John Campbell). William married Amelia Leech from Hampshire: they had seven children including John (1812) who married Elizabeth Lawley of Caistor and became a silk merchant in Newark, and Emily (1817) who married Robert Smith of Louth.

It would seem (from documents held by Medway Council) to be through William's marriage to Amelia that he became owner of a farm at Strood in Kent. Together with his property in Louth and share in the shop when he died in 1829 (then a widower), he would have been reasonably well off. This may explain why his brother Adam did not leave any legacies to William's children, as he did to those of his brother John and sister Ann (see page 30).

We can now return to the key figure in the Eve dynasty, the eldest son of James the foundling, Adam [3]. As he grew up in the mud and stud farmhouse in the small rural village of Scartho with its dilapidated church (which within some thirty years would have to be taken down and rebuilt), he would learn the story of his grandfather finding the baby in the churchyard. Adam and his brother John were close in age, but the next boy, Alexander, died in infancy when Adam was eight; the two sisters, Ann and Mary, were born when Adam was 10 and 14, and it would be another seven years before William was born.

Soon after that the wealthy lawyer George Tennyson of Market Rasen (grandfather of the future Poet Laureate Alfred) acquired nearly half of the parish of Scartho where Lord Yarborough was lord of the manor, and Trinity College, Cambridge was the next biggest landowner. However, farming was still on the medieval strip system, and the open fields would not be enclosed until near the end of the century (1795-98). One of the Commissioners then was John Parkinson of Asgarby, Steward of the Lincolnshire estates of Sir Joseph Banks of Revesby, who acted for more than thirty enclosures, and the Surveyor was Christopher Epworth of Grimsby. Both would act for the Louth enclosure four years later when their decisions would affect Adam's land holding.

Adam and John would learn to ride a horse, and help their father in the farming round and the rearing of sheep for wool, but Adam had no interest in becoming a farmer; that would be for John. Adam seems to have inherited a new gene which his father's bloodline brought into the Eve dynasty. He developed sporting and social interests and looked to the wider world beyond the village. In those formative teenage years he would hear of the opening of the Louth Navigation canal from Tetney Haven and the making of the turnpike road from Horncastle via Louth to Saltfleet Haven (both in 1770 when he was 15). Louth was already served by the Dexthorpe turnpike from the south (the present A16) and leading west to Gainsborough and Bawtry (the A631).

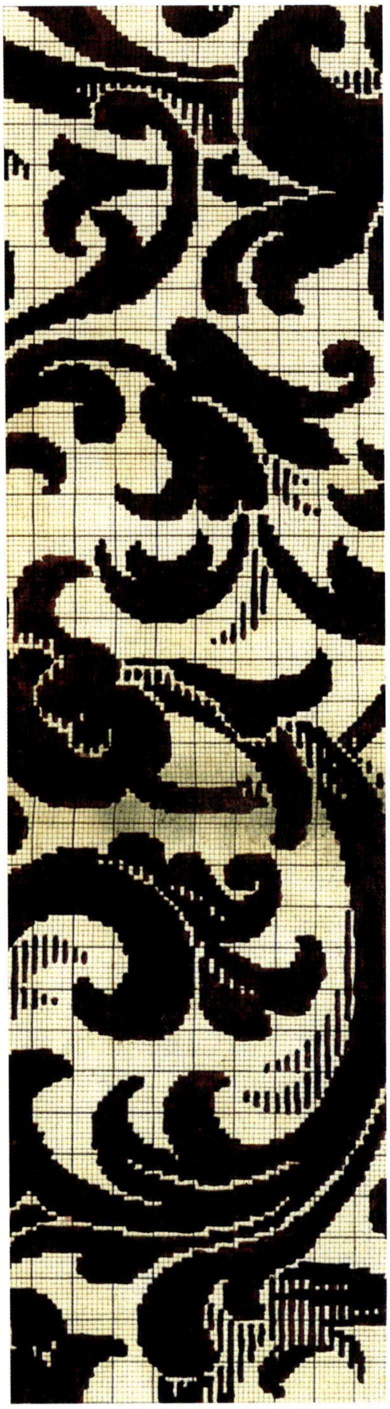

Part of a Louth carpet design, 1864
(see pages 128-129)

It is not known how the children of James and Mary at Scartho were educated – perhaps in a dame school in the village, although Adam might have been sent to a private academy in the nearby larger village of Waltham. One of the sons, William, who later lived in Louth would send his five boys to the Boys Grammar School. His nephew Adam [4], farming at Haugham, sent one son, Adam [5], to the same school, but James (born 1826) was sent to Grantham Castlegate School (an English and Commercial school established in 1814 by William Hardwick – from Goltho and brother in law to Thomas, John and William Espin – then run by his son John) and a governess was employed to teach the girls at Haugham.

When Adam left school at 13 (1768) his father put him to a seven year apprenticeship with Waltham draper and grocer Thomas Langley (who also owned 9½ acres of land allotted to him at enclosure of the parish in 1771). Langley was also a Quaker and perhaps Adam's father hoped that his son would receive a sound moral as well as business training. Adam probably lived with his uncle Edward in Waltham and completed his apprenticeship in 1775.

Nearby Grimsby, with but a small market and decayed port, held little attraction for Adam. It may be that he got a job as an assistant to Frederick L'Oste in Louth. The 'road' to Louth may have been mired and rutted in winter and dusty in summer, but Louth was the new port. Prospects for commerce were good. And Louth had a Mansion House, built by the Corporation in 1750, where there were social entertainments, and a theatre.

The road into Louth used by Adam when he travelled from Scartho
(Painted by J. Salmon)

Louth in the 1770s had finally awoken from the 'years of sleep', with commercial and industrial development stimulated by the canal, and by 1778 there were some five hundred families in the town. High status houses and shops were of brick and pantile, but most properties were still timber framed with earth walls and a thatched roof, and the streets were not yet fully paved. The Market Place was larger than now; the town pump there, the Aswell spring and the river were the main water supplies – distributed by a water carrier.

Nonetheless, Louth was a town on the move. The Corporation government of the town, the self-electing oligarchy The Warden and Six Assistants were enterprising and forward looking. The leading citizen was Frederick L'Oste (1723-1807), son of Revd Charles L'Oste who was Vicar of Louth 1711-1730. Frederick married Elizabeth Hill of Alford and six of their children survived to adulthood. He established himself as a grocer at No 1 Market Place in 1755 (the year of Adam's birth) and was Warden of Louth seven times (1765, 1772, 1778, 1783, 1790, 1796 and 1804) and when he died in 1807 he was referred to as the Father of the Corporation.

Border of Louth carpet c. 1850
(see pages 92-93)

Frederick's son Charles was five years younger than Adam. By 1781 Frederick had decided to retire and his son had taken over the shop as a mercer and grocer, but Charles had his sights on London. Adam was a risk-taker and saw an opportunity. In October 1781 he took a seven year lease of No 1 Market Place (to run from May 1782) to set himself up as a mercer and grocer. Charles departed to London where four years later he was listed as a man's mercer. The annual rent for the shop (with one room and a kitchen behind and two above) was £15 (about £900 today). Adam was betting on increased trade as the population of the town continued to grow – and he was right. He was 26.

Frederick L'Oste's wife died in 1790 and four years later, when age 71, he married Naomi King who at 23 was younger than any of his children. Meanwhile in January 1786 Adam, aged 30, had confirmed his social status by marrying Sarah Allenby (29), daughter of well-to-do grazier Daniel Allenby of Hallington. Allenby was a tenant of Charles Chaplin of Tathwell, a man of sporting interests who also owned all the land in Hallington and Raithby. As there was no longer a church at Hallington, the wedding was at St Peter's, Raithby (with Hallington), conducted by Revd Robert Chaplin (1768-1837), son of Charles and an older brother of George who became a close friend of Adam. [The present church at Raithby is a rebuild of 1836-37.]

One imagines that Adam's shop supplied the clothes for the men even if not the bride's wedding gown. It was a society wedding worthy of record in the *Lincoln Rutland & Stamford Murcury:* "Jan 12. Married Mr Adam Eve, an eminent mercer and draper in Louth, to Miss S Allenby of Hallington, an amiable and much-accomplished young lady, with a fortune of £1,500." [about £95,000 today]. He had built a profitable business in only five years and made a profitable marriage, but Adam was to find that Sarah was unable to bear children.

The story of the shop in the Market Place, the carpet factory and Adam's role in their success is told elsewhere, but here we need to sketch in other aspects of his personal life as background to that story. The same year Adam married, a turnpike was opened from Great Grimsby to Wold Newton church. This avoided the miry Marsh roads, and from Wold Newton the dry chalk road was used to near South Elkington on the Dexthorpe turnpike, thus improving travel between Louth and the family farm at Scartho. Three years later, in 1789, there was another improvement when Westgate Bridge was built over the River Lud. In 1802 the Louth-Scartho turnpike was opened (the present A16 but through all the villages), further helping Adam to maintain links with the village of his youth.

Adam acquired, rented or built property on the north side of Padehole or Finkle Street, which had been laid out in the late 1760s/early 1770s (now Northgate), towards the east end, and another new street was created and named after him: Eve Street. The making of Eve Street and James Street to give a more direct link from the town centre to the canal (Riverhead) was started in 1793 by James Dunn. [James Street was built on Corporation land, and most likely named after a monarch, as was later Charles Street. However, it is worth noting that on his 1873 plan of the town, Borough Surveyor T W Wallis used an apostrophe – James' Street, which would support the view that the street was named after the builder James Dunn.]

In 1794 Adam and Sarah set up home in Ivy House on James Street, rented from the Corporation on a 99 year lease, close to the wool spinning factory of which he had taken a lease three years before.

Ivy House, James Street, 1979

As part of the procedure for enclosing Louth's open fields in 1802, Adam bought 15 small plots of land to add to his own allotment in lieu of rights of common related to his two freehold properties. The Commissioners arranged them in one block of 4¼ acres on the edge of old enclosures in the triangle between Holme Lane Road (now High Holme Road) and Keddington Road (now Newbridge Hill). Clearly he was a man of some influence, but doubtless it helped that he knew one of the Commissioners John Parkinson of Asgarby, and the Surveyor Christopher Epworth of Grimsby, both of whom, four years before, acted in the enclosure of Scartho where his brother John lived.

About half of that land was later called Cricket Close: was cricket played there, and did Adam play? [The MCC (Marylebone Cricket Club) had been formed in 1788, rules established and the game became popular.] However, at some time Adam built stables and yards and supplied them with spring water, and that was where he kept his race horses.

The paintings of Adam's horses by Richard Jones (see next page) have not been traced. However, this painting (1845) by Louth artist Bennett Hubbard (1806-1870) is typical of the style of the time

The years across the turn of the century were ones of wars with the French. As defence of the realm the Volunteer Cavalry was formed in 1797, and in November 1803 Adam (age 48) was gazetted Cornet in the Louth Gentlemen and Volunteer Cavalry, and made Lieutenant in June 1812.

Adam the carpet maker's involvement in the sport of horse racing is revealed in a report in the *Lincoln, Rutland & Stamford Mercury* for 1 October 1813: "Match against time. On Thursday 30th for a bet of 40 guineas [about £1,400 today] a grey filly, 3 years old, 14 hands high, by Carpet Weaver, dam by Grog, the property of Mr Adam Eve of Louth, ran over the Doncaster course, two miles in 4 minutes 26½ seconds carrying 6 stone 2 pounds. The time allowed was 5 minutes". Adam owned two mares by Grog, a horse which figured in the early progeny of the famous Lottery, winner of the first Grand National steeplechase run over the Aintree course in 1839. Lottery had been bought at the Horncastle Great August Horse Fair, where earlier in the century ' the finest and best horses in the kingdom', bred on the Lincolnshire Wolds, were traded: a 4-year old hunter could command 80 guineas. In fact horse breeding on the Wolds had strong links with fox hunting. When the South Wold Hunt was formed in 1822 out of the Brocklesby (which had hunted the whole of the Wolds) one of the four kennels for the new Hunt was Dog Kennel Farm (built 1826) on Chaplin land at Hubbard's Hills. Whether Adam, then in his sixties, hunted with the South Wold is not known.

Flower pattern on a Louth carpet runner
(see pages 88-89)

However, his racehorses were clearly an important part of his life because he had paintings made of his appropriately named stallion Carpet Weaver and his mares by Grog. The artist was most likely Richard Jones (1767-1840), originally from Reading, painter of animals and sporting subjects, who exhibited at the Royal Academy in 1818, 1819 and 1820, and who lived near Adam in James Street in the 1820s and early 1830s. In his Will Adam left the paintings to his nephew Adam at Haugham. Jones also painted a portrait of Adam which was bequeathed to his adopted son Charles Paddison (see below).

Adam's other sporting interest was hare coursing where he mixed with the gentry. Poachers were interested in hares, as in the county song *The Lincolnshire Poacher* (in print by 1776) – 'We caught a hare alive, my boys ...' Hares on estates were guarded as game, coursed by the gentry and provided much sport. In November 1782 Robert Vyner (1717-1799), MP for Lincolnshire, of Gautby Hall wrote to William Burrell Massingberd of South Ormsby to say that he would be returning to Lincolnshire during the Christmas Parliamentary recess, and that 'Gautby was so dirty and dull at that season', and asked 'if it would not be inconvenient to you to lend me your house at Orsmby ... when I would be in reach of Mr Chaplin and in the neighbourhood of some society, who like myself, are simple enough to be amused with coursing a hare'. [This was rather strange as Gautby Hall was regarded as one of Lincolnshire's greatest mansions, built by his father Robert (1685-1777) from a family of London Goldsmiths and MP for Lincolnshire for fifty years, and important enough to be drawn for Sir Joseph Banks by the artist John Claude Nattes in 1791.]

The Chaplins of Tathwell and Blankney regarded their lands at Tathwell, Raithby and Hallington as a sporting estate. 'The country about Louth', wrote diarist John Byng (later Lord Torrington) during his Tour into Lincolnshire in 1791, 'is famous and preserved for coursing: Mr Chaplin of Tathwell is the grand leader of this diversion, which brings in winter a society to this place'.

The Louth Coursing Club was founded in 1806, among the first in England, an example of the influence of the Chaplins of Tathwell who bred greyhounds. The greyhounds of Lincolnshire were said to excel those of other counties. Two annual meetings, later reduced to one, were held at Tathwell. Recording of such events was one of Richard Jones's specialities and four coloured engravings – Going Out, Finding, Coursing and The Death – were published in 1827. **(See pages 22 and 23).** The extent of Adam's involvement in hare coursing is shown by the fact that the Louth Coursing Club had 'presented' to him – or more likely he had won with his own greyhounds – a silver tankard and a silver cup, which were left to his nephew at Haugham. The sport continued long after Adam's death: in 1869 there were five competitions, the most valuable being the £30 Tathwell Hall Stakes.

A more leisurely and bucolic pursuit was Adam's founding in 1804 (he was then in his 50th year) of the Louth Anacreontic Society. The name meant in praise of love and wine from Anacreon, a Greek poet of the 6th century BC who was noted for his poems of pleasure, and the fact that his death was said to be due to a grape pip sticking in his throat. The convivial nature of the Louth Society is captured in these lines:

Our toast let it be,
May our club flourish happy, united and free,
And long may the sons of Anacreon entwine,
The myrtle of Venus, with Bacchus's vine.

The frontage of the Fleece Inn (part of a drawing of the Market in 1815 by Thomas Espin), where the Anacreontic Society met, which became the Golden Fleece Hotel in Edwardian times (right)

Membership was limited to 21 businessmen and professionals, probably by Adam's invitation. They met every Saturday evening at the Fleece Inn, on the south side of the Market Place and appropriate bearing in mind that Adam's wealth derived from turning fleeces into carpets, for a convivial time placing bets on matters of small consequence such as the height of a room or the shortest distance between two places in the town. The stake was a bottle of wine, the loser to pay the rest to drink his health. However, the Society's minute book records more topical and time-limited wagers:

12 November 1812. John Espin [then Adam's partner in the carpet factory] bets Robert Paddison [solicitor] a rump and a dozen of wine that there will be a general peace in Europe within four years of the death of Bonaparte.

16 April 1819. John Espin bets William Hardy [coal and corn merchant] one bottle of wine that the town of Louth will be lighted with gas previous to the anniversary 1824. (Espin would have lost as the town was not lit with gas until 1826, but he died in 1822).

continued on page 25

Going Out

Engravings of paintings by Richard Jones (1767-1840)
Near Tathwell. Published 1827

HARE

Coursing

Finding

COURSING

One of the men is likely to be George Chaplin.
Could one of the others have been Adam Eve?

The Kill

THE CHRISTMAS BELLS.

Written on hearing the Louth Bells on the 12th of December 1829; and respectfully addressed to the Members of the Anacreontic Society,* who assemble at the Fleece Inn every Saturday Evening.

I.

In murmurs wild and cheerless sounds the blast,
The lamp of day no more in splendour shines,
Night's sable mantle round the heav'ns is cast,
The moon-beam on it's icy bed reclines;
The fleecy show'rs descend upon the plains,
Or hang suspended on the leafless trees,
The peasant in his straw-thatch'd hut remains,
Bearing his nursling children on his knees:
Whilst, echoing gently through the winding dells,
Are heard the distant village Christmas Bells.

II.

Now in their hall, where oft the joke goes round,
And where their welcome Neighbour† takes a seat,
The Grecian Poet's chosen sons are found,
Who here in harmony and friendship meet:
Here *Adam*,‡ oldest of Anacreon's race,
To all, his wishes for their health conveys,
Then, with the smile of youth upon his face,
Relates some frolic of his early days,
Or of some fav'rite greyhound's exploit tells,
Perform'd since last were heard the Christmas Bells.

III.

Next *Jackson*, leaning on his elbow chair,
Sends forth a whiff from best Virginia drawn,
Speaks of the humours of some Irish fair,
P'rhaps Donnybrook, where wondrous feats are shewn;
Whilst *Hardy* tells how he, a warrior knight,
March'd with his small but proud and fearless band,
With gilded epaulette and armour bright,
Himself the champion of Britannia's land:
Ev'n now his soul with thirst of glory swells,
Warm'd by the music of the Christmas Bells.

IV.

Campbell informs them that in Denmark's state
(The "Globe" declares it) there is something wrong,
But, lest the subject should excite debate,
Allen requests from *Bellamy* a song;
In notes sublime th' impassion'd strain he pours,
To loftiest sounds his dulcet voice extends,
Now, with the linnet, up to heav'n he soars,
Or with the lark, descending, he descends:
Such harmony the cloud of care dispels,
Whilst aided by the merry Christmas Bells.

V.

Then *Marsh*, with lòok serene and placid brow,
Takes up his glass and drinks unto his friends,
His observations all with candour flow,
He flatters none, and yet he none offends;
Espin some highly-finish'd plan displays,
Or *Bogg* explains the properties of heat,
Whilst *Paddison* upon the table lays
A fresh-grown sample of his Indian wheat:
And *Sutton*, who in melody excels,
Sits list'ning to the cheerful Christmas Bells.

VI.

Searle, with a veteran sportsman's warmth, declares
He never knew his dogs perform so well,
And of the havoc made 'midst birds and hares,
Norfolk and *Overton* proceed to tell;
Wilson and *Grant* converse about the chase,
Lucas and *Gray* their deeds of arms rehearse,
And *Lees* unbends his laughter-loving face,
Whilst *Wrangham* chants his brethren's fame in verse:
And *Wright* of Haarlem's matchless organ tells,
Excell'd by nothing but the Christmas Bells.

VII.

The hour is come when each in peace retires,
The low'ring bells sound softly through the vale,
Like mingled chords which flow from Hebrew lyres,
When borne along upon the western gale;
Or as the strain which o'er the water sweeps,
From barge, at ev'ning, sailing near the shore,
Which, as her steady course the vessel keeps,
Sinks in the distance and is heard no more;
Whilst on each note the ear with rapture dwells,
Till lost in silence are the Christmas Bells.

* Established in the year 1804, and consists of 21 Members.

† John Eve, who generally attends as a Visiting Member, though not an inhabitant of Louth.

‡ Adam Eve, the Founder of the Society.

Louth, 17*th Dec*. 1829.

[Jacksons, Printers, Market-place, Louth.]

4 June 1825. Mr Adam Eve bets Mr Dunn [James, the builder] one bottle of wine there is not a steam packet from Hull up to Louth by the navigation within seven years from this date. Also Mr Adam Eve bets Mr Dunn one bottle of wine that the tolls will not be reduced within seven years on the Louth Navigation from this date. (A marginal note records: 16 February 1828. Mr Eve lost the last bottle.)

28 May 1831. Mr Edward Bogg [maltster] bets Mr Allen [ship owner] one bottle of wine that there will be 7,000 inhabitants in the town when the next census is taken. (Bogg and three others who wagered the same lost: the figure was 6,927.)

The Anacreontic Society continued after Adam's death in 1831, but membership declined and the weekly meetings were changed to Thursday. By 1857 the sole remaining member was Thomas Jackson the printer. Clearly Adam's convivial leadership had been missed.

A published poem *The Christmas Bells* (opposite), written on hearing the Louth bells on 12 December 1829, was addressed to members of the Anacreontic Society, naming the members and referring to their character and exploits. It shows the range of Adam's business friends. He was then 74, and had lost his wife earlier in the year.

Louth Riverhead

The Neighbour was visiting member John Eve, Adam's younger brother who farmed at Scartho and was also a land surveyor. (John) *Jackson,* smoking a pipe of Virginia tobacco and telling the story of visiting an Irish fair, was a printer and bookseller in the Market Place (he and his brother had published Tennyson's first poems two years earlier, and they printed 'The Christmas Bells'). (William) *Hardy,* coal and corn merchant at the Riverhead, told of some army exploit.

There was (John) *Campbell,* by then sole proprietor of the shop Adam had founded (Adam's younger brother William having died earlier in the year), (George) *Allen,* ship owner and wharfinger at the Riverhead, requesting (John) *Bellamy,* hatter on Upgate, to sing a song, and (Thomas) *Marsh,* Clerk to the Court of Appeal and Collector of Taxes, took up his glass to drink with his friends.

(William) *Espin,* who ran the Priory Academy where he taught Adam's illegitimate boys (see below) and was also an artist and surveyor, showed his latest artistic plans, (Thomas) *Bogg,* maltster on Northgate, explained the properties of heat, and (Samuel) *Sutton,* a shopkeeper on James Street where Adam lived, had a good singing voice. (Thomas) *Paddison* was a cornmiller, hence the reference to Indian wheat; his watermill was in Maiden Row (now Church Street), the site later of the outdoor swimming pool.

(George) *Searle,* grocer and tea dealer on Mercer Row, declared 'He never knew his dogs perform so well', and (Robert) *Norfolk,* grocer, tea dealer, cheesemonger and tallow chandler on Mercer Row, and wine and spirit merchant (Thomas) *Overton* told of the havoc 'midst birds and hares' – all about coursing with greyhounds, while attorney (William) *Wilson,* Adam's solicitor who had married Elizabeth Chaplin of Tathwell, and (Richard) *Grant,* Adam's great nephew, conversed about the chase (fox hunting).

(Henry) *Lucas,* wine merchant in the Butcher Market, and coal and timber merchant (Stephen) *Gray* spoke of 'deeds of arms'. Others present were (John) *Lees,* ironmonger, (Charles) *Wright,* tailor, and (William) *Wrangham,* silversmith and glass and china dealer. And no doubt the landlord of The Fleece, Edmund Carleton, found those bucolic Saturday evenings profitable.

Coursing with greyhounds

The belief in the family descended from Henry Paddison is that this portrait is of Eleanor Paddison, the mother of Adam's three boys

As for Adam himself, 'oldest of Anacreon's race, to all his wishes for their health conveys. Then, with the smile of youth upon his face relates some frolic of his early days, or some fav'rite greyhound's exploits tells, performed since last were heard the Christmas Bells'. However, the poet – William Wrangham (it is in the style of his other effusions) – made no mention of Adam's extra-marital activities. It is only from his Will that they are known.

Ivy House where Adam and Sarah lived in James Street had dining and drawing rooms, good kitchens, ale and wine cellars, several 'sleeping rooms', an extensive yard, coach-house and stabling for six horses, dog kennels, a brewhouse and a 'productive garden'. There was a room for a nursery but there were no children.

When Adam decided that if he was to have an heir to run his carpet factory he would have to make 'an arrangement', and whether or not his wife gave her consent will never be known. But it was the year following their silver wedding anniversary in 1811 that his first illegitimate son, John, was born. He was followed by Henry (1815), Charles (1816), Lucy (1816/17) and Thomas (1819, who died in infancy). John, Henry and Charles were described in Adam's Will as sons of Eleanor Paddison, widow, 'by me begotten on her body and whom I have adopted as my own son'(s). Adam was 57 when the first boy was born and 64 when the last was born. But who was the mother?

Eleanor Seales was born in 1776 in Newark and married William Paddison (believed to have been a boot and shoe maker) there in 1805. When she was widowed and when (certainly before 1811) and why she came to Louth, or how she came to meet Adam Eve are not known. She was 36 (21 years younger than Adam) when John was born and 43 when Thomas was born.

In such an 'arrangement' it was usual for the mother to be a widow, ideally one who had already had a live birth. It was also usual not to adopt until the child was about 12 years old when it seemed clear that he would continue to adulthood. When did Adam adopt the boys? Where were they baptized? Was Sarah compliant with her husband's other family, and the adoption of the boys? Or were they not adopted until after she had died? It was not until then that Adam made his Will, and it does not say when the boys were adopted. Was there a scandal? The fact that Adam had illegitimate offspring, and who the mother was, would have been well-known. It would appear that in society then, such an arrangement was just accepted. Indeed, Eleanor had her portrait painted, almost certainly by Richard Jones and commissioned by Adam, but not until after Sarah's death.

Eleanor lived in James Street. The Rating Valuation lists for 1823 and 1838 show her living in one of the terrace houses Adam had built for his factory workers, on the south side between the river and Ramsgate (demolished after the 1920 flood). Coincidentally, at the 1841 census she was living close to another William Paddison, shoemaker (age 45 and not born in Louth) and his wife Susanna (same age but born in Louth) and their seven children (eldest 15 and all born in Louth). The youngest, Jabez, became a builder and lime burner, in the Grimsby Road pits, and his widow Sarah Jane continued to run Paddison's Noted Lime Pits into the 20th century. But William had been in debt. There is a letter surviving in the Eve & Ranshaw archives (now in Louth Museum) written in 1835 by John and Henry Paddison to the executors of Adam's Will, John Campbell and Thomas Oldham, requesting that the principal sum of £200 6s 6d (about £14,000 today) and an arrear of interest due from William Paddison of Louth, shoemaker, be 'altogether released and discharged'. Why should Adam have lent a shoemaker that amount of money, the precise amount of which seems to suggest a loan to buy a house/shop? Is it possible that William was Eleanor's first (illegitimate?) son before she came to Louth, and therefore that he was half-brother to John and Henry (and Charles)?

Boys playing cricket in the grounds of Espin's Priory Academy, about 1833. Drawn by Joy William Best, a Louth artist who lived on Westgate

It has to be assumed that Eleanor brought up Adam's children with his financial support. The boys were undoubtedly educated at Espin's Mathematical, Nautical, Architectural and Commercial Academy at Priory Cottage. Adam had known Thomas and John Espin since they came to Louth in 1790, and John became his partner in the carpet factory in 1811. Thomas had opened the school when John Paddison was six; when Thomas died in 1822, he was followed by his half-brother William (who would go on to manage the factory when Adam died). The practical curriculum, particularly perhaps the commercial content, would have appealed to Adam's desire for the boys to succeed in the business world, rather than the classical curriculum at the Grammar School. And there was the advantage of boarding accommodation which would have been helpful to the boys' mother.

Although the boys had not reached their majority (21) when Adam died (John was 19, Henry 16 and Charles 15), he had made provision for part of their legacies to be applied to placing them in trade or a professsion. Adam left Eleanor an annuity of £40 (about £1,800 today) a year payable by his trustees from rents on his properties on Padehole (Northgate) and Eve Street. The 1841 census recorded her as of independent means, living quietly on her own. Eleanor Paddison died in October 1847 and was buried in St. Mary's churchyard (Louth Cemetery did not open until 1855).

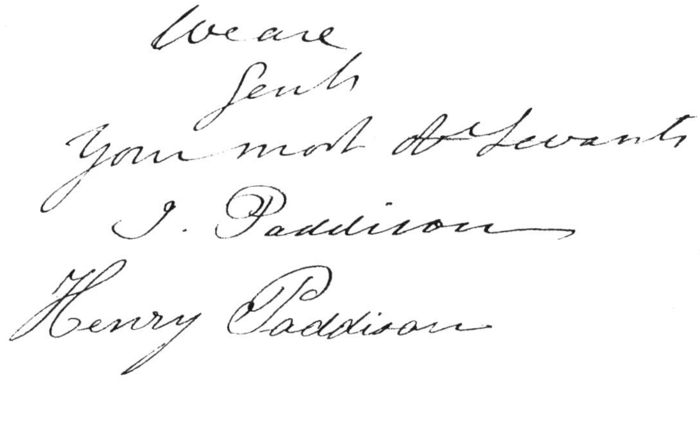
We are
Gents
Your most Obt Servants
J. Paddison
Henry Paddison

The signatures of John and Henry Paddison on their letter to Adam Eve's executors
(see opposite page)

John Paddison was allowed the use of some of his legacy of £3,000 (£135,000 today) when only 19 to be involved in the carpet factory with William Espin (see The Factory chapter). He married Ann Elizabeth Brickhills of Halton Holegate and they had one boy, William Brickhills, born 1836, who attended Louth Boys Grammar School. He was listed, among leading citizens of the town (including William Espin), as a subscriber to R S Bayley's *Notices of Louth* (1834) which contained a map of the town showing the carpet factory. John was a Wesleyan Methodist who joined the breakaway Wesley Reform Association (or Warrenites) when it was established in 1836. He was a Shareholder Trustee with ten shares when their chapel was built in Walkergate (Queen Street), now the Masonic Hall. The Secretary was William Brown who would later paint the famous Louth Panorama (1844-47). The occupations of other trustees shows the type of tradesmen with whom John mixed: William Brett and his son William, drapers, John Moody, tailor and linen draper, George Whelpton, cordwainer (who would go on to make a fortune with his purifying and stomach pills – laxatives), Francis Brown (William's son), cordwainer, Thomas Rayner, tailor, William Blakelock, saddler and harness maker, Abraham Marshall, bookseller, John Naull, ironmonger, and John Brett, surgeon. John Paddison died in 1838 at the early age of 26. His widow continued to live at the White House John had built on Grimsby Road.

Charles Paddison, the youngest of the three brothers, came into his inheritance of £3,000 in 1837. When John died, he took on the factory with William Espin, and on his own in 1838, after which Espin and his family returned to schoolteaching in Mansfield Grammar School in 1840. Charles did not marry but had an illegitimate daughter Ellen Brown, by his housekeeper Harriet Brown (from Claxby); Ellen later married Michael Hainey.

Reverse of a fragment of a Louth carpet
(see page 110)

Charles retired early (at 46) from the factory about 1861/62, when his brother Henry took up the reins briefly, and continued a bachelor life in the former factory overseer's house (see The Factory chapter), now 68 James Street. To judge from the provisions of his Will when he died after 'a long and lingering illness' in March 1874 aged 58, it would appear that the business had been reasonably successful. He made bequests of £500 (about £24,000 today) to each of his trustees – brother Henry and William Chatterton (farmer at Tathwell) – together with his properties. He left funds for the education and maintenance of his illegitimate daughter and a bequest of £500 when she reached 21, and an annuity of £20 to his sister Lucy (who had married Ellis Smith).

Charles also left £100 to Ellen Andrews, wife of Robert (maltster, brewer and farmer of the Old Phoenix Brewery in Walkergate, now Queen Street) together with the portrait of his mother Eleanor which he had inherited from Adam. Why? He also had his own portrait painted by Bennett Hubbard of Louth, which he left to his nephew Charles John Paddison (who turned out to be rather a black sheep). The portrait of Adam Eve by Richard Jones passed to Charles's brother Henry, and Adam's gold watch went to nephew Henry Russell Paddison.

Small bequests in his Will reveal how well he got on with his factory workers (these referred to as his servants): John Capes, wool sorter, then aged 73 (19 guineas), Samuel Burdett, foreman carpet weaver, then 53 (£5); and Thomas Cook, dyehouse labourer, then 63 (£5). His clerk, Thomas Preston, living on Newmarket, received 19 guineas, and he left £5 to Benjamin Crow (20 Lee Street) a solicitor's clerk who was Secretary to the Louth General Friendly Society and also Secretary to the Louth Mechanics' Institute (who then owned the Mansion House on Upgate); does this mean that Charles was a member of the Institute? An interesting sidelight was a direction that the mourning required on his death should be supplied from the shops of his friends – John Freeston, tailor and woollen draper, 6 Mercer Row, William Everett Oliver, linen and woollen draper, 77 Eastgate, and Edmund Brotherton, linen and woollen draper, 13 Market Place.

The story of Henry Paddison, the middle adopted son, seems to show that he inherited some of his biological father Adam's business acumen. As already noted, he and his brother John had been in partnership with William Espin; at that time Henry was boarding with William Fridlington in Brackenborough learning about farming. Although only 19, he was appointed to represent the parish on the first Board of Guardians for the new-built (1834) Louth Union Workhouse. Among the 88 Guardians were men with some connection to his father Adam: Adam Eve, nephew, Haugham, Richard Chaplin, Adam's friend, Tathwell, and Thomas Oldham, executor of Adam's Will, Saltfleetby St Clement.

When Henry reached his majority in 1836 and received his legacy of £2,000 (£190,000 today; why it was less than those to his brothers is not known), he set up as a gentleman farmer with two servants on a rented farm at Gayton le Wold. He was there at the 1841 census, and in 1844 he had his portrait painted by Bennett Hubbard. Then in 1845 he emigrated to South Africa, bought farmland at Colesberg, married Isabella Russell and had four children – Martha Annie (1848), Elizabeth (1851), Henry Russell (1853) and Charles John (1855). When Isabella died, aged 36, in 1859, Henry sold up and returned to England with his young children. Martha Ann would marry George Pirie in South Africa, Elizabeth would marry George Christian, have two children in South Africa and return to England, and Henry Russell would marry Harriett Mutton of St Ives (Cambs). Charles John would fail in managing the family farm in Essex, go bankrupt and in 1877, at only 22, return to South Africa.

Henry Paddison
Painted by Bennett Hubbard
March 1844

As for Henry himself, in the 1860s he was living at Eastfield House, Keddington near Louth. When brother Charles retired from the factory (1861/62), Henry went into partnership with Edward Hoff of Holbeach, but this was shortlived and wound up in 1863. Henry then moved to Wood Hall at Arkesden in Essex. He was 59 when he married again in 1874, to Sarah Ann Peacock (born in Suffolk) 16 years his junior, a governess who had been at Panton Hall (near Wragby). Interestingly on their marriage certificate Henry's father's name was given as Adam Eve Paddison. They settled at Bilsby Hall near Alford where he was a well-respected and successful farmer. When he died in 1897, after bequests to his family in South Africa he left his entire estate to his wife Sarah; she died in 1902.

Having traced the relevant parts of the Eve family tree, we can now turn to the last years of the life of Adam the carpet maker, the full stories of the factory on James Street and the shop in the Market Place being told in later chapters. His wife Sarah (73) and his younger brother William (53) had died in 1829, and later that year Adam made his Will, the contents of which show his considerable wealth: monetary bequests alone totalled over £11,000 (around £500,000 today). The executors and trustees of his properties were John Campbell, sole proprietor of the shop following William's death, Thomas Oldham of Saltfleetby House, a major landowner, and nephew Adam Clarke, linen and woollen draper of Market Rasen. For some reason which is not clear a codicil was added which removed Adam Clarke as executor and reduced his legacy from £300 to £200; the legacy to his great nephew Adam was also reduced from £500 to £300. The codicil was signed only seven days before Adam died on 11 February 1831.

In addition to the large bequests to his three adopted sons, Adam left £1,000 (£45,000 today) to his nephew Adam the farmer at Haugham, and £300 each to two of his great nephews Adam (13) and James (5). The three sons of his widowed sister Mrs Ann Clarke of Market Rasen – Richard, Marmaduke and Adam – received £200 each. He left £100 each to his nieces: Ann, wife of Thomas Grant of Louth, Mary, wife of James Martin, Elizabeth, wife of John Campbell, Ann, wife of William Wells, and Eve (unmarried). Also bequeathed £100 each were Ann Chapman, daughter of John Chapman the elder, formerly a grocer and draper at Newmarket (a horse racing connection?), Mary Storr of Boston and her 'natural son' (what did that imply?) Robert Anderson Storr, and his book-keeper William Farrow (the last subject to any amount still owing on a loan of £100 made in 1810). His servants Henrietta Andrews and William Balding (18, a distant relative of the author of this book) received £15 each. Adam also remembered his hare coursing friends George Chaplin (1760-1835) and his nephew Richard Chaplin (1801-1840) of Tathwell Hall with mourning rings.

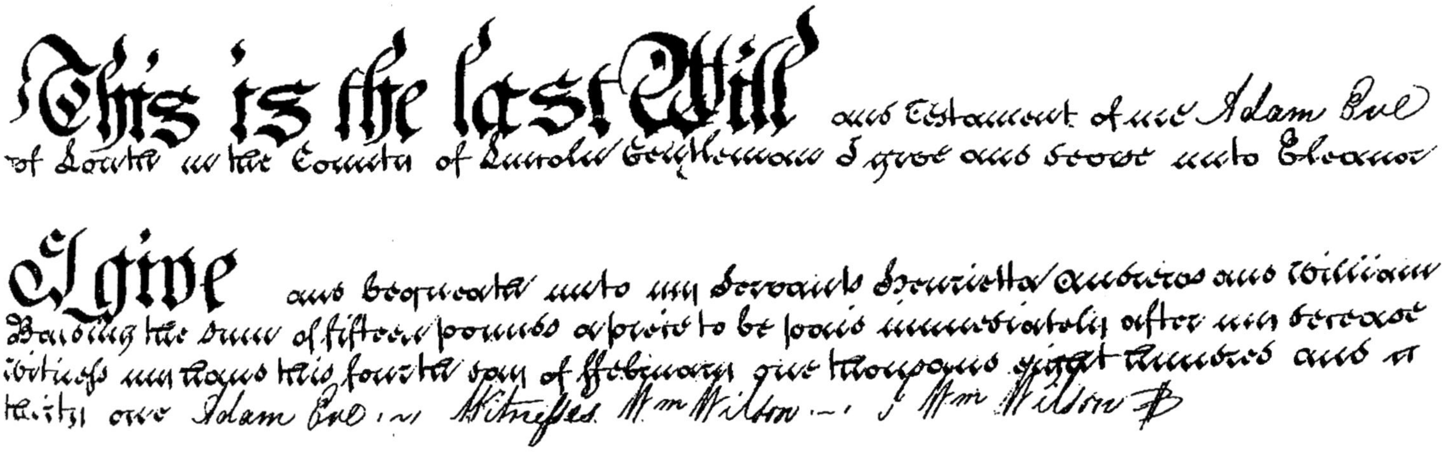
This is the last Will and Testament of me Adam Eve of Louth in the County of Lincoln Gentleman I give and devise unto Eleanor

I give and bequeath unto my servants Henrietta Andrews and William Balding the sum of fifteen pounds apiece to be paid immediately after my decease witness my hand this fourth day of February one thousand eight hundred and thirty one Adam Eve Witnesses Wm Wilson J Wm Wilson

The heading and second codicil of Adam Eve's Will

What are we to make of Adam's wife Sarah, that 'amiable and much-accomplished' lady to whom he had been married for 43 years, and of whom we know so little? Adam had portraits painted of himself, his mistress and his horses, but not his wife. What would he have done with his wealth if she had outlived him?

It is worth noting that the codicil was witnessed by solicitors William Wilson and his son James William Wilson, the latter also an accomplished artist who had received drawing lessons from William Espin and Richard Jones, and would go on to publish *Sketches of Louth* (1840) – another example of the range of Adam's business and social interconnections.

This is also shown by the fact that his obituary appeared in the *Lincoln, Rutland & Stamford Mercury;* "Died at Louth on Saturday last, Adam Eve Esq in his 76th year. About thirty years ago he established a carpet manufactory at Louth (the first of the kind in the county of Lincoln) and by his unremitting attention, skill and perseverance, brought it to such a state of perfection that his manufactured goods were in the highest estimation not only in this kingdom but in America, where for several years he had a regular and extensive contract. The town of Louth and the neighbourhood are indebted to him for many valuable improvements: he was indefatigable in his attention to the roads, bridges and other public works throughout the district, and gratuitously appropriated a considerable proportion of his time in that way. He was a kind and liberal benefactor to many who needed his assistance, and to his friends and acquaintances in general his hospitality was proverbial."

The emphasis on his carpet factory will be dealt with elsewhere. His indefatigable attention to public works is no doubt a reference to his being a Commissioner under local Acts – For Paving, Lighting, Cleansing, Regulating and otherwise Improving the Town and Parish of Louth, 1825 (with William Espin and John Campbell among many others), For improving and maintaining the Navigation from the River Humber to Alvingham and thence to Louth, 1828 (with his brothers John and William and others), and probably the Louth to Scartho Turnpike (1802). He also had shares, with his brother William, in the Louth Gas Company, founded in 1826; both were on the Committee with other leading businessmen for the ascent of Charles Green's gas-filled Coronation Balloon from Woolmart Yard opposite the Gas Works at the Riverhead in August that year to celebrate the opening of the Works and the supply of gas for the town.

Gravestone of Adam's parents – James (1725-1788) and Mary (1734-1822)

His proverbial hospitality was reflected in the activities of the Anacreontic Society noted earlier, but there is no record of his kind and liberal benefaction. What a pity that his portrait by Richard Jones cannot be found. Adam was buried adjoining the graves of his father and two younger brothers William and James (died 1800, age 21) under a large weeping ash tree (now gone) in the churchyard of St Giles, Scartho where his father had been found as a baby. (The wrought iron railings which surrounded the graves now form the church gates.)

The inscription on his gravestone reflects another aspect of Adam's business acumen – that is, the benefit to the town and district of the carpet factory: 'Here rests the mortal remains of Adam Eve, who died February 5th 1831 aged 75. As a tribute to his memory it is recorded that in the year 1798 he commenced at Louth the first Carpet and Blanket Manufactory that had ever been established in the County of Lincoln, and by his skill and perseverance it attained a degree of perfection which rendered it highly beneficial to the town and neighbourhood'.

Upper part of Adam Eve's grave slab

We can now turn to the water-powered wool spinning mill that Adam developed into a successful carpet factory.

Broken grave slab of William Eve (left) and Adam (right)

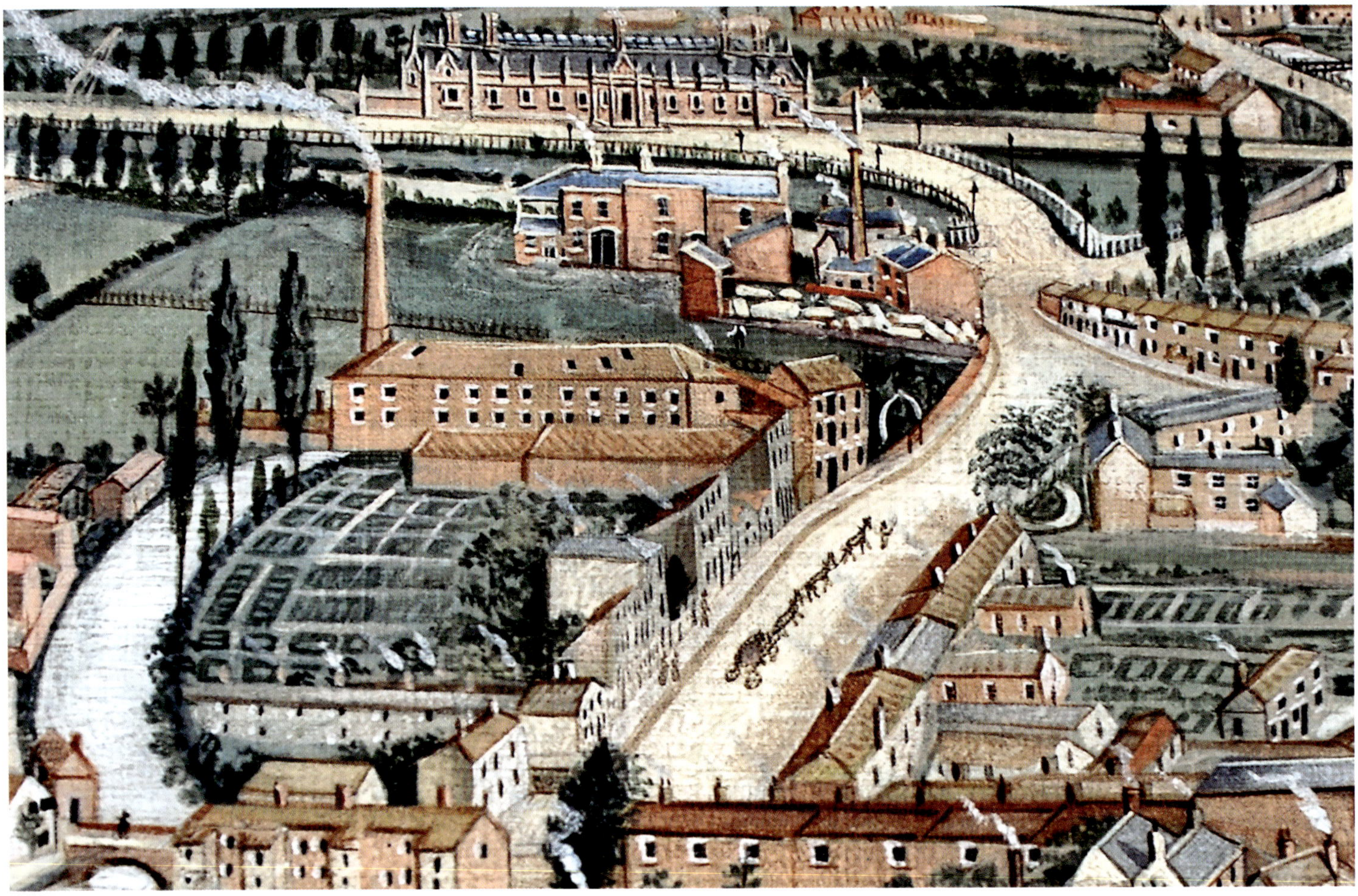

River Lud | Factory with tall chimney | James Street | Adam Eve's Ivy House (with curved carriage drive)

From William Brown's Louth Panorama, 1847

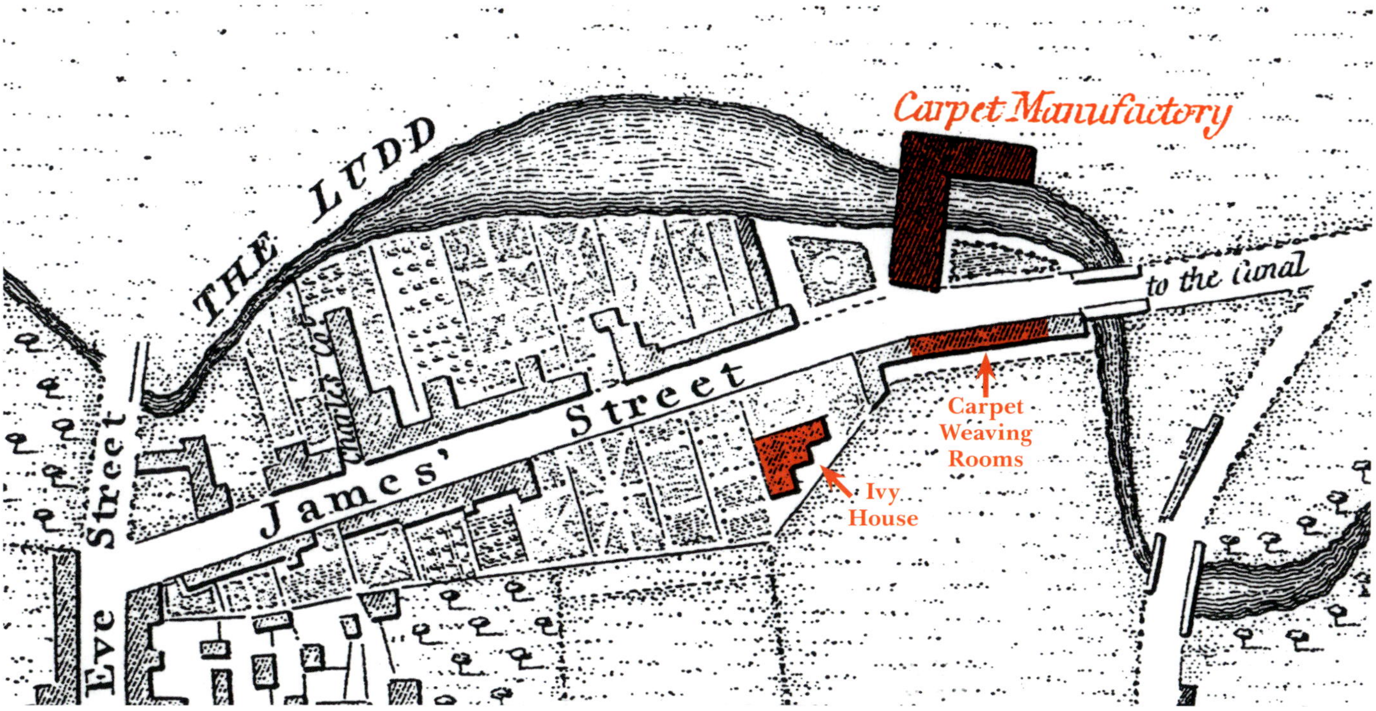

Part of an early map of Louth, by Thomas Espin 1808, showing the location of the Carpet Manufactory, the carpet weaving rooms and Ivy House on the opposite side of the street. Note the formal gardens down to the mill dam on the river. The garden area with a centre circle immediately west of the factory is where there was an ornamental fountain.
(see page 46)

Chapter 3

The Factory

THE YEAR is 1787. You are walking along Ramsgate from Eastgate (then Watery Lane). On your right is the small and already old House of Correction (now the site of the Orme Almshouses), beyond which are grass closes down to the river with a watermill (established in 1716 and later extended to become Bryan Hall's mill, and now flats). Downstream from there are the warehouses and manufactories on the Louth Navigation Canal at the Riverhead. On your left is a larger grass close belonging to merchant Gabriel Neve, on the town side of which is the recently built Manor House, and in the distance is the open North Field of the parish, still farmed in strips, the fallows luxuriant with thistles. [It will be 25 years before the Act of Parliament to enclose the open fields into the now familiar hedged pattern].

As you come to the (probably) wooden bridge over the river, to the left is another grass field called Wood's Close (rented to John Wood by the Corporation) and you are amazed to see rising from the greenfield site adjoining the tree-lined river (usually known as Beck West and once the site of a small watermill) a three-storey, 11-bay brick built factory with pantile roof and roof lights, hipped at each end. It is far bigger than any other building in the town apart from the parish church of St James, and dominates the rural scene. [James Street had yet to be laid out.] You have been told that its purpose is to spin wool by water-powered machinery, but what you don't know is that it will be empty and unused for some months.

This is the manufactory that in just a few years time would become Lincolnshire's only producer of carpets, and establish Louth as one of only three places in England, after Barnard Castle and Kidderminster, specialising in flat-weave floor covering. Its genesis, it could be said, started in 1771 with the arrival in Lincolnshire of an influential clergyman.

The Revd Reynold (or Reinhold) Gideon Bouyer (1741-1826) was born of Dutch Huguenot parents in London, educated in Holland and then Cambridge where he graduated as Bachelor of Laws in 1769, and was ordained Deacon in Norwich (1764). In 1771 he married Elizabeth Ponton of Little Ponton near Grantham and was installed Rector of Theddlethorpe St Helen with Mablethorpe St Peter and Rector of Willoughby St Helena under the patronage of the Duke of Ancaster, whom he served as Chaplain. The Bouyers lived at Willoughby where, according to John Byng on his Lincolnshire tour in 1791, 'The Rector Dr [sic] Bouyer, has lately built a good parsonage'.

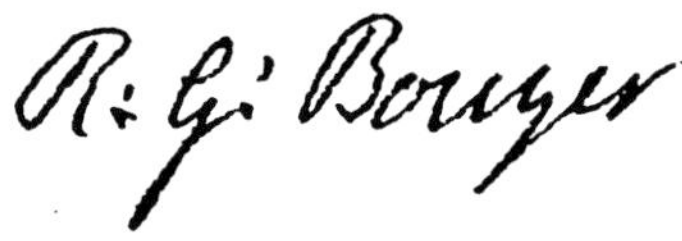

Gideon Bouyer's signature

Bouyer was soon actively involved in the religious and social life of his parishes, with particular concern for the poor and needy. With private means, and status as Chaplain to the Duke of Ancaster, he set about practical ways of improving attendance at church, reading the Bible and family prayers, and of relieving poverty. He would go on to lead a committee of clergy of the 'Deaneries of Louth Eske, and Ludburgh, Calcewaith, Horncastle, Gartree, Bolingbroke, Candleshoe and Hill' who were alarmed at neglect of attendance at worship (only a third of inhabitants attended), poor attendance at Sunday Schools, and almost total disuse of family prayers and reading the Holy Scriptures. About 1804 they published *Two Addresses on the Duty of Family Prayers and on Reading the Holy Scriptures, together with Occasional Prayers.* Two of the latter provide an insight into what motivated Bouyer: one about 'good works', and the other, for 'When the weather is unseasonable', which refers to 'the relief of the needy'.

The basic problem was that of keeping down the parish Poor Rate by creating employment for the needy rather than just providing charity, particularly employment such as spinning and weaving wool. The cost of providing a spinning wheel for a cottager to work at home was about six shillings (30p). Louth had a Jersey School to teach children to spin jersey or worsted from the 1660s which was supported by the (Old) Corporation (Warden and Six Assistants) by paying the rent and a teacher: in 1666 a Jersey man was paid ten shillings and sixpence for teaching seven children. The building was also referred to as the 'Workhouse', implying confinement: in 1743 the Corporation paid nine shillings and three pence for 'mending the Spinning House' and £3 7s 8d in 1748 for 'repairs of the Workhouse'. Also the Edward Bolle trustees employed Spinning Master Luke Phillips from 1762 to 1769 at £15 (about £1,000 today) a year to teach 'the poor of Louth in Spinning'.

CONSIDERATIONS

UPON THE

PRESENT STATE

OF THE

WOOL TRADE,

THE

LAWS made concerning that Article,

AND

How far the fame are confiftent with true Policy, and the real Intereft of the State.

BY A GENTLEMAN,

Refident on his Eftate in LINCOLNSHIRE.

Times were certainly hard for wool-growing Lincolnshire which felt the effect of the government policy of prohibiting export of wool in the interests of manufacturers. Landlords, it was said, were generally apathetic and 'wrapped up in their pleasures', and the poor suffered, although a meeting was held at the White Hart in Lincoln in October 1778 to make an application to Parliament for leave to export wool, under proper restrictions, where 'all growers of wool and persons of landed property were requested to attend'. In the 1770s the price paid to wool growers in the Marsh fell by up to 30%, according to John Bourne, agent to Tyrwhitt Drake on the Marsh near Skegness. And 'A Gentleman Resident on his Estate in Lincolnshire' [attributed to Henry Butler Pacey FRS MP of Boston; d.1785] wrote in a pamphlet *Considerations upon the Present State of the Wool Trade* (1781) that the price of long-combing wool had fallen by a half from the previous fifty years' average, with 'little demand ... and an accumulated quantity in the hands of the grower'. It was calculated that in the winter of 1781-82, some 250,000 tods of wool were unsold in Lincolnshire. A good price could be obtained on the Continent, and smuggling was rife.

That was work for the 'owlers' as they were known as they only worked at night. Small boats put out from Suine Haven (Grainthorpe) and Saltfleet to meet ships out at sea, and it was said that few ships left a Lincolnshire port without a few sacks of wool, perhaps labelled 'hops' surreptitiously stowed in the hold. And what more natural than to organise a return cargo of Dutch gin or hollands and tobacco – brought ashore on a moonless night and carted through gaps in the dunes at Theddlethorpe to be stowed away in cottage chimneys and farm barns.

Smugglers at work

Gideon Bouyer knew what was going on and what was being done to prevent it, not least through his friendship with young Henry Cracroft Marshall (1759-1789), the local Customs and Excise Officer, of Theddlethorpe Hall. He also knew of the efforts of Sir Joseph Banks (1743-1820), President of the Royal Society, with his main country seat at Revesby and with other land in the county (including in Fulstow), on the 'Lincolnshire Wool Committee' to enable the export of surplus long and coarse wool.

The 'open' Committee of Landowners of the County of Lincoln meeting at Lincoln Castle in October 1781 considered 'how far an immediate relief may be given to the present distress (occasioned by the low price of wool)' by exporting 'to the foreign market that surplus of wool which is now unsold and unsaleable at the home market'. When the Committee met again in February 1782 at St Alban's Tavern, London among the leading Lincolnshire landowners present were the Duke of Ancaster (Chairman), Sir Joseph Banks, Sir Peter Burrell, Robert Vyner, Charles Anderson Pelham, Dr Humphrey Sibthorp, Sir John Thorold and Revd Edward Walls, all of whom would four years later be subscribers to the spinning mill in Louth.

There was also a meeting at Louth and correspondence flowed between Banks and Charles Chaplin of Tathwell, and his eldest son Thomas published 'A letter from a Grower of Long Combing Wool to the Manufacturers of the valuable Staple'. Banks himself had published cogent arguments in favour of export.

The Petition put forward by the Committee was 'That leave may be given to bring in a bill for permitting an exportation of long and coarse wool, at such period after the normal time of clipping, with such duty and under such restrictions as Parliament shall think proper'. This brought a flurry of opposition pamphlets from the manufacturing interests of Yorkshire and East Anglia, such as *Plain Reasons against a general exportation of Wool* which was against the export of any kind of British wool, saying that it would be 'highly injurious to the trade and manufacture', and not willing to accept even limited exporting of long and coarse wool. The manufacturing interests won the day and the petition failed.

Part of a Louth carpet woven in the 1850s
(see pages 100-101)

In March, and somewhat prophetically, *A letter to the landed Gentlemen and Graziers of Lincolnshire* by a Friend and Neighbour was published, urging them to 'give greater encouragement to the invention and use of those machines by which one man or child may do the work of several'.

The Lincolnshire Marsh roads were near impassable for carts in winter and growers had to keep wool in store at home in the hope of better times, but storage tended to cause wool to become harsh and less pliable. Moreover the increased penalties for illegal export of wool imposed in 1786 and the increased efficiency of the Revenue Service – Riding Officers on land and Revenue cutters at sea – would make smuggling even more hazardous.

There was also the problem of the Poor Rates. The slump in the price of long wool and expenditure on relief of the poor reached an 'alarming level' at the beginning of the 1780s. At the conclusion of the American War of Independence (1783) the poor rates were so high and the poverty of the labouring classes so great in east Lindsey that the magistrates intervened in the administration of the Poor Law by publishing orders for purchase of raw materials and the teaching of all poor children to knit before they were six and to spin before they were nine years of age.

The late Pauline Robinson of Theddlethorpe Hall demonstrating spinning in 1976

The 4th Premium medal awarded to Ann Perryn age 11 in 1790. The inscription reads: Plenty & Peace are the Fruits of Industry & Subordination. On the reverse it records that the Society of Industry was founded on 30th November 1783.

At the Louth Michaelmas Sessions in September 1783, as a result of 'the alarming increase of Parish Rates, and the Want of Regard to the Employment of the Poor in general, and of the Infant Poor in particular', the magistrates issued Rules and Orders to Overseers of the Poor. They were to purchase wool, woollen yarn, hemp and flax, spinning wheels and other implements for the employment of the poor of every denomination, punish those who refused to work; paupers were not to be allowed any relief in money until they had done 'such work as they may be capable of' and 'no person was to be allowed any relief on account of any child above six years of age not able to knit, cases of sickness excepted', and similarly for a child over nine years of age not able to spin.

Gideon Bouyer was a Justice of the Peace and probably took a lead in persuading fellow magistrates of the need for such Rule and Orders. His personal response was to be the prime mover in the establishment the same year (1783) of the Society for the Promotion of Industry in the Southern District of the Parts of Lindsey. Its intention was to instil the 'habits of industry' into the younger generation, maintain the influence of the Established Church among the poor, and to provide an outlet for surplus wool. Raw wool acquired after the clipping in June could be combed, spun, woven into cloth or knitted into stockings and blankets and sold before it was necessary to balance the parochial accounts in March the next year.

The Committee of the Society who Bouyer drew together were clergy and gentry, many of them doubtless also magistrates. The influence of the business man, young Adam Eve who had taken the lease of his shop in Louth in 1781, would come later. Each parish paid an annual parochial subscription to the Society calculated as one percent of the Poor Rate the previous year: for Theddlethorpe St Helen for example it was about ten shillings (£30 today), where the Overseers of the Poor accounts, which were 'audited' among others by Bouyer, show payments for supplying spinning wheels, for spinning hemp, and for making stockings and woven cloth. The Overseers purchased a few pounds of combed wool for beginners, after which they became part of the general practice of wool-combers giving out wool and paying for the spinning. 'As soon as their worsted will reel into twelve or thirteen hanks to the pound, it may be very profitably worked up into stuffs for the use of the poor', reported the Society.

To encourage children under eight to take up knitting hosiery at home, the Society awarded annual premiums (222 between 1786 and 1790). To promote the spinning of yarn by older children there were Jersey Spinning Premiums of an article of woollen clothing. Rules for competitions included disqualification if found spinning before seven o'clock in the morning or after eight in the evening, and they were required to answer 'every question in the Church catechism, without hesitation'. The best were crowned King or Queen of the Spinners of each of four districts and for the whole division, and the Overseers of their parish were awarded the Flag of the Society to be hung in his parish church. Outstanding in 1786 and 1787 was 14 to 15 year old Susanna Langton of North Somercotes, who could spin two hanks, five lees, ten yards, worth 1½d, in an hour (one hank is seven lees and one lee is 80 yards, i.e. a total of 1,560 yards). The Trustees had a collection among themselves, totalling six guineas, to include 'some small piece of plate with a suitable inscription' for her. Over the years 1786 to 1790 the Society awarded 469 spinning premiums. A result of the availability of cheap yarn was that weavers were able to set up looms at home. However, the obstruction to the growth of worsted weaving was the expense of land carriage if the cloth could not be dyed and finished at home. This led to the Society subsidising a dyer and finisher at Louth (see the chapter on the Stuff Ball).

For the older children the Society established spinning schools or classes (at Legbourne and Grainthorpe for example) rather than encouraging children to spin at home. The reasons were the possibility of employing a 'reeler' or yarn winder; the opportunity for children from large families in small cottages; the greater volume of yarn than a spinner at home 'embarrassed by the continual bustle and various avocations of family concerns'; the quality of work improved by inspection by the master or mistress; to instill in children the 'habit of industry'; and the promotion of 'that emulation which naturally arises among numbers together in the same employment'.

The headquarters of the Society was at Alford, where they had annual meetings at the George Inn to consider competitors for premiums, followed by a dinner at the then fashionable hour of three o'clock. In 1796 the annual distribution of premiums began with prayers at eleven o'clock and a sermon by Revd Thomas Pennington (formerly Curate of Theddlethorpe St Helen, and then Rector of Sausthorpe and Vicar of Bilsby).

AN
ACCOUNT
OF THE
Origin, Proceedings, and Intentions
OF THE
SOCIETY
FOR THE
PROMOTION OF INDUSTRY,
IN THE
Southern Diſtrict of the Parts of LINDSEY,
in the County of LINCOLN.

Meanwhile, what was happening in Louth? In 1778 the Corporation had resolved to take in hand the provision of a wool manufactory for employment of the poor, and the Warden (John Inett) was instructed to take up a loan of £200 (about £13,000 today) for the purchase of materials and erecting a building. Nothing came of it. Then in 1780 the Corporation agreed to contribute (if necessary) £1,000 (£60,000 today) towards 'the establishment of a woollen manufactory', but the proposed scheme did not go forward and eighteen months later the resolution was rescinded. However, the Warden and Six Assistants expressed readiness to consider any more eligible plans that might be submitted to them.

In 1784 the newly formed Society attempted to enlist the support of Richard Arkwright, inventor of the 'roller spinning' process and the first to build a successful water-powered cotton-spinning factory at Cromford in Derbyshire (in 1771). However, he had not achieved success in adapting the machinery to worsted spinning, and he declined.

What caused the Corporation to reconsider its contribution to a woollen manufactory? It is possible to build up a picture of what was happening in the years 1785 to 1787 by study of documents in the Eve & Ranshaw archive, and in particular the names, status and inter-relationships of people therein, and other sources such as *The Sheep and Wool Correspondence of Sir Joseph Banks 1781-1820,* the *Lincoln Date Book* (1866) and *Louth Old Corporation Records* compiled by R W Goulding.

Louth Mansion House or Assembly Rooms on Upgate where the Warden and Six Assistants held their formal meetings. From drawing by T. W. Wallis, made before the building was refronted and the ball finials removed in 1849.

First, the members of the Corporation who met at the Blue Stone Inn (Upgate) on 11 October 1787, to seal a lease to Richard Brumfit of Leeds of the land and water mill 'lately erected thereon' for the purpose of spinning long and coarse sheep's wool by machinery, and five days later met at the Mansion House to seal a conveyance by feoffment (grant) of the ground and water mill to Sir Joseph Banks and Robert Vyner. The members were:

Robert Neve (born 1755), merchant (son of Robert Neve of Saltfleet), Warden in 1788; he owned land just south of the factory site;

Nicholas Wrigglesworth (1725 -1803), surgeon, who lived for thirty years in the house which is now Lloyds TSB bank on Mercer Row and was Warden seven times including 1787; he was doctor to Charles Chaplin of Tathwell and attended the death of his eldest daughter Diana (19) in 1782; and he corresponded with Sir Joseph Banks about wool growing;

Dr Charles Clarke, Doctor of Physic, 45 Westgate, who was Warden six times including 1786;

John Inett, surgeon, Warden five times;

and **John Robinson** (died 1811) who was Warden six times.

The Town Clerk was attorney Thomas Phillips (died 1804 and followed by Edward Bellwood) who made an alphabetical list of the 32 subscribers to the Spinning Machine and Acct of each Subscription: 'One year and a half Interest thereon at 3% C1 (calculated) up to 1st July 1787'. This indicates that the subscriptions were made by the end of 1785, after the first Stuff Ball on 17 November (see chapter The Stuff Ball). The list was copied in December 1793 and used to mark when Adam Eve bought out the subscribers (see below). The names and amounts were taken from the Grant to Banks and Vyner where the order is according to the amount subscribed. It is no surprise therefore to find that the subscribers, or rather investors or shareholders hoping for a return, were 'society', that is aristocrats and land gentry with a vested interest in the growing of wool and the market price, and clergy, with a concern for the welfare of the poor, most of them supporters of the Society for the Promotion of Industry in their part of the county, and of course of the Stuff Ball. The list below gives information where known of the subscribers, and (in brackets) the value of their subscription/investment today:

The Warden and Six Assistants of the Town of Louth and Free School of King Edward the Sixth in Louth	£300	(£18,000)
The Most Noble Brownlow Duke of Ancaster [the leading Lincolnshire family, of Grimsthorpe, also owning land in east Lincolnshire; Lord Lieutenant of Lincolnshire]	£100	(£6,000)
Sir Joseph Banks Bart [1743-1820; of Revesby where he was to be found in the autumn; President of the Royal Society and chief mover and facilitator in promoting the growing, local use and exporting of wool; few matters of significance in Lincolnshire happened without his approval, and most were supported from his purse]	£100	(£6,000)
Sir Peter Burrell [of Eresby near Spilsby; his wife Priscilla was Baroness Willoughby D'Eresby and the daughter of the Duke of Ancaster; Sir Peter was made Lord Chamberlain of England in 1781, became MP for Boston in 1782, and made Lord Gwydir in 1779]	£90	(£5,400)
Charles Anderson Pelham [of Brocklesby, MP; created Lord Yarborough in 1794]	£90	(£5,400)
Charles Chaplin [1730-1795; Tathwell Hall; large landowner with sporting interests and leading sheep breeder; corresponded with Sir Joseph Banks; High Steward of Louth 1782-1795; lessee of the tolls of Louth Navigation Canal, towards the construction of which he had subscribed £500 (£30,000 today) twenty years earlier; he had 15 children by his wife Elizabeth nee Thoroton]	£50	(£3,000)
Gilbert Caldecot [of Lincoln; racehorse owner]	£50	(£3,000)
Willoughby Wood [Thoresby House, South Thoresby and owner of most of the parish; son-in-law of Sir John Thorold (below); Gentleman of the King's Privy Chamber; died 1807]	£50	(£3,000)
Revd Edward Walls [Boothby Hall, Welton le Marsh; Lincoln Longwool tup breeder; later critic of Sir Joseph Banks and drainage of the East Fen]	£50	(£3,000)
Revd Reynold Gideon Bouyer [Willoughby; Secretary (almost certainly) of the Society for the Promotion of Industry]	£50	(£3,000)
Thomas Livesey [Stourton Hall]	£50	(£3,000)
Samuel Dashwood [Well Hall, near Alford]	£50	(£3,000)
Charles Chaplin [1759-1816; Blankney; nephew of Charles Chaplin of Tathwell]	£50	(£3,000)
Sir John Thorold [Syston Park, near Grantham]	£50	(£3,000)
Dr Humphrey Sibthorp [Canwick Hall near Lincoln; Doctor of Physic]	£50	(£3,000)
Revd Dr Francis Willis [1718-1807; Greatford, near Stamford; physician who treated the 'madness' of King George III 1788-89]	£50	(£3,000)
Dr Charles Marshall Clarke [1755-1830; Thorpe Hall, South Elkington; Doctor of Physic; son of Dr Charles Clarke – see Corporation members above)	£40	(£2,400)
Robert Vyner [1717-1799; Gautby Hall; (son of Robert Vyner 1685-1777); MP for Lincolnshire; stepfather to Charles Anderson Pelham, first Lord Yarborough through marriage to Eleanor, widow of Francis Anderson. Owner of land in Withern and Authorpe; his cousin Revd Dr Robert Vyner (1753-1804) was Rector of Authorpe]	£30	(£1,800)
William Burrell Massingberd [South Ormsby Hall; died 1802, age 84]	£30	(£1,800)

William Welby [Denton Manor; died 1790]	£25	(£1,500)
Thomas Chaplin [1756-1804; Tathwell: eldest son of Charles Chaplin of Tathwell; sheep breeder]	£20	(£1,200)
Henry Cracroft Marshall [1759-1789: Theddlethorpe Hall; Customs & Excise Officer]	£20	(£1,200)
Revd John Emeris [1766-1797; Headmaster Louth Grammar School]	£20	(£1,200)
John Ansell [North Ormsby Abbey]	£20	(£1,200)
Revd John Goodwin [Vicar of Utterby but, like other local clergy, living in Louth where the social life was]	£20	(£1,200)
Mrs Elizabeth Lee [Bath; widow of Robert Lee, (d.1779) Warden of Louth 1776 and after whom Lee Street in Louth is named]	£20	(£1,200)
Thomas Phillips [Attorney; Louth Town Clerk]	£20	(£1,200)
Bentley Bennett [Keddington]	£20	(£1,200)
George Maddison [Stainton le Vale; died 1810, aged 100]	£10 10s	(£630)
Revd Edward Brackenbury [Skendleby]	£5	(£300)
William Brackenbury [Halton Holegate]	£5	(£300)
Revd William Massingberd [South Ormsby]	£5 5s	(£315)
	£1, 540 15s	£92,445

The land measuring 68 yards by 53 yards (= approx three-quarters of an acre or a third of a hectare) cost £70 1s 1d (£4,203) and the building of 'the water mill and machine and fixing wheels and other necessary works' amounted to £1,470 13s 11d (£88,242).

The piece of land was at the east end of Wood's Close, with the river on the north and east, and Gabriel Neve's land on the south. The western limit of the plot was where James Street now makes a slight change in direction. Access was a short track from Ramsgate/Ramsgate Road (then the only way from the town to the canal) and a wooden bridge over the river (remember there was then no James Street).

Did the Corporation realise that part of the rest of Wood's Close upstream of the factory would be flooded by the mill dam? However, the Corporation was quite astute: they subscribed £300 and got back just over £70 by selling the land to give access to the building site.

In the absence of further documentary evidence about the actual building of the manufactory, but with the aid of engravings, paintings and maps, using information about the building of the dyehouse and hot-press at the Riverhead in 1787 (see chapter The Stuff Ball) and the *Universal British Directory* 1792, together with looking at the Indenture of 9 April 1791 which contains the name of Adam Eve, it is possible to deduce or confirm the sequence of events of the first five formative years of the factory.

Building work must have started in spring 1786, the subscriptions having been made by then. The Corporation had taken the initiative in inviting subscriptions, through the Town Clerk Thomas Phillips and perhaps with the help of Gideon Bouyer. It is interesting that the total of subscriptions (£1,540 15s) was exactly the cost of buying the land and building the factory, which implies that the Corporation had obtained quotations from a builder and a millwright based on plans already drawn up. There is no record of who drew up the plans, but it is logical to believe that it must have been someone with experience of the layout of a spinning factory. Did the advice come from Richard Arkwright (with whom Bouyer had communicated in 1784), or was it a factory owner merchant or manufacturer from Leeds? Such men would be known to wool growers and staplers of Lincolnshire, to Louth businessmen buying products from Yorkshire – trading vessels plied regularly from Nell's wharf at the Riverhead to Leeds and Wakefield, and to Sir Joseph Banks whose advice would doubtless have been sought. Certainly three Leeds merchants did eventually become involved in the running of the Louth factory.

A Louth carpet design, 1865
(see pages 136-137)

Who built the factory? It must have been William Dunn – he had supplied bricks for the Louth Canal twenty years earlier, went on to build the dyehouse and hot-press at the Riverhead and was the only builder listed in the 1792 directory. The bricks and pantiles came from a local source, but it is not known exactly where, and there are no clues on Thomas Espin's map of the town in 1808. It is worth noting that there was a tax on bricks, raised in 1783 (and not repealed until 1850) to help pay the costs of the War of American Independence. William Dunn employed his son James and others as bricklayers. John and Thomas Coulam were carpenter/joiners (the early days of a reputable firm still in business in Louth over eighty year later), and Thomas King was the only glazier listed in the directory.

The indentures use the term 'mill machine' as an alternative to 'building', and then go on to identify 'the water wheel pitt [sic] wheel the upright shaft and the horizontal shaft'. In other words one wheel in one of the two arches on the southern side, the northern arch being for the bypass sluice. The wheels and shafts were probably made by one of two millwrights in Louth at that time – Thomas Marrows and William Scargal. The water wheel would have been made of oak with wrought iron buckets or paddles. Later replacement wheels would have been cast iron, and almost certainly by John Sanderson of Louth. The T W Wallis paintings of 1897 show one wheel in the central arch, and to one side a wheel which had been taken out of the southern arch. (See page 66) The width of the first wheel was 8-10 feet with a diameter of 12-16 feet, low breast shot, with an efficiency of 50-60 percent.

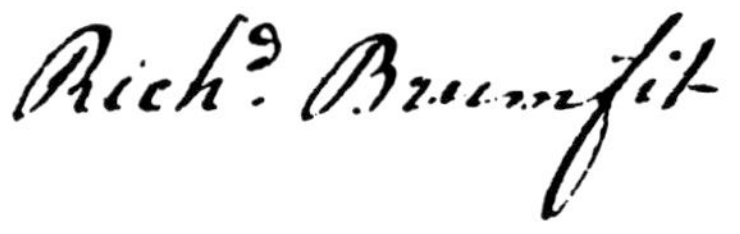

On the same axle as the water wheel, and inside the building, was the pit wheel or wallower with iron cog gears to transfer the power to the iron upright shaft. This in turn transferred power to the iron horizontal shaft in the upper floor used to drive any machinery by rope belts (leather belting came later). If such rope belts were made in Louth, there were two ropers – Elmit and Austin Brown, and William Oliver. However, it would be at least a year after completion of the building before there were any spinning or weaving machines to be driven by water power.

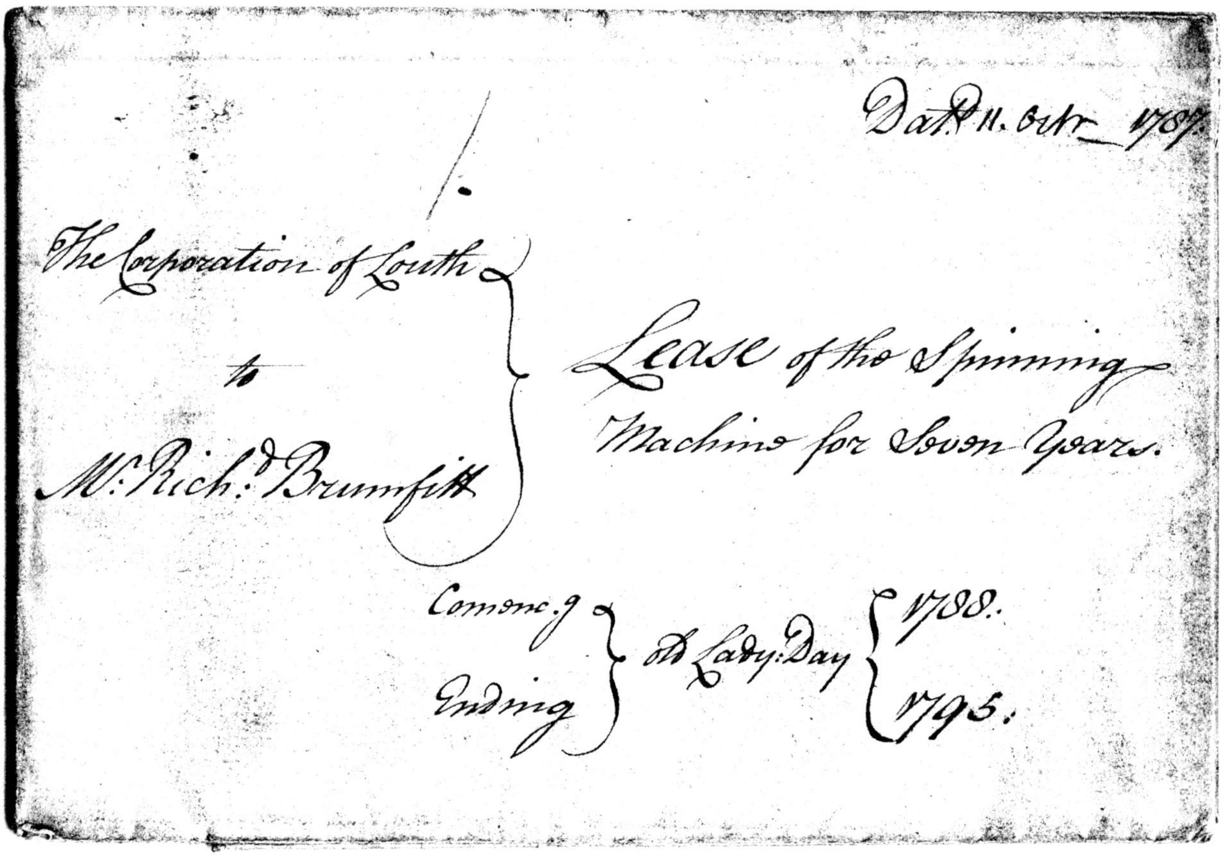

Dat:d 11. Octr 1787.

The Corporation of Louth
to
Mr Richd: Brumfitt

Lease of the Spinning Machine for Seven Years.

Commenc:g } at Lady Day { 1788.
Ending } { 1795.

Examination of the lease of 11 October 1787 of the factory 'for the purpose of spinning long and coarse Sheep's Wool by Machinery' by the Corporation to Richard Brumfit (spelt with two ts in the lease but the signature has only one t) identifies that it had been in the tenure of Thomas Clarke but was 'now unoccupied'. Clarke (b.1759) was the second son of Dr Charles Clarke, a member of the Corporation and Warden in 1786, and his tenure seems to have been an interim arrangement. Richard Brumfit was a Leeds carpet manufacturer. Under the terms of the seven year full repairing lease at an annual rent of £20 (£1,200 today), payable half-yearly in April and October, not including rates, he had to install necessary spinning, weaving and other machinery and remove or sell it at the end of the lease. It specified twelve looms or weaving frames (no mention of spinning), and that the carpets had to be made of long and coarse sheep's wool *only*. There was a clause which gave Brumfit the opportunity at the end of seven years to extend the lease for a further 14 years at an annual rent of £50. And there was also a get-out clause if he was not 'able to establish a Carpet Manufactory' within the first three years, provided he gave six months notice. In effect he had only two and a half years.

Having taken that action, the Corporation turned its attention to matters of financial management. On 17 October 1787 Sir Joseph Banks and Robert Vyner signed and sealed a 'Declaration of Trust to the Subscribers to ye Mill erected in Louth for the purpose of Spinning Sheep's Wool by Machinery'; that is they would act on behalf of the subscribers, the money having already been spent on building the factory. The arrangement would be administered by Town Clerk Thomas Phillips, with payment of a nominal ffee [sic] farm (ground) rent of two shillings and six pence (25p) payable to the Corporation. The parchment document was signed at Horncastle in the presence of Richard Clitherow, attorney, and his clerk Richard Babington (Horncastle being the more convenient place for Banks and Vyner).

Sir Joseph Banks

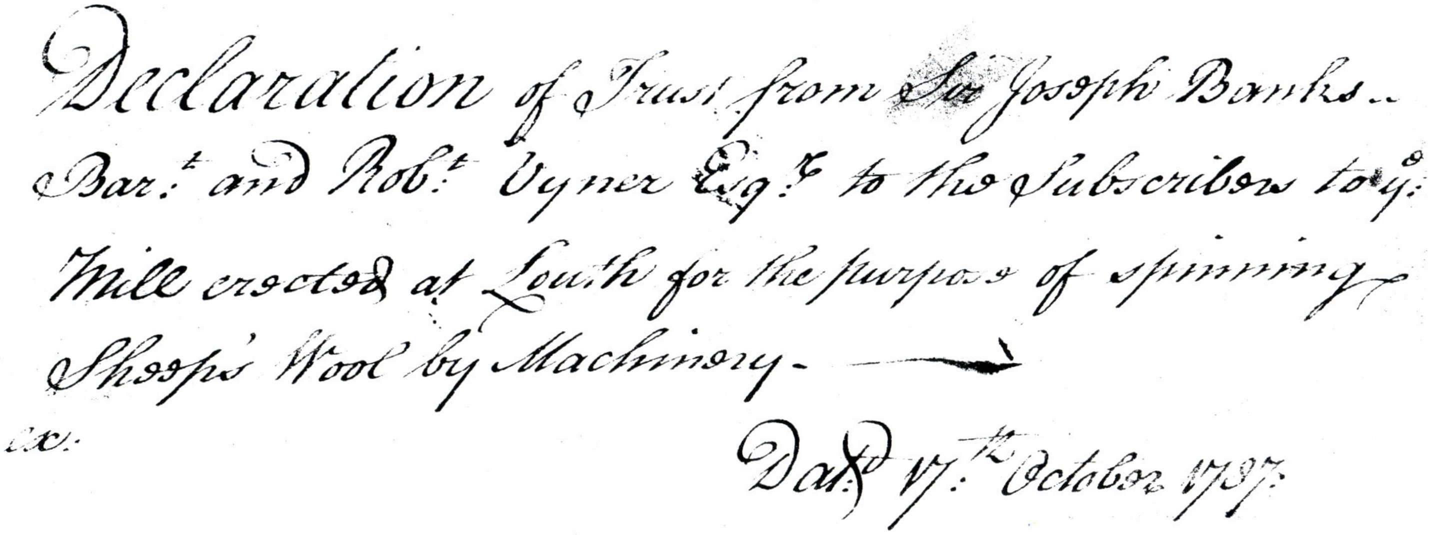

Declaration of Trust from Sir Joseph Banks Bar.t and Rob.t Vyner Esq.r to the Subscribers to y: Mill erected at Louth for the purpose of spinning Sheep's Wool by Machinery

ex:

Dat.d 17.th October 1787

Brumfit installed scribbling (coarse carding or teasing) and carding and other machinery. There is no record of whether the latter were weaving looms, or of the workforce, or if in fact any carpets were made (unlikely). It would seem that he was struggling and likely to take advantage of the get-out clause in his lease. According to Arthur Young in his *General View of the Agriculture of Lincolnshire* for the Board of Agriculture (1799) there had been 'great difficulties' and 'the man broke' – that was Brumfit.

It is clear however that Adam Eve was taking a close interest in the factory, awaiting an opportunity to take it over, the businessman in him sensing the growing demand for locally produced and reasonably priced carpets (see chapter The Carpets). It was to take ten years for Adam to gain full control, and it started with negotiations with Brumfit which led to Adam taking over the lease under Articles of Agreement on 3 June 1790.

Articles of Agreement had made covenanted concluded and fully agreed upon this third Day of June one thousand seven hundred and ninety Between Richard Brumfitt of Leeds in the County of York Carpet Manufacturer of the one part and Adam Eve of Louth in the County of Lincoln Mercer and Draper of the other part as follows

It was a bold move. Adam must have felt sufficiently confident with the success of his shop, together with the £1,500 his wife had brought into the marriage four years earlier. Not even the bad weather of 1790 deterred him, when the previous winter's snow did not finally melt until August. Under the terms of the Agreement, Adam bought the carding and other machines for £180 (£10,000 today), but Brumfit kept and removed any wool and woollen yarn. Adam was astute therefore in making the agreement in June, the time of clipping (shearing) when supply of raw wool would be readily available; for example it was said that Charles Chaplin of Tathwell had all his wool spun into yarn for carpeting – but where was it spun?

Chaplin's Watermill at Hubbard's Hills, built about 1788 as a cloth mill for spinning wool.
(Painted by John Mogford in 1867)

In fact, Chaplin, in addition to his subscription for the Louth factory, had aspirations of his own with watermills at Raithby and Hallington for his wool. At the same time as the Louth factory was being built Chaplin created his own watermill in Hallington parish at the northern end of Hubbard's Hills. Valuation for the Royal Exchange Fire Insurance Policy of 14 February 1788 records a water cloth mill (£100), dyehouse (£40) and dwelling house (£200). When it was for sale in 1802, the advertisement in the *Lincoln, Rutland & Stamford Mercury* noted that 'the stream is very powerful, has a large fall and might be advantageously employed in spinning wool by machinery'. By that time Charles Chaplin had died (1795) but the property remained in Chaplin ownership (until 1905). It had been converted to a corn grinding mill and continued as such until damaged by the flood 29 May 1920. The property was purchased by the Pahud Trustees in 1907 to form part of the Hubbard's Hills gift to the town of Louth.

Turning again to Arthur Young's *General View of the Agriculture of Lincolnshire* (1799), we find that 'Mr Chaplin established a machine at Raithby near Louth, a Big Ben for combing wool, invented by Mr Edmund Cartwright; he lost a great deal of money; a fire engine (steam engine) there for it; all now gone and done with'. Valuation for the Sun Fire Insurance Policy 1 March 1792 records a wool spinning mill with 'going gears and machinery' and a house £4,500, utensils and stock £2,000, workshop and offices £700, steam engine £600 and six cottages £300: total £8,100 (£470,000 today). In other words, even allowing for any difference between building cost and insurance valuation, Chaplin's outlay on the Raithby mill was something like four times the cost of the Louth factory!

The workforce was to include children, and an advertisement was placed in the *Lincoln, Rutland & Stamford Mercury:* 'Wanted several children. They are taken (with a certificate from the Parish) from Eight Years of Age to Thirteen for five years. They are Brought up (with great Attention to their Morals and Manners) to spin the growth of the country, which has already contributed to the advance of Wool. Any parish officers or persons with large families having children to provide for, may place them there immediately, to great Advantage; and may at any time see the children and the Manner in which they are kept and managed – No premium is required. They must be well clothed, and will be returned so. Such as are diligent and attentive to the Business will be kept in employment after the Expiration of Five Years. A Sunday School is kept for Children, they must all attend Church on Sunday. Apply to Mr Chaplin, Raithby Mill'.

Doubtless the intention was for the moral and religious care of the children to be responsibility of the Rector of Raithby, Revd Robert Chaplin; he was the third son of Charles, was also Vicar of Tathwell, where he lived, and Minister at Haugham.

The watermill, steam engine and cottages were along the east side of the beck downstream from the road bridge at Raithby. The enterprise was shortlived, the mill being advertised for sale in the *Lincoln, Rutland & Stamford Mercury* in August 1799: 'To be sold at Raithby mill, near Louth. A large waterwheel 25ft diameter and 4ft 6ins breadth, with wrought iron bucket plates 4ft 2ins long and 15ins deep. Also a wheel of 16ft diameter with two rows of iron cogs (the pit wheel). The wheels are both made of the best oakwork and are very little the worse for wear. The wheels have never been exposed to the water. Apply to Mr Farr at Raithby mill'. No wonder Arthur Young wrote 'he [Charles Chaplin] lost a great deal of money' – in the failed enterprise at Raithby, leaving his sons to try to recoup something by sale of the property. It is most likely that there was no buyer, and that the buildings were taken down and the materials sold.

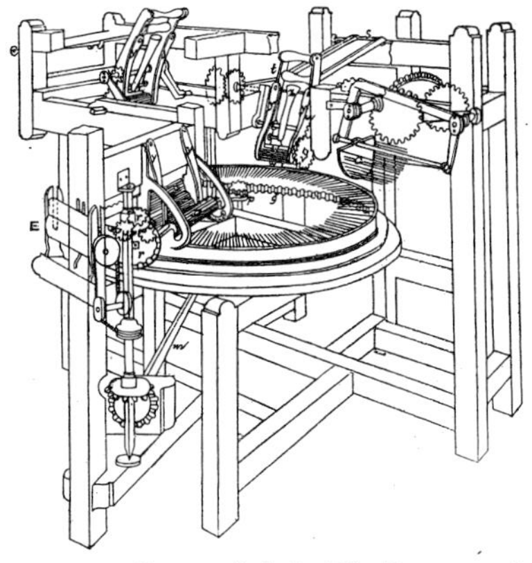

Cartwright's Big Ben wool combing machine installed by Chaplin at Raithby.

The Big Ben wool combing machine was invented by Revd Dr Edmund Cartwright (1743-1823). He studied at Oxford and wrote poetry, took Holy Orders and was a curate in Derbyshire and Leicestershire. In 1785 he patented a power loom and built a spinning and weaving factory at Doncaster after inheriting property there from his wife's family. He then patented the wool combing machine (1790-92), a circular revolving principal comb and clearing combs with draw off rollers. The feeder roller to the principal comb was operated by the action of a crank lasher; this movement suggested that of a pugilist – hence the name 'Big Ben' after a celebrated prize fighter.

Doncaster organised a procession to commemorate the 4th century Christian martyr Bishop Blaize, the patron saint of woolcombers, which generated a poem with the lines:

Come all ye master combers, and hear of our Big Ben,
He'll comb more wool in one day than fifty of your men.

Chaplin heard about it and ordered one for his Raithby mill but, as elsewhere, it did not prove capable of combing wool as effectively as by hand. It would be some years before a satisfactory machine was built. Cartwright claimed that his Big Ben could be worked by an overlooker and ten children – which would explain Chaplin's advertisement for children.

Meanwhile and by contrast Adam Eve continued to be optimistic, rather more practical, and determined to make a go of the Louth factory. Using his business connections in Yorkshire he formed a partnership with two Leeds merchants – John Cookson and Joseph Fawcett, and negotiated a new 21-year lease of the factory, land and use of the river from Sir Joseph Banks and Robert Vyner which was signed and sealed on 9 April 1791. Under the terms of the lease they could erect other buildings if required 'for the carrying on of the trade or business of spinning carding or manufacturing long and coarse Sheep's Wool ... and not for any other purpose whatsoever'. The annual rent had gone up to £77 1s (£4,200 today). It is believed that Adam and his partners called themselves the Louth Spinning Mill Company; later it was Adam Eve & Co.

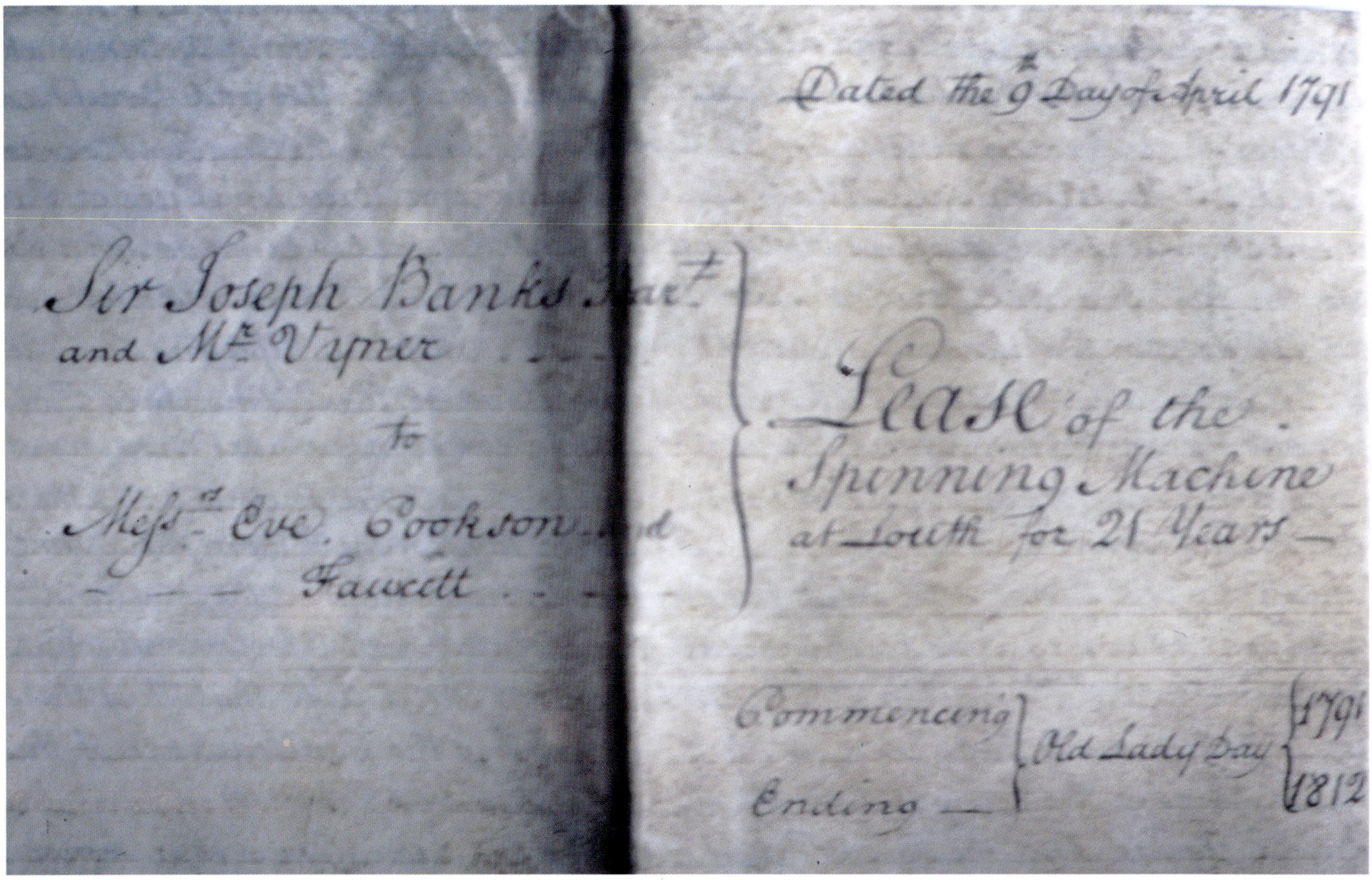
Dated the 9th Day of April 1791

Sir Joseph Banks Bart and Mr Vyner to Messrs Eve, Cookson and Fawcett

Lease of the Spinning Machine at Louth for 21 Years

Commencing / Ending — Old Lady Day — 1791 / 1812

When John Byng (later Lord Torrington) was in Louth on Saturday 19 July that year (1791), he visited Adam's shop and his companion bought 'a piece of Lincolnshire Stuff'. Their guide was Dr Samuel Carter Pettener (1748 – 1831), apothecary and surgeon who lived in Kelsey House, Mercer Row (now Peter Rhodes electrical appliances), a member of the Corporation and Warden seven times. Members of the Corporation were well known to Adam, and his aim was already to gain full control of the factory. The following year (1792) he began buying out the subscribers or shareholders: the first were Thomas Phillips, Town Clerk, and Revd John Goodwin. Vicar of Utterby, £20 each.

The next year (1793) he paid Thomas Chaplin, by that time at Somersby, £20 for his share and ten guineas to George Maddison (Stainton le Vale) for his, and was able to negotiate reduced amounts with William Burrell Massingberd (South Ormsby) five guineas for his £30 share, and Revd William Massingberd four guineas for his five guineas. Total nearly £80 (about £4,300 today). The signed and sealed parchment assignments for the payment made in 1792 and 1793 are in the Eve & Ranshaw archive.

Thomas Chaplin Esq.re & others

to

Mr. Adam Eve

Assignment of three Subscriptions to the Spinning Machine./

Dated 27th Novem.r 1793.

The factory was still accessed only by a track from Ramsgate. Moreover the only route between town and canal was by Eastgate, Ramsgate and Ramsgate Road. There can be no doubt that Adam was influential in the Corporation's decision in 1793 to lease the remainder of Wood's Close to the builder James Dunn on the understanding that he laid out £1,000 (about £50,000 today) to build the 'new intended road from Padehole [now Northgate] to the Navigation'. That involved demolishing buildings on Northgate to lay out what is now Eve Street (more evidence of the Adam influence) and the line of James Street with the slight change of direction where it joined the former track near the mill. The other evidence of Adam's influence was the building of Ivy House for him to rent on the south side of the new street, the closest he could get to 'his' factory. Ivy House, a substantial property in its own grounds was the most prominent dwelling in the street. It was about status.

Tho.s Chaplin

Thomas Espin's town plan of 1808 (page 33) shows the properties built by Dunn on James Street, including Charles Court. There were three storey buildings with a single pitch roof from front to back on the north side (see image from the Louth Panorama), at least one of which is reputed to have been a barracks for Volunteer Yeomanry during the Napoleonic Wars. There were also designed gardens, particularly those extending to the mill dam. Just west of the mill the plan shows a separate garden area with a central circular feature. This was the site of the public fountain, with wall, steps, stonework, rail and posts, as described in the Schedule to the 1825 *Act for Paving, Lighting, Watching, Cleansing, Regulating and otherwise Improving the Town and Parish of Louth.* The fountain was where townsfolk could go on a Sunday afternoon stroll to marvel at the largest commercial building in Louth – the 'Palace of Industry'. The Corporation were still the biggest shareholders, and it was as much a show-off for them as it was for Adam.

'The Palace of Industry' in later years – about 1860

For the next two years Adam had to trim his sails and consider how best to run both shop and factory. He was not without competitor in the county, to judge from an entry in the *Lincoln Date Book* for June 1794: 'Manufactory of blankets, carpets, yarn etc at Brant Broughton. John Hubbert thinks it necessary to inform his friends and all who may please to encourage his manufactory that the summer season will afford an opportunity of exploiting their business, which induces him to request such as are inclined to send their wool will please to do so as soon as convenient'. The summer weather was bad in 1795, with the death of many new shorn sheep. And the following winter had hard frosts from 24 December to 14 February 1796.

In 1795 Adam paid Revd William Brackenbury (Halton Holegate) £4 for his £5 share and Revd John Emeris (Headmaster of the Grammar School) £17 for his £20 share. The same year Adam's younger brother William, who in his early teens had joined him in the shop, became a partner.

During 1796 Adam paid out £354 10s (£14,000 today): £16 10s for the £20 share of Bentley Bennett (Keddington), £4 for £5 share of Revd Edward Brackenbury (Skendleby), £40 for £50 share of Charles Chaplin of Blankney, £16 for £20 share of Mrs Elizabeth Lee (Bath), £40 for £50 share of Willoughby Wood (South Thoresby), £20 for £25 share of William Welby (Denton) paid to his son William Earle Welby, £40 for £50 share of Revd Edward Walls (Spilsby), and £16 for £20 share of Henry Cracroft Marshall (Theddlethorpe), paid to his brother William as Henry had died seven years earlier. He also paid £160 to Dr Charles Marshall Clarke (Thorpe Hall) for his £50 share and those he had acquired from Charles Chaplin of Tathwell (£50; he had died that year), and Sir Joseph Banks (£100). A composite Assignment was drawn up for the payments made in 1795 and 1796, with signed receipts on the back.

Two years later Robert Vyner let Adam have his £30 share for £24, and Lord Yarborough (formerly Charles Anderson Pelham) his £90 share for a nominal five shillings and in exchange for an 'Oyster Scalp or ground and fishery' at Cleethorpes which Adam had just purchased from Lord Middleton. What was that all about – had Adam seen the chance of a 'profit' on the deal? And what would his Lordship want with an oyster bed on the foreshore at Cleethorpes, then a small fishing village with a few summer seabathers? Perhaps as his own source of oysters to serve guests? It is interesting to note that witnessing the signatures to the Indenture for the deals with Yarborough, Vyner (signed by his executor son also Robert – which means that he could not have signed until the next year because his father did not die until 1799), and William Marshall, executor for his deceased elder brother Henry, was John Campbell, then a 16-year old apprentice in Adam's shop (see chapter The Shop).

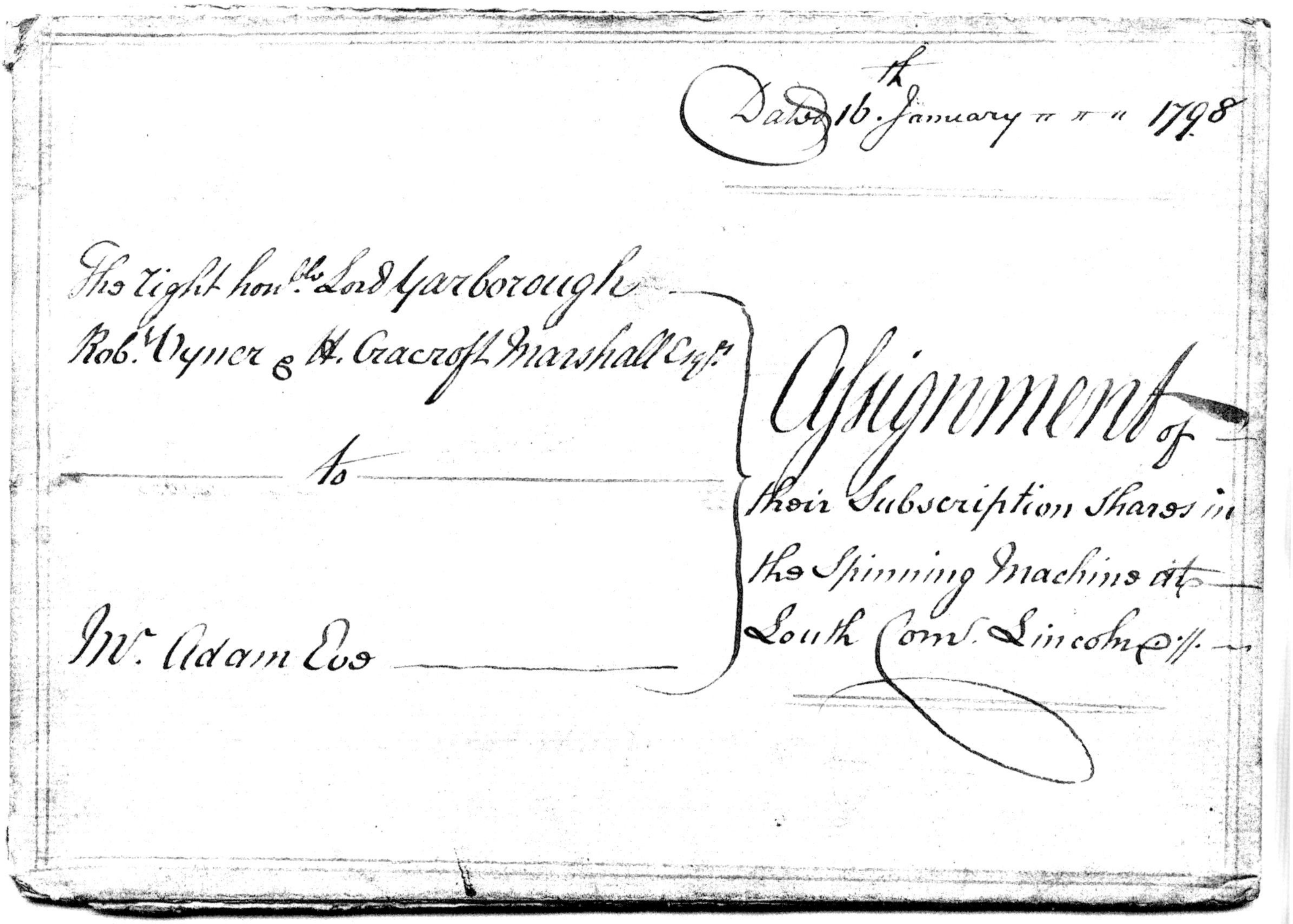
Dated 16th January " " " 1798

The right honble Lord Yarborough
Robt. Vyner & H. Gracroft Marshall Esqrs
to
Mr. Adam Eve

Assignment of their Subscription Shares in the Spinning Machine at Louth Com. Lincoln

Adam may seem to have been a successful wheeler-dealer, but there are indications of difficulties in 1798/99. In May 1798 he had to borrow £200 from his brother John (still at Scartho) and a further £100 in May 1799 – neither of which were repaid until 1825. These were in the form of IOUs on scraps of paper, now in the Eve & Ranshaw archive along with other IOUs as we shall see. Then in October 1799 Adam's partnership with John Cookson and Joseph Fawcett was 'dissolved by mutual consent' and a notice to that effect posted in the *London Gazette*. Adam wanted to do things his way.

Factory workers and working conditions will be discussed in the next chapter, but the first glimpses came in 1799 when John Cragg of Threekingham, land valuer, enclosure commissioner and compiler of information about Lincolnshire, visited Louth. 'We went to see Mr Eaves [sic] woollen manufactory. The machines were very curious to see worked, there were about 20 machines in two buildings which carded, spun and reeled the wool, almost all turned by water, they employ many children and other persons to manage them, the smell of the oil and wool I thought very unpleasant. We afterwards went to see the carpet manufactory which is not far off. We saw several looms employed in weaving those curious pieces of furniture'.

The 'two buildings' implies a division within the factory and the use of two waterwheels, confirmed by the sketch plan of 1852. It is interesting to note carpets referred to as furniture, but what does 'the carpet factory, which is not far off' mean? In the Schedule to the 1825 Act mentioned above, there is a section about the north-west corner of the west weaving room of the carpet factory on the south side of James Street projecting 2ft 4ins into the footway. Those fragments of information and the typical industrial-type multi-pane windows at two levels still extant identify the location of the weaving rooms, with hand-operated looms and then open to the roof, as now dwellings Nos 1-4 The Mews towards the eastern end of James Street. They were built adjoining the house next to the river which was for the overseer of the factory, William Foggitt, and probably just before the rest of James Street was laid out, that is about 1792.

The former carpet weaving rooms on James Street. The white house at the end, next to the river, was that of the factory overseer, and later that of owner Charles Paddison.

Returning to Adam's buying out the subscribers, 1801 was the key year when he was able to pay the Corporation their £300, which gave him the controlling interest and made the lease, which still had eleven years to run, redundant. Also in 1801 he paid John Ansell (North Ormsby) £17 for his £20 share, Samuel Dashwood (Well) the full £50, as also to Gideon Bouyer – but not acknowledged until 1817 (!) from Durham where he went when he left Lincolnshire in 1810.

Other payments Adam made, for which there is no date documentation, were £100 to the Duke of Ancaster, and £50 each to Gilbert Caldecot (Lincoln), Thomas Livesey (Stourton Hall), Dr Humphrey Sibthorp (Canwick), Sir John Thorold (Syston Park) and to Revd Dr Francis Willis (Greatford).

That left Lord Gwydir (formerly Sir Peter Burrell) who required interest on his subscription and Adam could not/did not pay him £130 until August 1816. The parchment Indenture for that payment records The Right Honourable Peter Lord Gwydir, Baron Gwydir of Gwydir in the County of Denbigh, Deputy Grand Chamberlain of England, and Adam Eve, Merchant, and the original subscription share of £100 (not £90 as on the original document of 17 October 1787) with the interest due (of £30). This was the only buy-out on which Adam paid an interest; there must have been some hard bargaining. The Indenture was signed, including receipt of £130, Gwydir, and witnessed by his two valets Joseph Blades and John Donmall. Attached to the Indenture are two slips of paper, instructions from Adam to pay Lord Gwydir £100 and £30, dated a month before the payment would be due, to Messrs Cook Townsend & Co, Crown Court, Cheapside, London (his city bankers). In Louth he banked with Claypon, Garfit and Claypon, Mercer Row (now Lloyds TSB). The London connection suggests the extent to which Adam had built up his business, including export of carpets to Europe, particularly after the final defeat of Napoleon in 1815, and to America. According to Joseph Noble's *Gazeteer of Lincolnshire* 1833, Adam's carpets were 'of extensive note throughout Europe'.

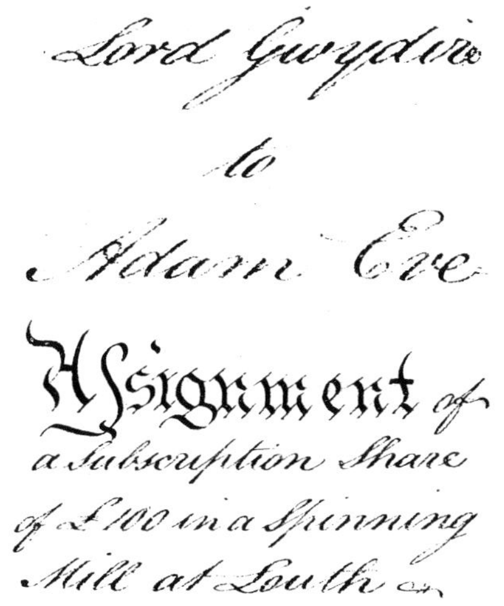
Lord Gwydir
to
Adam Eve
Assignment of
a Subscription Share
of £100 in a Spinning
Mill at Louth &c.

The only invoice known for supply of carpets by Adam was to Hyde & Oldrid (now Oldrids) of Boston in 1804. For manufactured goods such as carpets, transport was by stage carrier on turnpikes (now A16) to Boston. In the 1820s the journey to London took a week; Gibberson & Co's stage wagon left the Bluestone Inn, Louth on Saturday mornings at three o'clock, and arrived at the White Bear on Basinghall Street, London in the early morning of the following Saturday. In the 1830s Joseph Cash of Louth was a Common Stage Carrier to Spilsby, Horncastle, Grimsby, Hull and London, and in the 1840s Robert Smith of Louth ran a daily service to Grimsby, Spilsby, Boston and Horncastle, and longer distance services to Liverpool, Manchester, Halifax, Bradford, Huddersfield, Dewsbury, Wakefield, Leeds, York, Darlington, Selby, Hull and London. There was also water carriage from Louth Riverhead to Leeds and Wakefield, but that would be for bulk raw materials; for example wool at four pence per tod in the 1820s.

Robert Smith's stage wagon, 1840s

1805 was a pivotal year for Adam: he decided to pass the running of the shop to his brother William (then 29) and concentrate on the mill and factory. In April their partnership was dissolved 'by mutual consent': the notice posted in the *London Gazette* said that any debts due to the partnership should be paid to William, and that he was to meet any demands due from the partnership. Later that year William married Amelia Leech from Hampshire, and entered into a partnership with John Campbell (23) who had come from Howden as a young teenage apprentice and later married Adam's niece Elizabeth Clarke. With John they traded as Eve & Campbell. (The story of their successful partnership is told in The Shop chapter). A surviving billhead of 1815: Bt of Eve & Campbell Wholesale and Retail Woollen & Linen Drapers Grocers etc and showing an image of the Carpet & Blanket Manufactory suggests a continuing business link with Adam and his factory. The bill was for 12 pairs of blankets at 18 shillings a pair and 6 double rugs at 11s 6d each, supplied to the Louth House of Correction. For information about blanket making see The Workers chapter.

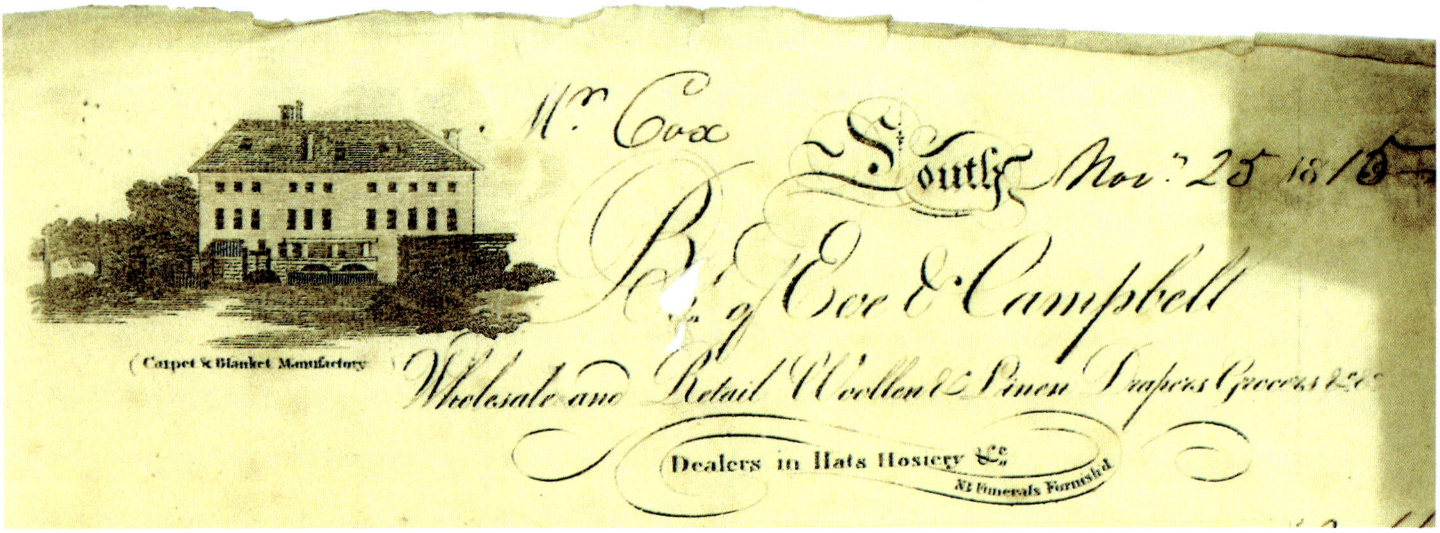

The 1823 Valuation records William with a house, stable, granary and garden on Northgate and owning three plots of land totalling 12-13 acres; and the 1826 directory lists him living on Foster's Terrace. He was also active in local works: he and Adam had shares in the Louth Gas Company and they were both on the committee organising the balloon ascent when the gas works opened in 1826, and in 1828 both were Commissioners for the Act to improve the canal. William died in 1829. When Adam died two years later he made bequests to the children of his brother John and sister Ann, but not to those of his brother William. One wonders why.

However, it seems that Adam, having invested in the weaving rooms and looms and buying out shareholders, was encountering financial difficulties in running the factory on his own. In May 1805 Adam had to borrow again from his farming brother John, this time for a larger sum, £400, and again not repaid until 1825. In fact John lent Adam a total of £700 (the equivalent of about £27,000 today) for a period of 25 years! Also in May 1805 Adam and one William Parkin borrowed £100 from William Crossgill, and in December 1806 Adam gave an IOU to his brother-in-law Richard Clarke, draper at Market Rasen, for £500 (£20,000 today).

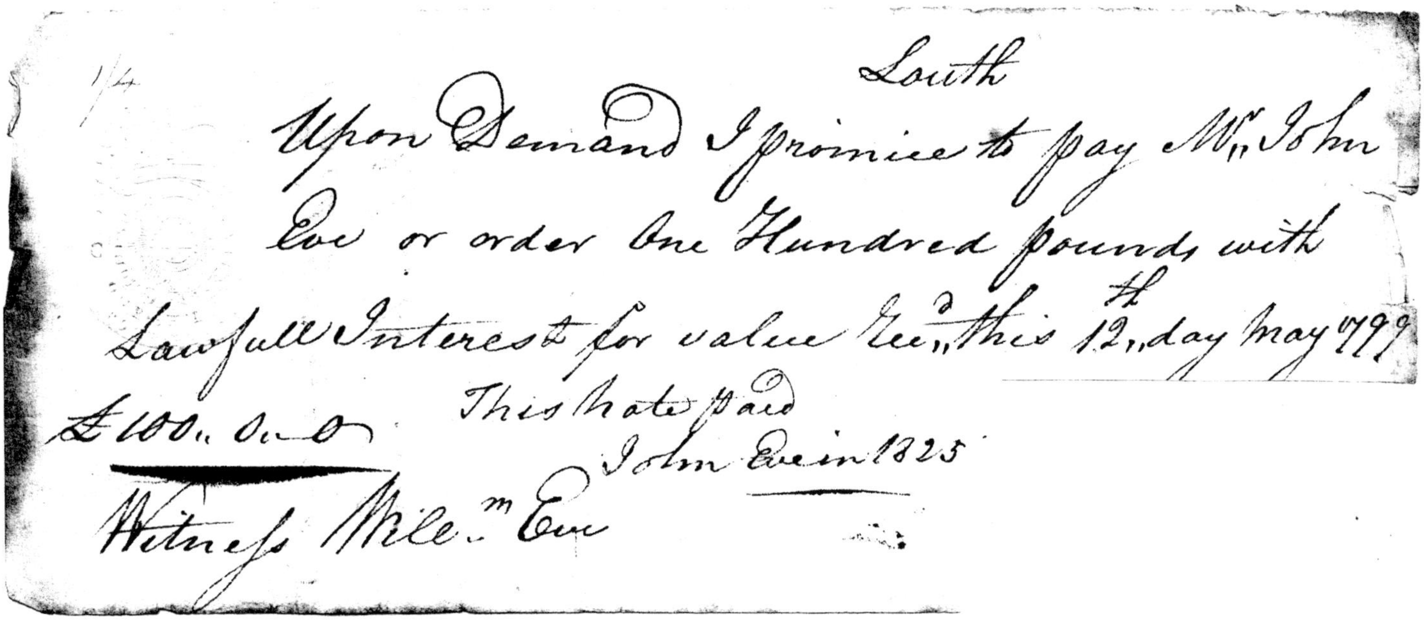
1/4

Louth

Upon Demand I promise to pay Mr John Eve or order One Hundred pounds with Lawfull Interest for value Recd this 12th day May 1799

£100..0..0 This Note paid John Eve in 1825

Witness Willm Eve

Judging from the promissory notes in the Eve & Ranshaw archive, 1809 and 1810 were again years when Adam was juggling his finances. In July 1809 he borrowed £90 (about £3,000 today) from his carpet factory overseer William Foggitt. A year later he repaid £10 with interest, but not until 1819 did he repay another £10. What salary or remuneration, one wonders, was he paying Foggitt? By the time of the next repayment of £10 in September 1825, Foggitt had died and it was received by his widow Mary. There were further repayments of £5 in October and December, the balance of £50 having been paid in November.

Adam's second promissory note to his brother John

In January 1810 Adam repaid, with interest, the loan from William Crossgill, but only with the aid of a loan of £50 from John Holland (he ran the corn-grinding mill on Bridge Street) who in turn needed a payment of that amount from William Parkin! Then on 13 May Adam lent £100 to his book-keeper William Farrow, a near neighbour on James Street; after Adam's death he became a land and road surveyor and lived on Walkergate (Queen Street). On 25 May Adam and William Holland made an agreement to indemnify each other to repay Edward Croft £200 (£7,000 today) in association with William Parkin. The book-keeping for those IOUs on top of income and expenditure for the shop and the factory (no records surviving except stocktaking for the shop) suggest that William Farrow earned the bequest of £100 in Adam's will – even then it was subject to any repayments still due on the loan!

Book-keeper William Farrow's promissory note to Adam Eve

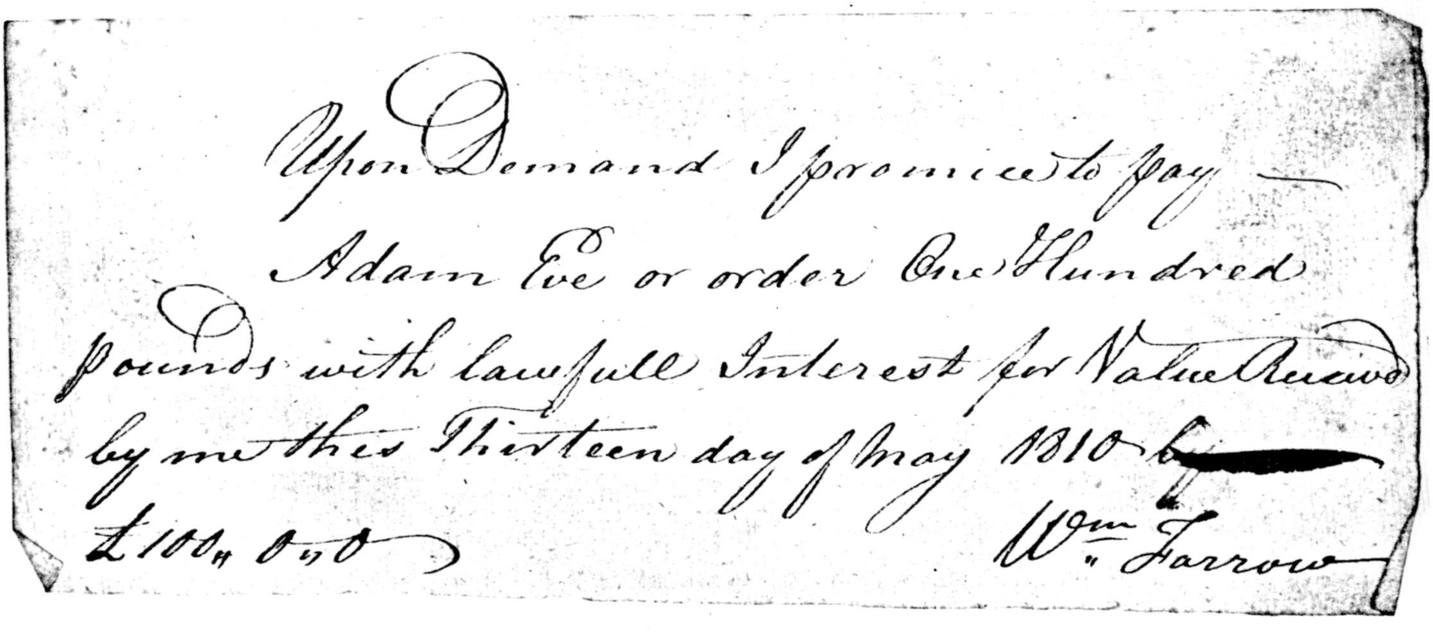
Upon Demand I promise to pay Adam Eve or order One Hundred pounds with lawfull Interest for Value Received by me this Thirteen day of May 1810

£100..0..0 Wm Farrow

What were all those deals about and why were they necessary? What seems curious about them is the dilatory way Adam repaid his own overseer, and that the amounts were relatively small compared to the large bequests he was to make to his illegitimate/adopted sons in 1831.

A likely explanation of Adam's financial dealings is to be found in what one of his carpet weavers, John Green (see next chapter), wrote in his 'autobiography' about 'trade being very uncertain and subject to continual change' and that some weavers had 'little more than half employment'. That was in 1815. Carpet weavers were piece workers, there were seasonal fluctuations (perhaps depending on wool supplies after clipping) and slack periods with fewer orders, and perhaps a weaver might have to wait for dyeing a particular colour of yarn. The period 1816 to 1828 saw a marked increase in England's export of carpets to America, but little change in trade with Europe, despite the end of the Napoleonic Wars, and from 1828 to 1840 exports stagnated. For an explanation of factors affecting the later decline and demise of the Louth carpet factory see The Carpets chapter.

Phoenix Fire Insurance plaque which was on the carpet factory

Among the IOU slips in the Eve & Ranshaw archive is one for money owing to Adam: 'Memorandum I owe Mr A. Eve Thirty Nine Pounds for Rent due the 13th May 1815 by me ... Louth 28 Oct 1815' (all in Adam's handwriting) and signed with a strong literate hand William Swallow Evison. On the reverse is a note that £31 1s 6d had been paid and that £7 18s 6d 'remains due to A. Eve but Evison is Transported' (!) Evison is not on the published list of Lincolnshire convicts transported to Australia, so it leaves us with intriguing question marks.

Whilst Adam was turning the spinning mill into a commercial venture, the *Universal British Directory* (1792) had included the following under a description of Louth: 'A manufactory has lately been set up by a Society of Gentlemen for the employment of the poor in spinning jersey, which has been found of great service to many distressed families, and reflects much honour on the Revd R G Bouyer, the original promoter of it'. Gideon Bouyer left Lincolnshire for Durham in 1810 to become Vicar of Eglingham, but he had already been made Rector of Howick, Northumberland and Canon of Durham Cathedral in 1792. He became Archdeacon of Northumberland where he established at his own expense parochial libraries in every parish. He died in 1826, aged 84, and was buried in the Chapel of the Nine Altars in Durham Cathedral. Without Bouyer's concern for the poor, drive and philanthropy there might never have been the mill in Louth which Adam turned into a carpet factory and a profitable enterprise.

We have already noted (in the last chapter) connections with the Espins, Thomas (the teacher) and John (his younger brother) coming to Louth in 1790. Both were skilled topographical artists and surveyors. Thomas designed a new town hall (1795) to be built in the Market Place (but it never was) and produced a plan of the town in 1808. He and John travelled the county making drawings (1799-1800) for Louth-born Bartholomew Howlett to engrave for his *Views in the County of Lincoln* series. That of the ruins of Louth Park Abbey by John includes himself as the artist.

Sketching the ruins of Louth Park Abbey. Artist John Espin is seated on the left

Thomas never married, but John did (to Susanna Dalton in 1794), and at Enclosure John had nearly three acres of land on the north side of Holmes Lanes (High Holme Road). The first information we have of John's involvement, as a partner with Adam, in the factory is the year following the sudden death of John's wife in 1810. A notice in the *Lincoln, Rutland & Stamford Mercury* in June 1811 (clipping time) was addressed 'To the Growers of Wool: Messrs Eve and Espin beg leave to inform the farmers that they intend taking in at their manufactory in Louth, and give price agreeably to qualify – Those who will make them clean and good colour will have a price agreeably to Wakefield market. NB No other person is authorised to take in any on their account but at the above premises'.

Bales of wool on their way to the factory
(Depicted by William Brown on the Louth Panorama)

No evidence has emerged as to who was designing the carpets, but it is reasonable to suspect that John, as an artist, could have been as the benefit he brought to the partnership. When the partnership ended with John's death in January 1822, he was described as 'carpet manufacturer'. At that time Adam was 67, and his factory overseer had died about the same time, which implies that for his last eight or nine years Adam was running the factory himself. Certainly, in 1825, he obtained a patent for an improved method of flat-weaving (see The Carpets chapter).

The earliest image of the factory

The earliest image of the spinning mill, in fact the only one before installation of steam power and the addition of a chimney (in 1834), is on the Eve & Campbell billhead of 1815 (mentioned above), and shows the mill about twenty years after it was built, and still a greenfield site, noting the trees on the north side. The view is the upstream side, looking east. In the foreground is the mill dam, the bypass channel with vertical sluice gate and steps up to the level to operate it on the left, and debris grills across two arches – which implies two waterwheels. It is three storeys high, and the arrangement of the windows suggests vertical internal divisions; there also appear to be roof lights.

The plan of the building as depicted on the Enclosure Award map 1805 and Thomas Espin's plan of the town 1808 show an L-shaped building, labelled carpet factory, with eastern extension on the north side of the river: that was the drying shed. The wool was washed twice in the river, before spinning and after dyeing. When the weather was good the drying could be done on posts in the adjoining paddock, but at other times the shed was essential. Espin's map also shows the weaving rooms and overseer's house on the south side of James Street opposite the factory. (See page 33).

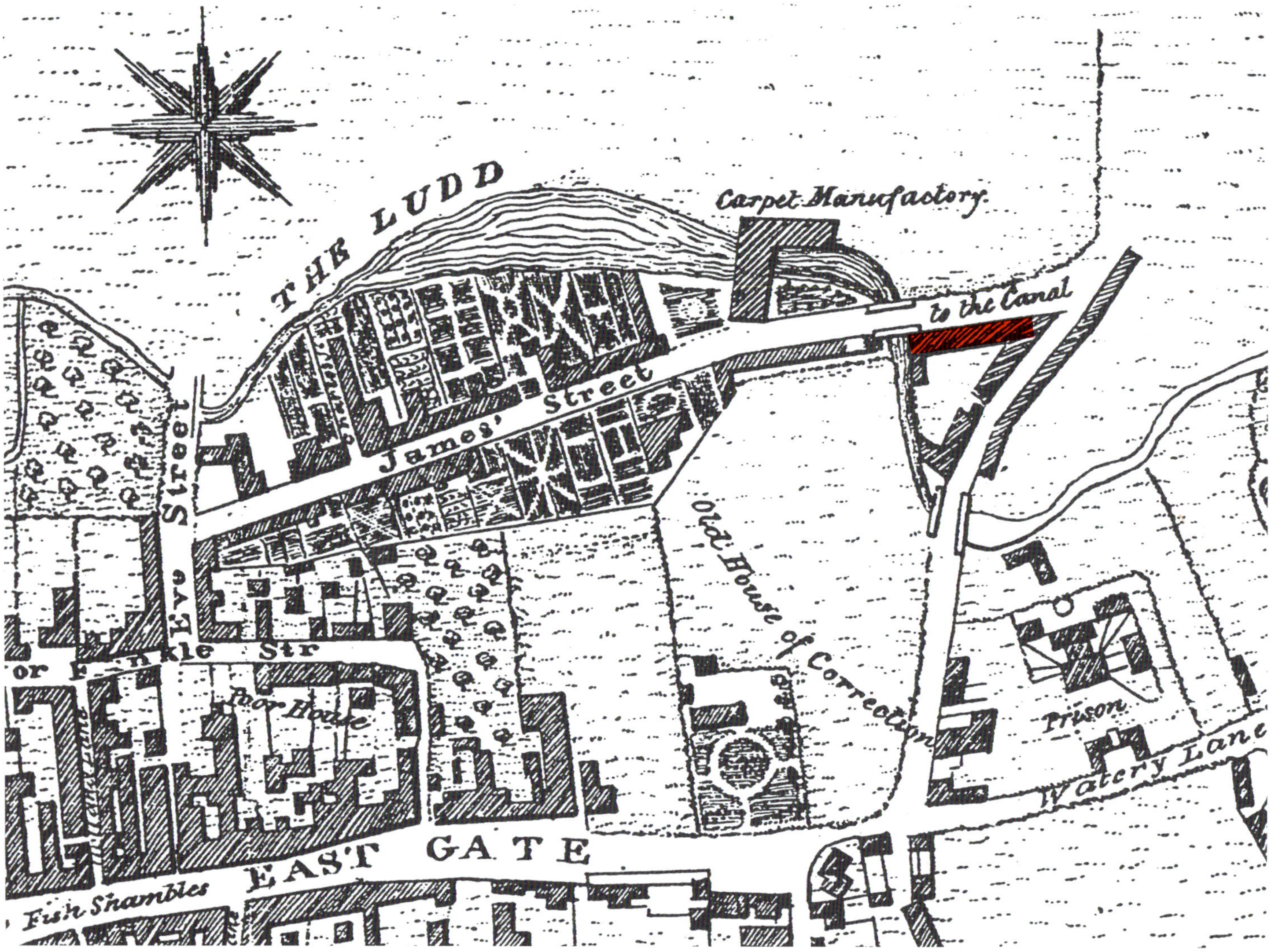

Part of Bayley's map of Louth in 1834. The terraced houses Adam built for his factory workers are shown in red

A later town plan, of 1834, from R S Bayley's *Notices of Louth* shows terraced houses on Ramsgate and also on the south side of James Street between Ramsgate and the river. Both terraces were demolished after damage in the 1920 flood. The twelve two-down-and-two-up terrace on James Street was built by Adam, probably between 1815 and 1820, for his workers who came to Louth from other manufacturing towns, as we shall see in the next chapter. The 1823 Valuation rated the houses at £2 10s (£125 today) and the occupiers of five can be identified as working in the factory – a wool sorter, a wool comber, a yarn scourer and two carpet weavers. Adam's house (Ivy House) was rated at £20 (£1,000 today) and the mill, manufactory, dyehouse and other buildings at £100 (£5,000 today).

Population in town and countryside was on the increase; Louth itself had grown rapidly in the first twenty years of the 19th century from 4,760 in 1801 to 6,970 in 1831. That meant an expanding market for carpets, rugs and blankets from the factory.

1825 was a key year in the history of the factory. The ban on the export of wool, the root cause of events which led to the building of the spinning mill, was lifted. The Jacquard (punched card) system of weaving was introduced to the factory (see next chapter) and Adam was granted a Patent for 'Certain Improvements in Manufacturing Carpets'. The detail of the Patent will be described in The Carpets chapter, but the interesting point here is the name of the person who communicated the idea to Adam; his name was William Augustus Prince, 'residing abroad'. It is highly likely that he was an American and is an indication of how Adam developed a successful export business to the USA, on a contract basis according to his obituary. Clearly Adam had extensive business connections, but unfortunately there are no records to substantiate the statement in his obituary about that overseas trade. And it raises the question of how the carpets were delivered to the port of export. The use of stage waggons along turnpikes to London has already been noted, and it also seems possible that export started at the Riverhead, along the canal, up the Humber and the Trent and then the Trent-Mersey to Liverpool.

Also in 1825, in June, the Corporation opened 'a commodious building', the Wool Market (Wool Mart, now John Taylors auction rooms on Kidgate); another example of stimulating the economy of the town. (The building would later be bought by the Eve and Ranshaw shop as a warehouse). The successful working of the economy depended on people paying on time. A formal promissory note with embossed stamp One Shilling Six Pence reads 'Upon Demand I promise to pay Adam Eve or order Eight pounds with lawful Interest for Value received this 19th day of June 1826 by me' and signed John Knowles. One hopes he honoured it.

We have noted the death of John Espin, Adam's partner in the factory, in January 1822. On 14 December the same year his brother Thomas, Master of the Commercial and Mathematical School at the Priory Cottage, died (and was buried in the mausoleum he had built for himself in the grounds). The trustees of the Mapletoft School, of which he was also master, took immediate action and appointed Thomas's half-brother William, who was 25 and teaching in Mansfield. Clearly William had drive, ambition and ideas and before the end of December had made plans for the school, detail of which appeared in the notice in the *Lincoln, Rutland & Stamford Mercury* on 3 January 1823: to completely repair and considerably enlarge the Priory School 'for the reception of younger gentlemen as boarders', and that the 'various branches of English Education … will be combined with Drawing, Planning, Book-Keeping etc for those pupils whose friends require it'. Adam would certainly require it – for his illegitimate/adopted boys John (10), Henry (8) and Charles (6) Paddison.

Eight years later, when Adam died in February 1831, the boys were still under age: John 18, Henry 16 and Charles 14. There was no obvious way of enabling Adam's unwritten desire for at least one of the boys to carry on the business. During the next four months there were discussions involving Adam's executors John Campbell and Thomas Oldham, William Espin and the three boys which resulted in a written agreement setting out the future of the factory. However, first the executors had to put the major part of Adam's properties on the market, and an advertisement addressed to 'Merchants, Manufacturers, Capitalists and others' was placed in the *Lincoln, Rutland & Stamford Mercury* in March for an auction sale at the Fleece Inn on 15 April at 7 o'clock in the evening, with three lots.

A fragment of the border of a Louth carpet
(see page 108)

Lot 1 was the freehold pasture of 2½ acres on the north side of the town known as Cricket Close, with yards, stables and other buildings and a pump of 'fine spring water', enclosed by brick walls and 'thriving quick (hawthorn) hedges', 'delightfully situated for building, being in an elevated situation, commanding an extensive prospect of the German Ocean' (North Sea). The location today is in the triangle between High Holme Road and Newbridge Hill, now occupied by 21st century housing.

Lot 2: 'All that very extensive Carpet, Blanket and Worsted Manufactory, situate upon the River Ludd [sic], a never-failing stream of water, by which the machinery is worked. It was established more than thirty years ago by the late Mr Eve, who during the whole of that time carried on a very profitable business, which is now continued under the direction of his trustees. It contains spacious rooms for Spinning and Weaving, Dyehouses, Combing Shops, Wool Warehouse, Two Tenements for Workmen, and all other suitable accommodations for carrying on the above business to a considerable extent. This lot is partly freehold and partly leasehold under the Corporation of Louth – The machinery belonging to the manufactory to be taken at a fair valuation.'

The inclusion of the wool warehouse, an extension to the mill on the south side of the river (now a private residence) is curious as it is not shown on Bayley's 1834 plan of the town, but is on the 1839 map and is clearly seen on the Panorama 1844-47. On suspects that it was an omission from the 1834 plan and was in fact built during Adam's time.

The Wool Warehouse

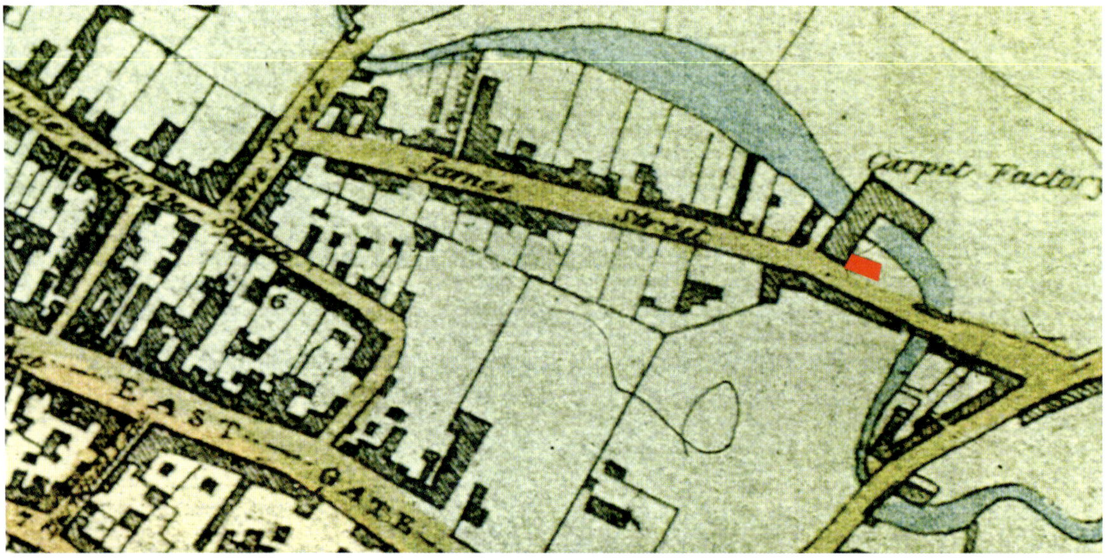

Marked in red on the 1839 map

The aftermath of the flood of 29 May 1920

When occupied by Car-men Spares Ltd

Now a private dwelling

The hand-operated hoist for unloading wool bales from the street is preserved on the top floor

Lot 3 was Ivy House, described as very well built and newly erected (in fact 38 years!). Accommodation was dining and drawing rooms, good kitchens, excellent ale and wine cellars, several good sleeping rooms, with an extensive yard, a spacious coach house, stabling for six horses, a brewhouse, dog kennels and other offices, with a very productive garden. It was noted as under lease from the Corporation with 61 years to run. The solicitors acting for the trustees were William Wilson and Field Flowers Goe.

Cricket Close was sold and Frederick Lucas, Town Clerk, took the lease of Ivy House, followed by his widow Elizabeth. Their son, Charles Edward who also lived on James Street, on the north side, ran C E Lucas & Bros, wine, spirit, ale and porter merchants, Rosemary Lane. Later, between 1882 and 1885, Adam's great nephew John Bowmar Eve was able to move from Temple Terrace into Ivy House with his family. His wife Elizabeth was a Ranshaw, and her two brothers Thomas and George came to Louth to manage the shop – hence Eve & Ranshaw, as we shall see in The Shop chapter. On a dining room window in Ivy House are scratched two names: 'F B Eve & C M Eve Oct 1892'. They were two of John Bowmar and Elizabeth's family, Frank Bowmar and Catherine Maud, then aged 26 and 28. Their elder brother John Frederic did not marry, managed the shop and continued to live there with his brother Frank Bowmar the veterinary surgeon. The latter took on a junior partner, Arthur Heane Adams, in 1922, who took over the practice three years later, and bought Ivy House in 1928 when the Corporation sold their remaining properties on James Street.

We can now return to William Espin and those first few months of 1831. (The previous year he had ridden his grey horse to the Market Place for the Proclamation of William IV.) Whether William had aspirations to run the carpet and blanket factory (did he bid at the auction?), whether he was asked by Adam's trustees, whether it was the wish of the boys, or whether Adam had told his executors that if he died before John came of age they should ask William, we shall never know. His decision may also have been influenced by 'indifferent health' at the time. The fact is that within a few days of the auction, when it would appear that the factory had not been sold, William had resigned from the Mapletoft School, 'wishing to retire in consequence of having engaged in another line of employment', and his Priory School was taken by Alexander Tallents Rogers as a Classical and Commercial School. By 25 May William had concluded an Agreement signed by John Campbell (for the trustees) and John Paddison.

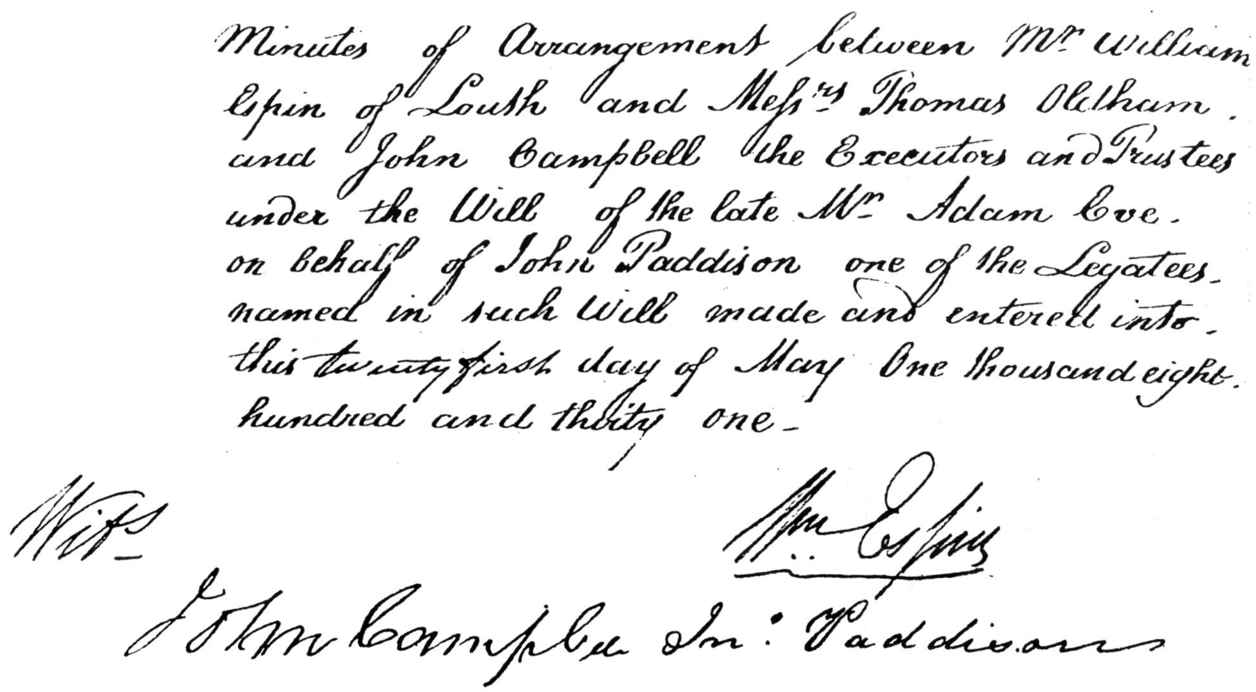
Minutes of Arrangement between Mr William Espin of Louth and Messrs Thomas Oldham and John Campbell the Executors and Trustees under the Will of the late Mr Adam Eve on behalf of John Paddison one of the Legatees named in such Will made and entered into this twenty first day of May One thousand eight hundred and thirty one -

Wm Espin

Wits

John Campbell Jno: Paddison

Under the terms of the Agreement William would take on the freehold and leasehold of the factory and a dwelling house (the former overseer's house, opposite the mill, into which Adam moved after the death of his wife), to retain the same as sole owner until Charles Paddison reached his majority, with such whole or part of the purchase money as he might require (at 4½% interest); William had some capital of course from the sale of the Priory. The business was to be carried on by William Espin aided by John Paddison, the 'best exertion' of each to be used for 'the improvement of the concern', with Espin taking all the profits until Paddison was 21, after which any profit would be shared equally under the firm of Espin and Paddison.

As an inducement to that arrangement 'for the advancement in the world of John Paddison' the trustees advanced £500 of his legacy (as allowed for in Adam's Will) to Espin as an interest-free loan until John was 21, at which time it would be treated as capital in the co-partnership. John was to be allowed £20 a year salary paid by Espin for ' keeping the books ... taking journeys to transact business ... or otherwise employing himself at all reasonable times ... in the management, conducting or execution of the business'. A further sum of £1,000 was advanced from John's legacy, the premium on the cost of an insurance policy to cover that amount being met out of John's salary; when John reached 21, the £1,000 would be similarly treated as capital. What these arrangements meant was that William Espin would be lent £1,500 which could be used by him for 'the improvement of the business'. It was also noted that when John reached 21, he would inherit the remaining £1,500 to invest in the business for the equal benefit of himself and Espin. Should John die before 21, Espin would have to repay the first £1,500 with interest.

Part of the underside of a Louth carpet with Greek key design
(see pages 98-99)

Other clauses were: an annual rent of 7½% of the cost price of the manufactory (we don't know what that was) to be paid to Espin as landlord by the co-partners; external repairs to be done by the owner; machinery to be found and repaired and all other repairs to the mill and works to be done at the expense of the co-partners. Finally, and enlightening in its implications, was a clause about an equitable allowance to be made to John Paddison in the event of dissolution of the partnership 'before an adequate remuneration shall have been drawn by the co-partners for money expended in any new wheel or from any material amendment in the existing wheels or in the race'. The implication is that Adam had not done much to the mill in his later years and that improvements were required, not least in the condition of the waterwheels. The Agreement provided the advance of £1,500, to enable those improvements to be made.

There is no mention of Henry Paddison in the Agreement, but he did join the co-partnership while still under age (as noted in The Eve Dynasty chapter). So the firm was Espin and Paddisons, but the partnership did not last long. A notice in the *London Gazette* in June 1835 announced that the partnership of William Espin, John Paddison and Henry Paddison had been dissolved by mutual consent. The firm was described as Carpet, Rug, Blanket and Worsted Manufacturers and Wool-Dealers. Henry went on to farming, Espin became Borough Surveyor, leaving John, then 23, to run the factory himself. But not for long, as he died in 1838 at the early age of 26.

NOTICE is hereby given, that the Partnership lately subsisting between us the undersigned, William Espin, of Louth, in the County of Lincoln, John Paddison, of the same place, and Henry Paddison, of Brackenborough, in the said County, Carpet, Rug, Blanket, and Worsted-Manufacturers and Wool-Dealers, carried on under the firm of Espin and Paddisons, was, on the 11th day of June instant, dissolved by mutual consent.—Witness our hands this 20th day of June 1835.

Wm. Espin.
J. Paddison.
H. Paddison.

Notice in the London Gazette 26 June 1835

However, the partnership had achieved one major objective in the operation of the mill – the installation of a steam engine in 1834 to supplement or replace what had clearly become defective waterwheels. The boiler house and tall chimney were built onto the northern end of the mill, with gearing connections to the internal machinery. And coal of course was readily available via the canal. Despite the claim in the advertisement for the sale of the factory about 'a never-failing stream of water', there were times in hard winters when the mill dam might freeze over. In fact in December the following year (1835) Louth and the Wolds had the heaviest snowfall for years which paralysed transport on the turnpike and frosts would have affected the flow of the Lud.

The Carpet and Blanket Manufactory, still in semi-rural setting in 1841

During his time in Louth, William Espin had three children – Thomas Espinell (1824 – 1912) born at the Priory who went on to be Professor of Theology at Queen's College, Birmingham and later Chancellor of the Diocese of Liverpool, John who became Chancellor of Grahamstown Cathedral in South Africa, and Annie Sarah. During his involvement with the factory William lived in the former overseer's house in James Street, which he had to vacate when Charles Paddison reached his majority. He also rented from the Corporation 3½ acres of land in James Street and owned six acres called the Poor Close at the Riverhead. On the dissolution of the partnership with John and Henry Paddison, he became Borough Surveyor, having acted as Surveyor for the old Corporation in the 1820s. He probably helped Charles Paddison to take on the factory after John died in 1838, before he returned to Mansfield as Master of the Grammar School there until his death in 1865.

John Paddison's short management of the factory was not particularly successful. He had used the balance of his legacy to build the substantial White House on Grimsby Road, and his poor health was probably a contributory factor. When he died his son William was only two, and he would die when only 18. Moreover there appears to have been a reduced workforce (see next chapter).

The three Paddison brothers were rather different characters. John aspired to living in some style on the income from the carpet-making business Adam had built up, but he had neither the drive nor the good health. Henry had no real interest in making carpets, and probably Adam knew that, which would account for Henry's smaller legacy. Charles turned out to be the one prepared to make the business work. He had his legacy and a house – that of the former overseer and kept for him by William Espin under the terms of the Agreement. He was 22. In the 1842 Directory he described himself as carpet, rug and blanket manufacturer, wool agent and stapler. The engraving of 1841 shows the factory still in a semi-rural setting (see previous page).

Charles took advantage of the Design Act 1842 to register as copyright new carpet designs (in 1845 and 1850 – see The Carpets chapter) and more than doubled the number of weavers in the factory. This meant increased output, with additional looms in the main factory. The most productive period of the factory was when Charles ran it (see The Workers chapter). Adam would have been proud of what he achieved.

Part of a new Louth carpet design, 1845

The size of the factory stands out on William Brown's Panorama (1844-47), and shows just beyond it a whalebone arch entrance to the garden opposite Charles's house. (See page 32) The East Lincolnshire Railway opened in 1848, providing improved export possibilities. In the long term however the railway would work against the factory as it became possible to import higher quality carpets from large manufacturing centres.

The plan of the factory and grounds in 1852 shows the new Wellington Street being laid out and developed, with an access, the Factory Road, on the north side of the river. The south end of the mill is designated the Old Mill, which suggests that production was concentrated at the north end, nearest to power drive from the steam engine, and perhaps limited use of water power.

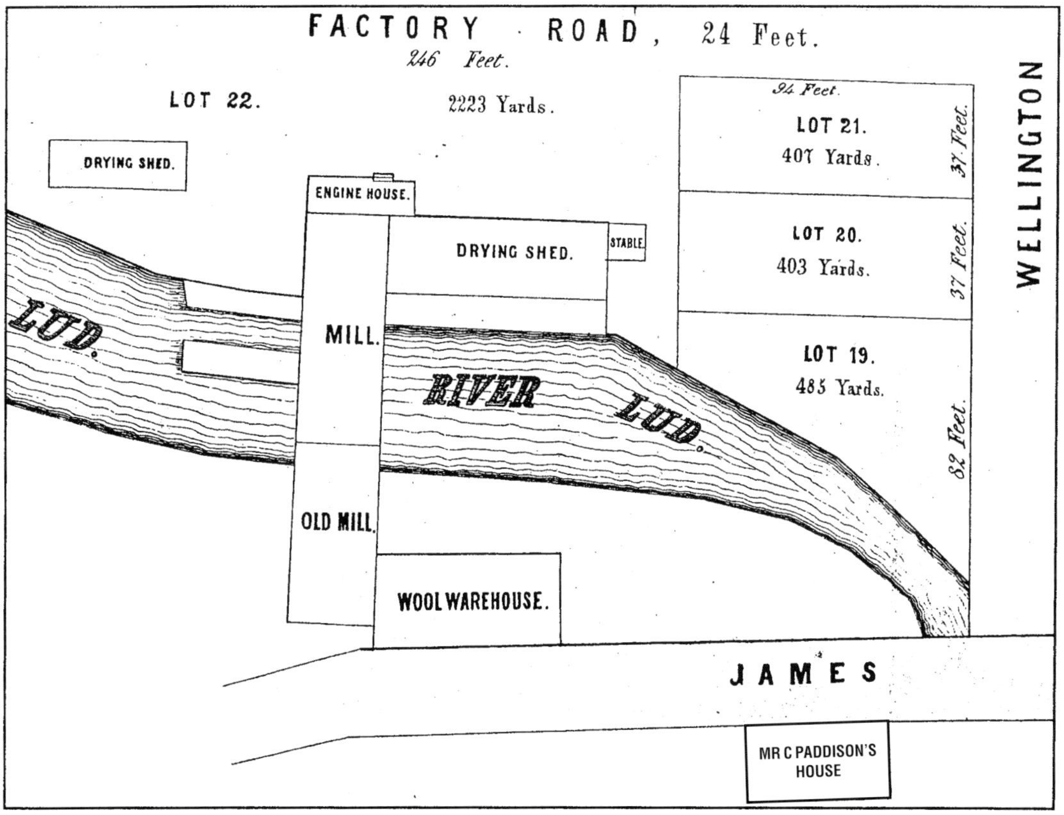

Plan of factory and grounds, 1852

Charles ran the factory for 24 years, during which time the population of the town grew to over 10,500, but then stabilised. When the census was taken in 1861, his brother Henry was a visitor, recorded as 'Farmer, Cape of Good Hope'. As we have seen, Henry had returned from South Africa two years earlier. One can perhaps imagine them discussing their respective futures. The outcome was Charles wishing to retire early because of poor health, and Henry agreeing to take over temporarily and bring in new partners – Edward Hoff (1819 – 1884), formerly a grocer and draper in Holbeach, and his son Robert William (b. 1840). How Henry had come to be acquainted with Edward Hoff is not known (although Edward had a relative, William, a farmer at Halton Holegate), but it would appear that Edward had some capital to invest in carpet making. The Paddison and Hoff partnership was short-lived, dissolved by a notice in the *London Gazette* in August 1863. Henry was then living, for a short time, at Eastfield House, Keddington (before moving to Essex).

Edward Hoff lived at The Grove, on the corner of Ramsgate Road and what is now Victoria Road, with his wife Elizabeth and daughter Anne (b.1854). In the 1871 census his full name of Edward Brown Smith Hoff is recorded and his unmarried daughter's name as Anne Elizabeth. Edward's son Robert William lived at 73 James Street (on the north side not far from the factory), and they traded as Hoff & Son.

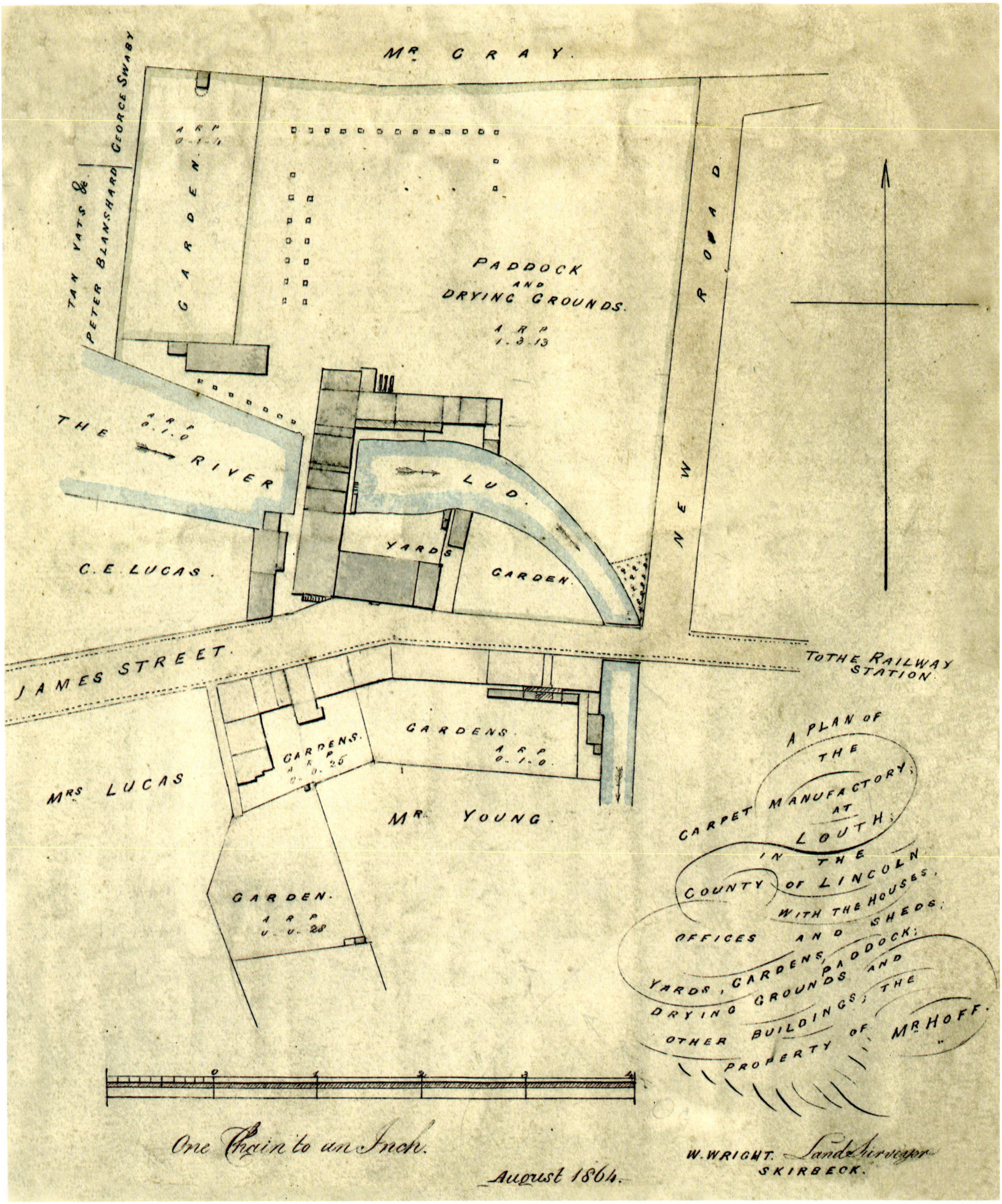
MR. GRAY.
GEORGE SWABY
TAN YATS &c.
PETER BLANSHARD
GARDEN
PADDOCK AND DRYING GROUNDS.
A R P 1.3.13
NEW ROAD
THE RIVER LUD.
A R P 0.1.0
C.E. LUCAS.
YARDS
GARDEN.
JAMES STREET.
TO THE RAILWAY STATION
GARDENS.
GARDENS.
A R P 0.1.0
MRS LUCAS
MR YOUNG.
GARDEN.
A PLAN OF THE CARPET MANUFACTORY, AT LOUTH; IN THE COUNTY OF LINCOLN WITH THE HOUSES, OFFICES AND SHEDS; YARDS, GARDENS, PADDOCK; DRYING GROUNDS AND OTHER BUILDINGS; THE PROPERTY OF MR HOFF.
0 1 2 3 4
One Chain to an Inch.
August 1864.
W. WRIGHT. Land Surveyor
SKIRBECK.

The partnership was active, registering nine new carpet designs in 1863-65, and in 1867 their carpets were Highly Commended at the Paris Universal Exhibition. In the 1860's and early 1870s their factory foreman, John Oliver Burdett, was also the carpet designer (see The Carpets chapter). In August 1864 the Hoffs engaged the services of William Wright, land surveyor of Skirbeck, to produce a Plan of the Carpet Factory and other property then in the ownership of Edward Hoff (opposite). This shows the lines of posts in the paddock drying grounds where the woollen yarn was hung to dry after washing and after dyeing. The plan of the factory buildings on the town survey by Borough Surveyor Thomas Wilkinson Wallis in 1873 shows only minor changes.

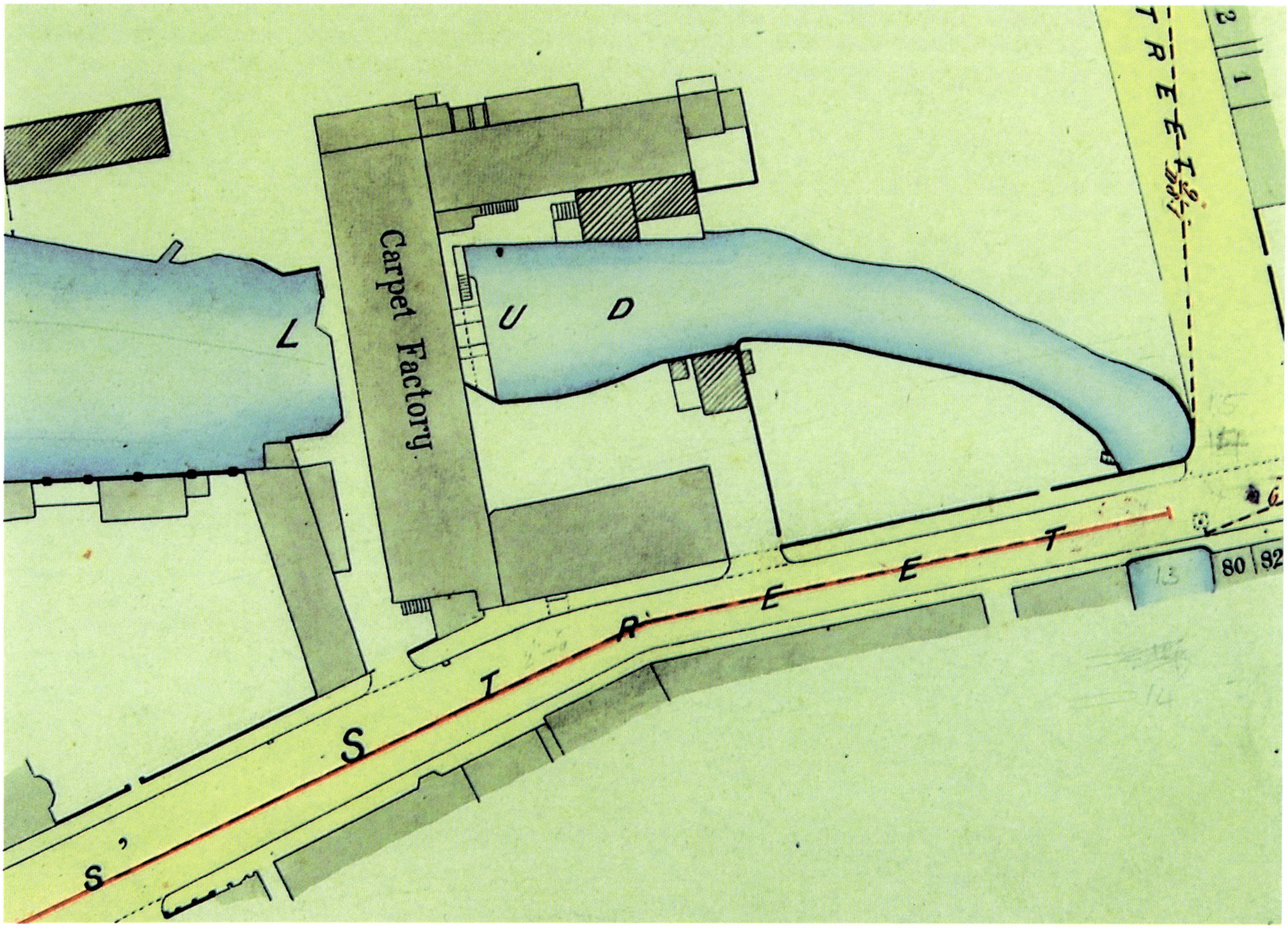

Part of Borough Surveyor T W Wallis's town plan showing detail of the factory buildings in 1873

The Hoffs took an active part in town affairs: father and son were both Borough Councillors in 1871-72, and Edward was still a Councillor in 1876. The carpet business seemed to be flourishing, and a national list of hand looms making flat-weave and similar carpets compiled in 1874 recorded Hoff & Son with 34 (but probably an over-estimate). The firm also had London offices at 32 Newgate Street.

However, White's *Lincolnshire Directory* for 1872 lists Hoff & Son as also manufacturing linseed cake, bagging etc. Was that diversification in the light of a declining market for flat-weave carpets? And there was growing competition in the supply of floor coverings. The same Directory carried an advertisement by Chiles & Co of London: 'The New Solid dustproof, draughtproof, waterproof and washable Carpets and Matting, are the cleanest, the most healthy and the most economical coverings extant'. And the *Post Office Directory for Lincolnshire* 1876 had an advertisement by Cardinal & Harford, Importers of Turkey, Persian and other Oriental Carpets, Rugs, Mattings etc, of High Holborn, London.

Louth's population peaked at 10,827 in 1881 and then declined rapidly in the next ten years. But success for the carpet factory did not depend on local demand. The wider market now looked to pile carpets. The days of a single, isolated factory making flat-weave carpets were numbered. And so were those of Hoff & Son. Matters came to a head in 1880 when an attempt was made to save the factory and the jobs of the employees. A group of local businessmen, led by architect Alderman James Fowler, then Mayor of Louth (for the third time). They formed the Louth Carpet & Woollen Factory Limited with a nominal capital of £5,000 in shares of £10 each (about £500 today). The subscribers were James Fowler (25 shares), John Lewis Fytche, Lindsey Magistrate, Thorpe Hall (30), John Sanderson, millwright (25), Joseph Cusworth, grocer and Borough Magistrate (10), John Woodrow Dennis, chemist and Borough Councillor (5), Isaac John Colbridge, grocer (5) and John Gildon Tupholme, printer (2). Total £1,020.

Memorandum of Association of The Louth Carpet and Woollen Factory Limited

The main objects of the Company were to purchase from Hoff & Son and their mortgagees the mill, warehouses, weaving shops, machinery, fixtures, stock in trade, offices, cottages, dwelling house, gardens and paddock; and to carry on the business of manufacturing carpets, hearthrugs and blankets. Other clauses related to financing the venture. The Memorandum of Association was dated 29 December 1880. Edward Hoff was made manager with Robert Hoff as commercial traveller. The normal pattern for a commercial traveller in carpets was to travel with new designs from September, taking orders for delivery in early spring the next year. Summer months were seen as 'between seasons'. Being a travelling salesman may have been part of Robert's role from the 1860s. The survival of small firms often depended on offering a range of designs. White's Directory for 1882 recorded a new name for the factory: the Luda Carpet Works. Signs of hope perhaps, but it was too late.

A summary of capital shares on 9 May 1881 listed 243 shares taken up at £7 each, made up of £1,567 paid and £134 unpaid. Total still only £1,701 (£88,400 today). Shareholders were listed as: James Fowler (25), John Lewis Fytche (30), Isaac John Colbridge (5), William Hyde (20) and Joseph Sutton Brown (5) (Hyde & Brown, solicitors acting for the Company), Mark Smith, chemist (2), Charles Michell Nesbitt, Manager Louth & Lindsey Bank and Borough Magistrate (10), John Woodrow Dennis (5), John Salmon, cabinet maker (2), Charles Mason, auctioneer (5), Charles Parker, printer (2), Alfred Ingoldby, bank manager Garfit, Claypon & Co (5), John Bowmar Eve, draper (Adam's great nephew) (20), John Cusworth (10), John Gildon Tupholme (2), Thomas Henry Burditt, printer (2), John Sanderson (20), William Robert Emeris, Lindsey Magistrate (grandson of Revd John Emeris, an original subscriber to the mill) (2), William Henry Smythe, Elkington Hall (30), Thomas Darnill, plumber (3), Garfit, Claypon & Co, bankers (20), Charles Thomas Ennals, surgeon (5), Thomas Maxey, builder (whose family would take over the building after the 1920 flood) (5), Charles Titley, innkeeper, Marquis of Granby, and brickmaker on Charles Street (3), and Richard Chaplin (relative of Adam's friend Richard Chaplin of Tathwell) Westgate House (5). What an interesting range of businessmen, bankers and gentry hoping to save what they clearly regarded as a reputable industry and employer in the town.

A revised summary of 5 March 1883 added Edward Hoff (25) and Robert William Hoff (20). Total shares value: £2,880 (£153,000 today). It was not enough. On 7 May the subscribers, chaired by Fowler, met at the factory office and passed a Special Resolution which was confirmed at an Extraordinary General Meeting at the offices of the solicitors, Hyde & Brown (58 Upgate) on 25 May to confirm 'That the Company is wound up voluntarily, and that James Fowler … and John Woodrow Dennis … are hereby appointed Liquidators for the purposes of such winding up'. That process was completed and the property disposed of by 13 January 1886. It was 95 years since Adam Eve had taken a lease on the Mill.

SPECIAL RESOLUTION

(*Pursuant to Companies Act,* 1862, *ss.* 51, 129, *&* 133)

OF THE

LOUTH CARPET & WOOLLEN FACTORY LIMITED.

Passed the 7th day of May, 1883. *Confirmed the 25th day of May,* 1883.

At an Extraordinary General Meeting of the Members of the said Company, duly convened, and held at the Office of the Company, James Street, Louth, in the County of Lincoln, on the 7th day of May, 1883, the following Special Resolution was duly passed; and at a subsequent Extraordinary General Meeting of the Members of the said Company, also duly convened, and held at the Offices of Messrs. Hyde & Brown, No. 58, Upgate, Louth, on the 25th day of May, 1883, the following Special Resolution was duly confirmed:—

RESOLVED—

"That the Company be wound up voluntarily, and that James Fowler, of Louth, in the County of Lincoln, Architect, and John Woodrowe Dennis, of the same place, Chemist, be, and they are hereby appointed Liquidators for the purposes of such winding up."

JAS. FOWLER,

Chairman.

Dated this 31st day of May, 1883.

'The Factory'
(from The Pictorial Record and Illustrated Advertiser, September 1898)

To quote from *Industries of the Eastern Counties: A Guide to Leading Commercial Enterprises* c.1890: 'Louth carpets until a few years since enjoyed a very high reputation through the country for their excellent weaving qualities and their manufacture gave employment to a large number of weavers, but in consequence ... of competition of the large centres of the carpet trade, with their facilities of railway communication and lower tariffs, the production by hand looms became unprofitable, and the works were finally closed in 1883'. 'The Factory', as it became known, was taken on by William Frederick Hoggard, timber merchant, Windsor (folding) chair maker, cabinet turner and toy chair manufacturer.

Upstream

T W Wallis paintings of the factory 1897

Downstream

The Ordnance Survey map of 1888 (revised 1905) shows the building labelled Saw Mill, with a timber yard on the north side, accessed from Wellington Street, and a house (Brookside) where once had been a garden adjoining the wool warehouse. In 1897 T W Wallis made watercolour paintings of all the bridges over the Lud, including the Mill. One was from upstream showing calm water in the mill dam and the three arches, and the other the downstream side showing the bypass channel (right), the remaining waterwheel still turning in the centre arch to drive Hoggard's machinery, and far right the waterwheel removed from the southern arch.

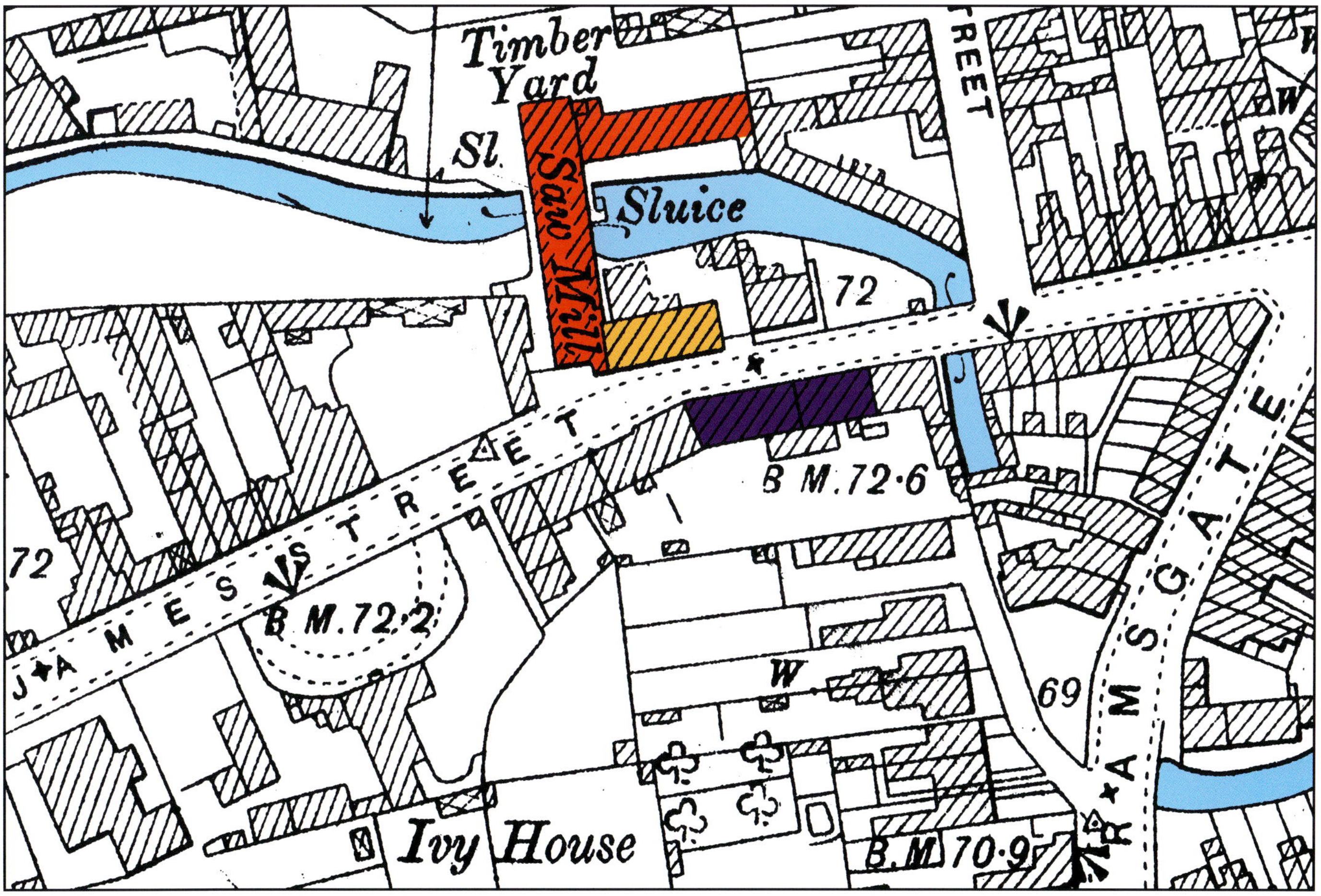

OS map 1888

Colours mark the original use of buildings

Spinning Mill and Drying Shed

Wool Warehouse

Carpet Weaving Rooms

On the occasion of the disastrous Louth Flood at teatime on Saturday 29 May 1920, the three arches were unable to cope with the volume of water, which backed up, flooded houses in James Street to ground floor ceiling height and added to the torrent of water flowing along the street. And tree trunks were washed out of Hoggard's timber yard and jammed between the houses on Wellington Street. The whole building was still standing in 1956, but by the time the next OS map was published in 1968 the central section of the mill had been taken down and a footbridge connection made between the remaining blocks. There was also a new saw mill, powered by electricity.

Today nothing remains of the original spinning mill except footings in the river banks and a slight change in level of the river bed. The wool warehouse and the carpet weaving rooms are now private dwellings. There is a Louth Civic Trust Blue Plaque on the original Wool Warehouse (see next page). Adam's Ivy House and the overseer's house are still occupied. However it is still possible by following property boundaries to trace the original plot of land in Woods Close marked out by the Old Corporation in 1786 for building a mill to spin long and coarse sheep's wool by water-powered machinery.

LOUTH CARPET
MANUFACTORY
established 1787
for spinning
long and coarse
sheep's wool
by machinery.

The underside of a Louth carpet. Date not known.
(see pages 106-107)

Chapter 4

The Workers

SPINNING YARN from long and coarse wool was the original prime purpose of the mill. The object was to increase the output of yarn for local weavers and so extend the purposes of the Society for the Promotion of Industry. There is no mention of weaving in the lease documents relating to the mill, but the first, and as it turned out unsuccessful, lease was to a carpet manufacturer, Richard Brumfit of Leeds. He installed machinery for scribbling (coarse carding or teasing) and finer combing of wool preparatory to spinning. It was not until the late 1790s, by which time Adam had control of the mill, that machines to prepare wool for the handloom carpet weavers worked satisfactorily. However, not all stages of the process could be mechanised.

When the raw wool arrived from the grazier it had to be washed – in the river – to remove dirt and then hung out to dry. The wool sorter separated the best parts of the fleece, on the back and flanks, from the coarser fibres on the fringes and towards the neck and tail. A scribbling machine did the coarse carding before it passed to the wool combers who used flat steel-toothed combs to prepare hanks of wool for the spinning machines, and the final stage of dyeing and reeling. The yarn then passed to the dyer using a limited range of colours from vegetable dyes (chemical dyes from 1850s). The yarn was washed in the river, doubtless generating colour patterns downstream. The washings were done below the mill on the north bank where the drying sheds and grounds were. Finally the dyed yarn was reeled onto bobbins or shuttles ready for the carpet weavers.

Wool combers in the later 19th century

The first information we have about the machinery in the mill is from Cragg's visit in 1799 when he noted 20 machines, most of them turned by water power. Another source mentions 60 people working there which included women and children. After the building of the Louth Union Workhouse in 1838, workhouse children were taken to work in the factory, girls usually employed in winding and reeling. Cragg remarked on the oily smell of wool, but the atmosphere would be dusty, and there was the noise of machinery driven by rope belts (leather came later) from the main horizontal shaft. The interior of the mill was lit by windows on both sides, but evening and winter working required light from tallow candles. Gas light was probably not installed until the 1840s or later, when it could be afforded.

The first hand looms were in the two weaving rooms on the other side of James Street from the mill. The main ground colours made up the warp of 1,300 threads, different strands of which had to be lifted in the correct sequence for each throw of the shuttle, the weft, to produce the required pattern. The combinations of warp threads were connected to heddles, one for each line of the pattern, which were lifted by pulling a cord – that was the job of the drawboy. The handloom therefore required two to operate it – the weaver and the drawboy, the latter paid out of the weaver's earnings. The drawboy was often a member of the weaver's family. The job of the weaver was made easier by Kay's flying shuttle, that is with a peg and string attached to each end of the shuttle which enabled it to be both thrown and pulled. This increased the rate of weaving, but was harder work for the drawboy. The standard width of carpet woven was 27 inches (three-quarters of a yard), the Flemish Ell, but could also be woven to 36 inches wide. Lengths were normally sewn together by the retailer to meet a customer's requirements.

The underside of a trellis pattern Louth carpet
(see pages 96-97)

From 1825 Adam introduced the Jacquard punched-card mechanism for lifting the heddles, which did away with the need for a drawboy. Joseph Marie Jacquard, a French silk weaver, had invented the system about 1804, but it did not come into general use until the 1820s. Each row of holes in a punched card represented a line of the pattern. The mechanism was mounted on top of the frame of the loom. It is likely that Adam placed the new looms in the main factory where the rooms were high. The introduction of the Jacquard enabled more complicated designs to be woven.

Power looms for carpet making, invented by American E B Bigelow, were in use in England by the 1840s, but rarely used for flat-weave carpets because of the capital cost and the fact that there was plenty of skilled labour available for hand looms. None of the Louth carpet looms was power driven.

The working day in a carpet factory was normally 6am to 8.30pm, with a quarter of an hour for breakfast, half an hour for dinner and 15 minutes drinking time; Saturday afternoon and Sunday were leisure time. The Factory Act 1833 limited the hours of children working: 12 hours a day for 11-18 years, eight hours for 9-11 years, and under 9 years were banned. Weavers were on piece work rates and could work irregular hours, depending on orders. They could weave five yards in 12 hours, or 36 yards a week – Thursday to Thursday or Saturday to Saturday, the 'fall days' when payment was made. The rate was about one shilling (5p) a yard, out of which the weaver had to pay his drawboy and provide his own candles.

It was hard work for the drawboys, and some were still working on handlooms in the 1840s and 1850s. Giving evidence to the Royal Commission on Children's Employment in 1841, an eleven-year old Kidderminster boy said, 'I don't much like getting up at night. I would rather get up in the morning and stay late. When I have done work I am very tired, when we "fall" I am hardly able to crawl along the streets to get home, and sometimes I go without food all the morning'. Perhaps conditions were not that bad in Louth where maybe Adam and the Paddison brothers, and later the Hoffs had a more benevolent attitude to their workforce, where there was no local competition and they could concentrate on quality rather than quantity. There were however strict rules for apprentices in the shop, as we shall see in The Shop chapter.

When Adam took control of the mill in 1791, he needed the skills and help of his partners John Cookson and Joseph Fawcett in using the machinery, but the supply of manual labour was local. However, when he started making carpets in 1798, there was a need for skilled weavers. As we shall see, a considerable proportion were inward migrants from other manufacturing districts, but Adam also took in apprentices. One example was John Green.

A loom with Jacquard punched card mechanism mounted on the top for lifting the heddles (see opposite page)
From The Penny Magazine, August 1843

Green was born in Nottingham in 1790 to Louth parents who returned when he was six months. They were of the family of the Greens who were members of the first Methodist chapel in Louth. His father died when he was four, and at 13 his grandfather (quite probably a trustee of the Louth chapel) put him as an apprentice at the factory, living in with the overseer William Foggitt (who preached at that chapel). After three years (1806) he absconded, served on a privateer out of Hull to the Shetlands but received no pay, and returned to Louth. He was reprimanded by Adam as a runaway apprentice, and vowed 'not to work any longer in Louth'. He walked most of the way to Leeds and got a job in Richard Brumfit's carpet factory; however when Brumfit met him the next day and realised Green was an apprentice elsewhere he refused him work. So he got work at Mr Howard's small carpet factory at Nether Mills but was there for only three weeks. The materials were bad and he received but little wages: 'I had been used to work upon good stuff at Mr Eve's factory', he wrote.

On a journey into Leeds to get his winder's wheel mended Green was persuaded to take the King's shilling and become a soldier. He was sworn in for seven and a half years before Mr Justine Sheepshank who told him, 'I know your master, Eve, very well'. He was enlisted in the Durham Light Infantry, fought in the Peninsular War under the Duke of Wellington, was badly wounded by a musket ball at San Sebastian, invalided to England and discharged with a pension of nine pence a day (£13 13s 9d a year; £550 today).

THE

VICISSITUDES

OF A

SOLDIER'S LIFE,

OR A SERIES OF

OCCURRENCES FROM 1806 TO 1815;

TOGETHER

WITH AN INTRODUCTORY AND A CONCLUDING CHAPTER:

THE WHOLE

CONTAINING, WITH SOME OTHER MATTERS,

A CONCISE ACCOUNT OF

THE WAR IN THE PENINSULA,

FROM ITS COMMENCEMENT TO ITS FINAL CLOSE.

BY JOHN GREEN,

LATE OF THE 68TH DURHAM LIGHT INFANTRY.

LOUTH:

PRINTED FOR AND

SOLD BY THE AUTHOR, AND BY J. AND J. JACKSON;

AND IN LONDON BY

SIMPKIN AND MARSHALL, STATIONERS'-COURT.

1827.

Green returned to Louth in 1815, became a book hawker but with little success and decided to leave Louth again. However in April that year his aunt died and left him some property. Adam took him on again as a carpet weaver and in June he married Mary of Theddlethorpe, but 'in consequence of our trade being very uncertain' he also fixed himself 'in a small way of business' – listed as wholesale worsted dealer in the 1826 directory. At the 1841 census he and Mary were living at 58 Northgate with a growing family including his first son, George, who also became a carpet weaver. In 1861, aged 70, he was recorded as a Chelsea Pensioner and carpet weaver, with George (48) still living at home, two unmarried daughters and a grandson, Joseph, age five (probably illegitimate who was later committed to the Union Workhouse, described as an imbecile from birth). John Green died in 1863, with the musket ball from Spain still inside him.

This unusual story of a Louth carpet weaver has been gleaned from the book he wrote: *The Vicissitudes of a Soldier's Life* or *A Series of Occurrences from 1806 to 1815 … containing a concise account of the War in the Peninsula, by John Green 68th Durham Light Infantry,* published by J & J Jackson, Louth 1827. [The same year Jacksons published *Poems by Two Brothers* – Alfred and Charles Tennyson].

A VALUATION

OF THE

MESSUAGES, TENEMENTS, LANDS, AND PROPERTY

SITUATED IN THE PARISH OF LOUTH,

IN THE COUNTY OF LINCOLN,

RATED FOR THE RELIEF OF THE POOR, PURSUANT TO ORDERS OF THE SELECT VESTRY:

TOGETHER WITH THE

OLD VALUATION,

AS PREVIOUSLY USED FOR THE SAME PURPOSE.

LOUTH:

PRINTED BY AND FOR C. A. WATSON, IN THE BUTCHER-MARKET.

1823.

In order to discover the names and origins of carpet weavers and other factory workers, it was necessary to trawl the occupation column of the census returns for Louth from 1841 to 1881. To narrow the search it was assumed that workers lived near the factory, which essentially turned out to be the case – James Street, Eve Street, Northgate and Ramsgate. It was also possible to work backwards using the 1823 and 1838 Rate Valuation lists and the Church Rate Poll Book 1834, searching for names recorded in the 1841 census. Moreover, where the head of a family had migrated to Louth and their children, or some of them, were born here, it was possible to work out an estimated date of their arrival. One family of whom ten worked in the factory and spanned eighty years of carpet making were the Spiveys – and there are still descendants in and around Louth.

Thomas Spivey (1770 – 1847) was a wool sorter living at Liversedge in the Spen valley west of Dewsbury in Yorkshire. By 1800 he and his wife Ann (1771 – 1841) had four surviving children: twins Martha and Mary (1791), Abraham (1795) and Rebekah (1799). Their next child Hannah (1801) was born in Louth, as were Isaac (1803), Jacob (1805), Reuben (1807), twins Joseph (died in infancy) and Benjamin (1809) and Frederick (1813). Therefore Thomas and his young family moved to Louth in 1800. Why? He was a member of the Liversedge Lower (Independent) Chapel, and in 1795 the newly appointed minister with Calvinist leanings required members to sign a Confession of Faith, with which Thomas appeared to have difficulty. That may have had some influence on his decision to move, but local economic hardship among the industrious poor and hearing, as he undoubtedly did on the local grapevine, about Adam Eve's new carpet factory in Louth which needed skilled labour and the chance of a better life, were most likely the main reasons. Indeed he and his family were able to occupy one of Adam's terraced houses on James Street close to the factory.

The journey from Liversedge to Louth was both exciting and tiring for the children, then aged nine, five and one, travelling by long distance carrier or stage van, which could carry a few passengers. Such transport plied regularly between south Yorkshire towns and Lincolnshire along the Great North Road to Bawtry and then by the Dexthorpe turnpike crossing the Trent by the new-built bridge (1790) at Gainsborough. The journey would have taken about three days with overnight stops at inns.

Thomas's new neighbours on James Street included John Storr, yarn scourer, Thomas Wilkinson, carpet weaver, Reuben Wilman, wool comber, Samuel Sutton, carpet weaver and Thomas Kew, carpet weaver who had come to Louth from St Pancras, London (and would become grandfather of H H Kew, hairdresser and taxidermist at 5 Eastgate which from the 1800s to 1920s was advertised as 'The Louth Museum'). Moreover, Thomas was close to the house of the factory overseer William Foggitt: when Foggitt came to Louth in 1797 he was already a Methodist preacher of twenty years standing and was a member of Louth's first (Wesleyan) Methodist chapel in Rose's Passage (behind the present Lloyds TSB bank on Little Eastgate). With Adam's business connections made on his visits to Leeds, Wakefield and other south Yorkshire towns, it is reasonable to suggest that he recruited Foggitt (a Yorkshire name) to be his factory overseer as part of his plan to start making carpets. And with Foggitt's nonconformist status, maybe he was the link that brought the Spiveys to Louth.

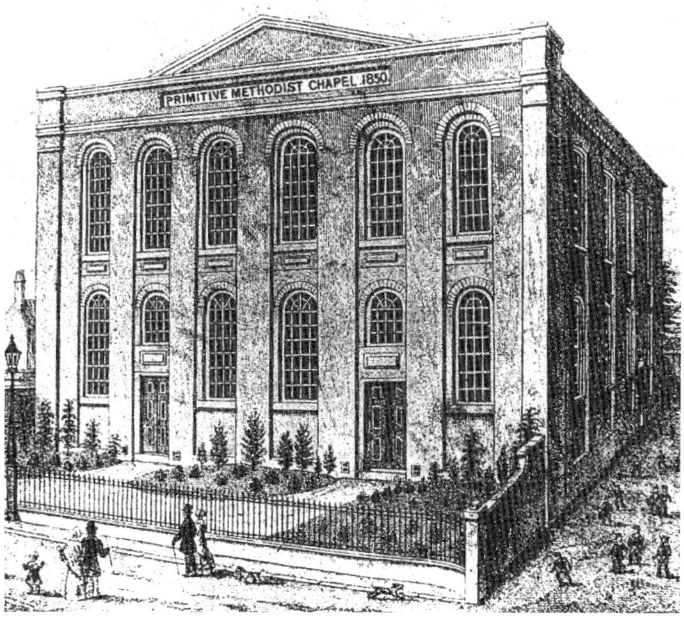

Primitive Methodist Chapel on Northgate where the carpet weaving Spiveys and their families were members. See next page. *(Drawing by William Brown).* **Now the site of Louth Library**

Of Thomas's three boys born in Louth, Isaac (1803 – 1840) became a carpet weaver; Isaac and his wife Martha would have five children and one of the girls, Fanny, became great grandmother to descendants in and around Louth today. The next boy, Jacob (1805 – 1889) worked in the factory as a teenager, became a carpet weaver and outlived the factory, retiring to live at 50 Newmarket where he died age 84. He had married Elizabeth Bratley of Withcall, lived in James Street and attended the Primitive Methodist chapel on Northgate (first built in 1820 and enlarged in 1836 and 1850; now the site of the Library). They had two boys, William (born 1839) and Charles (1840): both were spinners in the factory when only 12 and 11. William then became an apprentice joiner, but went on to become a Primitive Methodist minister, as did his brother.

William's obituary refers to his parents as the 'industrious poor' who 'did their best to give their children a good elementary education by sending them to the Day School and keeping them there as long as they possibly could before sending them out to business'. The Day School was the undenominational British School, which opened in 1841 (now Kidgate County Primary School). The boys also attended the Primitive Methodist Sunday School.

Thomas's son Reuben (born 1807), who worked as a tailor and was also a Primitive Methodist, became involved in the temperance movement and in the 1840s was running the Temperance Hotel on Eastgate (now the site of Wilkinson Hardware Store). Reuben's eldest brother, Abraham, was a carpet weaver and a Primitive Methodist. In 1817 he married Elizabeth Wilkinson of Biscathorpe, lived in Vickers Lane and they had eight children. John (born 1819) married Sabrina Ostler in 1838 at the newly (1835) enlarged 1,600 seat Wesleyan Chapel on Eastgate (now Louth Methodist Church) and lived in Titley's Yard off Northgate; their eldest son Abraham (born 1840) became a Primitive Methodist Local Preacher. John and Sabrina were both carpet weavers.

It was unusual to find women carpet weavers, but that was the case with another branch of the Spiveys. Abraham Spivey (born 1816) came to Louth from Birstall near Leeds, and both he and his wife Elizabeth (born in Louth) were carpet weavers in the 1850s and 1860s, as was their son Abel (born 1835). Other husband and wife weavers were Francis and Rebecca Blanchard, Henry and Elizabeth Rayner, John and Rachel Ruthven (specialising in hearthrugs), and William and Hannah Swingler, all in 1861.

The simple pattern of one side of a bed rug of the 1850s, perhaps woven by the Ruthvens?

Another family who migrated to Louth and became established was the Burdetts from Market Harborough. Samuel Burdett (born 1821), his wife Elizabeth and daughter Jane (born 1843) arrived between 1844 and 1847, as it was in Louth that their other children were born – Joseph Samuel in 1848 and Elizabeth Hannah in 1850. The 1851 census records them living on the southern edge of town in a row of labourers' cottages at the top end of Long Lane, with near neighbour carpet weavers Joseph Fieldhouse from Kidderminster and John Walker from Dewsbury. (Long Lane was renamed Church Street after the building of St Michael's Church, designed by James Fowler, in 1863.) By 1861 the family had moved to James Street. Samuel also brought with him to Louth his younger brother John Oliver, born in 1831 at Market Harborough and then in his teens.

Carpet making at Market Harborough had started in the early 19th century when the demand declined for tammies (high quality worsted), but the carpet industry there collapsed in the 1840s: that was why the Burdetts moved to Louth. The middle brother, Richard (born 1825 and also a carpet weaver) tried Halifax first, where he and his wife Adelaide had a daughter, also Adelaide, in 1849, before coming to Louth where their next daughter Mary was born in 1855. The family lived first in Eve Street and then Carpet Row on James Street. Daughter Adelaide was a winder in the factory and son Henry (born 1864) was a carpet weaver by the time he was 17.

Richard and Henry were still weaving carpets when the factory closed in 1883. The 1891 census shows Richard still in James Street, age 66 and 'living on own means' with his wife Adelaide (60) and their daughter Alice (17) a dressmaker. The entry about 'living on own means' raises the question as to whether a 'redundancy' payment was made to factory employees at closure.

Samuel Burdett rose to become foreman carpet weaver to Charles Paddison by 1861, but before the next census (1871) he and his family had moved to similar employment in Kendal, where his son Richard (born 1854 in Louth) also became a carpet weaver.

The youngest brother, John Oliver, remained in Louth, married Elizabeth from Leeds in the early 1860s, had two children, Jane Oliver and John Oliver, and lived at 9 Vickers Lane. By 1871 he had risen to foreman carpet weaver (after Samuel had gone to Kendal). More interestingly he was also recorded as a carpet designer. See The Carpets chapter for his designs for the carpets which were highly commended at the 1867 Paris Exhibition. However, the 1872 directory lists him as a carpet designer and dealer and in 1876 as a carpet dealer; in other words he had left the factory and set up on his own account. Perhaps he sensed the impending decline of the factory. Thereafter and until 1900 he had a carpet warehouse at 120 Eastgate. He then retired to Leicester House, Eastgate where he died in 1922.

Four other carpet weavers who abandoned Market Harborough for Louth were Thomas Lockington (born 1812), James Lockington (born 1818) and William Swingler (born 1826) and his wife Hannah (born 1824). They lived in Ramsgate, where their son John (born 1852) was drowned in the 1920 Louth Flood.

Incomers from south Yorkshire were brothers Joseph and William Bentley (Heckmondwike), James Bould, Samuel Daly and Richard Dyson (Dewsbury), Frederick Goodall (Liversedge), Charles Hollinsworth (Halifax) and Henry Rayner (Huddersfield), all carpet weavers. Of the Buckley family from Heckmondwike, father Matthew was a carpet weaver as was David; Mary Ann and Julia were wool yarn winders, and John a labourer at the mill. Enoch Cooper from Dewsbury was a wool spinner, Thomas Lee and his son Jeremiah from south Yorkshire were dyers. Louth also received two carpet weavers and a wool spinner from Kidderminster and two weavers from Barnard Castle, both centres for flat-weave carpet production. Others came from as far afield as Barnstaple and Bannockburn. Clearly Louth's standing in the trade was widely recognised.

An analysis of workers who have been traced shows some 80 family names, two-thirds of whom were immigrants: 12 in the early years, 16 in the 1840s, 21 in the 1850s, six in the 1860s and 10 in the 1870s. Half of those from Yorkshire arrived in the 1850s, those from Market Harborough in the 1840s and 1850s, and those from Durham and Kidderminster in the 1860s and 1870s (the latter perhaps a reflection of the introduction of power looms there). During the time the factory was operating over ninety weavers found work there. Other trades were wool sorter, wool comber, wool spinner, wool winder, dyer and general factory labourer.

Part of the underside of an Art Square Louth carpet
(see pages 90-91)

Good weavers were the key to success, and the Louth factory prided itself on quality before quantity. As an isolated factory away from main production centres, that was a sound policy. The number of weavers employed at any time was an indication of the number of looms in the factory. Checking all sources, including census returns for owners which gave the number of employees, a pattern of change emerges.

In **1823**, the year of the Rate Valuation and the first time where names of workers can be identified, Adam Eve, aged 68, was in sole charge, his business partner John Espin and factory overseer William Froggitt having recently died, there were ten carpet weavers:

John Athway (37)	from Hull
Charles Cooper	
Benjamin Furnish (57)	immigrant
John Green (33)	the returned soldier
Thomas Kew (32)	from St Pancras, London
Abraham Spivey (28)	from Liversedge
Isaac Spivey (20)	brothers of Abraham
Jacob Spivey (18)	brothers of Abraham
Samuel Sutton (42)	
Thomas Wilkinson	

Benjamin Furnish and Samuel Sutton, along with wool sorter Thomas Spivey (53) were among Adam's earliest employees. There were also four wool combers and a yarn scourer. Ten weavers implies ten looms – in the weaving rooms on the other side of James Street – and also implies ten drawboys. There would also have been girls reeling and doing general cleaning in the factory.

The 1826 directory describes the business as an 'extensive carpet and blanket manufactory'. We have already noted an invoice of 1815 for a pair of blankets at 18 shillings a pair, the standard price for common blankets then, but this had risen to £1 by the 1820s. Did the list of weavers include those making blankets, or were there also those specialising in blanket weaving? Unfortunately there is no direct information relating to blanket weavers. There is a reference in 1830 to employment of 28 men plus women and children. The women were probably employed on the (presumed power-driven) wool spinning machines, and some of the additional number of men, in pairs, could have been blanket weavers, particularly as blanketing was made on a broader (6 feet wide) loom than those used for carpets.

Handloom blanket weaving at Witney in the early 20th century, much the same as it was in Louth in the 19th century

Because of its coarseness, Lincoln longwool, called 'dag-locks' by the weavers of fine Witney blankets, was used for common low quality blankets. The short flocky wool, or noils, left in the combs was used for the weft. Weaving was continuous with coloured yarn in the weft, or shoots, to indicate the length of blankets (7½ feet), the cut ends bound with tape. The blankets than had to be fulled or dressed and stretch dried on tenterhooks. Blanket weaving was normally summer work for the coming winter and largely for local consumption. There were also periods of increased demand for common blankets for the army during the Napoleonic wars. Blanket making in Louth was always secondary to carpet weaving, and ceased in the early 1840s.

LIST OF VOTERS

On the Question of a

CHURCH RATE, AT LOUTH,

TAKEN

ON THE 3rd, 4th, & 6th OF OCTOBER, 1834.

The *List of Voters on the Question of the Church Rate* in October **1834** gives the occupation of every voter. William Espin (37) and the young John Paddison (22) were running the factory and both voted for the Rate. All their employees except two voted against. The implication is clear: the large majority of the factory workers were nonconformists. The list identifies 19 factory workers, living in James Street, Northgate and Ramsgate. The weavers were:

John Athway (48)
Robert Carter
Charles Cooper
George France (33) from Birstall
Benjamin Furnish (68)
John Green (44)
Thomas Kew (43)
Abraham Spivey (39)
Isaac Spivey (31)
Jacob Spivey (29)
Samuel Sutton (53)
Samuel White
Frank Whittaker
Thomas Wilkinson

Thomas Spivey (63) was still sorting wool, the wool combers were Reuben Wilman (58) and his sons David and Joseph, John Elvin, William Green, William Smith and Jonathan Tenant, and John Storr was the yarn scourer.

William Espin's involvement in the factory ended in 1835, and John Paddison ran it on his own until his death in 1838 when his younger brother Charles, then 21, took over. The list of weavers taken from the **1838** Rate Valuation list indicates some contraction of the workforce (and with only one new name, John Harrison) under John Paddison's management.

John Athway (52)
Robert Carter
George France (37)
Benjamin Furnish (72)
John Green (48)
John Harrison (37)

ANNO SEXTO

GEORGII IV. REGIS.

****

Cap. cxxxvii.

An Act for establishing a Company for lighting with Gas the Town of *Louth* in the County of *Lincoln*. [10th *June* 1825.]

There is no evidence as to when gas lighting was installed in the factory and weaving rooms, but it was probably during the ownership and management of Charles Paddison

6 Geo. IV.—Sess. 1825.

AN

A C T

FOR

Paving, Lighting, Watching, Cleansing, Regulating, and otherwise improving the Town and Parish of *Louth* in the County of *Lincoln*.

[Royal Assent, June 10, 1825.]

It was information in the Schedule to the Act for Paving, Lighting etc which revealed that carpet weaving rooms were on the opposite side of James Street to the factory *(see page 48)*

Thomas Kew (47)
Abraham Spivey (43)
Isaac Spivey (35)
Jacob Spivey (33)
Samuel Sutton (57)
Thomas Wilkinson

Within three years of taking charge, Charles Paddison was making a difference, having taken on seven new weavers, four of them under 25. The full list from the **1841** census was:

John Athway (55)	
Benjamin Bailey (65)	immigrant
Francis Blanchard (19)	born at Salfleetby
John Emerson (20)	
George France (40)	
Benjamin Furnish (75)	the oldest hand and still weaving
John Green (50)	
George Green (25)	John's son
James Green (40)	
John Harrison (40)	
Thomas Kew (50)	
Edward Sleight (40)	
Abraham Spivey (45)	
Isaac Spivey (38)	
Jacob Spivey (35)	
John Spivey (20)	Abraham's son
Samuel Sutton (60)	

Also, immigrant Caleb Simpson (20) was in prison (the House of Correction). Thomas Spivey (70) the wool sorter was still working. Two immigrants from Yorkshire – Thomas Lee and his teenage son Jeremiah – were dyers.

Over the next ten years Charles Paddison built up a thriving concern, recruiting and training more young weavers, ceased making blankets and made more rugs, registered new carpet designs in 1845 and 1850, and was using broad looms for Art Square carpets (see The Carpets chapter). Unfortunately we do not know the name of the designer. By the **1851** census he was employing 50 men, 6 women and 20 children. There were 40 weavers; this does not necessarily mean 40 looms as two men were needed to work the broad looms. In fact there were never more than 34 looms. The carpet weavers including 16 new immigrants, were:

John Athway (65)	the oldest and most experienced
Obadiah Athway (27)	John's son
Francis Blanchard (29)	
Matthew Buckley (44)	from Heckmondwike
Samuel Burdett (30)	from Market Harborough
John Burdett (21)	Samuel's brother
James Crabtree (23)	from Halifax
James Dunham (24)	born at Cadwell
Christopher Fawn (14)	
James Fieldhouse (37)	from Kidderminster with son William (11) as his winder
George France (50)	
Sandy France (34)	from Scotland
Joseph Frankish (20)	
Frederick Goodall (35)	from Liversedge
John Goodall (44)	from Alford
George Goodall (24)	John's son
John Green (60)	Chelsea Pensioner but still working
George Green (35)	

Richard Haigh (24)	from Bury
John Harrison (50)	
Charles Hollinsworth (24)	from Halifax
Thomas Kew (60)	
George Locke (24)	from Halifax
Thomas Lockington (39)	from Market Harborough
Henry Popham (21)	from Barnstaple
Edward Sleight (50)	
Thomas Sleight (25)	Edward's son
Henry Smith (18)	
Abraham Spivey (55)	
Abel Spivey (17)	apprentice: Abraham's son
Jacob Spivey (46)	
John Spivey (32)	
John Stainton (51)	from Ludford
John Storr (29)	from Dewsbury
Charles Sutton (31)	
William Swingler (25)	from Market Harborough
William Townsend (17)	
John Walker (28)	from Dewsbury
Thomas Whymont (32)	from Clipstone, Northants

John Elvin (40) was still sorting wool, and Thomas Lee (39) was in charge of dyeing the yarn with Morriss Brownlow (20) from Selby, William Fatton (23) from York, James Mahoney (22) from Southwark and Robert Rose (45) from Brighton.

At the Louth Petty Sessions in April 1851, Matthew Buckley's unmarried daughter Elizabeth (21) charged John Hatfield, carpet weaver, with being the father of her bastard child and 'prayed the court to make an order on him for its maintenance' at 1s 6d per week.

Ten years on and into the 1860s the enterprise was described as an 'extensive carpet manufactory employing a great number of hands'. The number of weavers had further increased to 42 and included 17 new immigrants. Charles Paddison may have done more recruiting, but it would also appear that Louth was seen as a good place to work. Carpet weavers in there **1861** census were:

Robert Allmar (20)	from Barnard Castle
Joseph Bentley (31)	from Heckmondwike
William Bentley (26)	Joseph's brother
Francis Blanchard (39)	
Rebecca Blanchard (35)	Francis's wife, born at Fanthorpe
Matthew Buckley (54)	
Daniel Buckley (18)	Matthew's son
Samuel Burdett (40)	Foreman
John Burdett (31)	
Richard Burdett (35)	from Halifax; brother to Samuel & John
Adelaide Burdett (29)	Richard's wife
Francis Dales (38)	born at Saltfleetby
Samuel Daly (24)	from Dewsbury
Richard Dyson (28)	from Dewsbury
Joseph Fieldhouse (47)	
James Gardner (34)	from Bannockburn
Thomas Halt (22)	from Wigfield, Yorks
James Hargreaves (30)	from Kidderminster
Charles Heal (16)	from Hull
James Lockington (43)	from Market Harborough
Walter Parrish (19)	born at Theddlethorpe
Henry Rayner (32)	from Huddersfield
Elizabeth Rayner (38)	Henry's wife

Charles Rushforth (24)	from Leeds
Edward Sleight (60)	
Thomas Sleight (34)	Edward's son
Abraham Spivey (65)	
Abraham Spivey (45)	from Birstall
Elizabeth Spivey (46)	Abraham's wife
Abel Spivey (26)	Abraham's son
John Spivey (41)	
Sabrina Spivey (41)	John's wife
Jacob Spivey (56)	
Elizabeth Spivey (49)	Jacob's wife
James Spriggs (41)	from Clipstone, Northants
Charles Sutton (41)	
William Swingler (37)	
Hannah Swingler (37)	William's wife
David Wilman (22)	son of wool comber
Christopher Wilson (17)	apprentice

Plus John Ruthven (42) and his wife Rachel (36) who were hearthrug weavers, and two carpet weavers (24 and 20) whose names in the census were indecipherable. John Capes (60) from Saltfleet was sorting wool, and wool spinner Enoch Cooper (34) had arrived from Dewsbury. Matthew Buckley's daughters Mary Ann (24) and Julia (13) were yarn winders; other winders were John Emerson (45), and John Clifton (13) who lived with his widowed mother from Halifax. Freeman Clifton (43) and his wife Sarah (44) were dyers and their son Thomas (15) was a labourer in the factory; Thomas Cook (52) from Legbourne and his wife Judith (44) were dyehouse labourers. There was also a spinner, Ellenor Griffin (50) from Ireland.

The total traced was 43 men and 14 women, which does not quite match with the number of employees recorded against owner Charles Paddison (44 men and six women); perhaps some of the wives were not working full time. Note that there were no children under 13. Also of interest is the fact that there were 14 families who made up 70% of the workforce. Some of the families were husband and wife weavers: if they or some of them were working together, it implies a dozen or so broad looms making Art Square carpets.

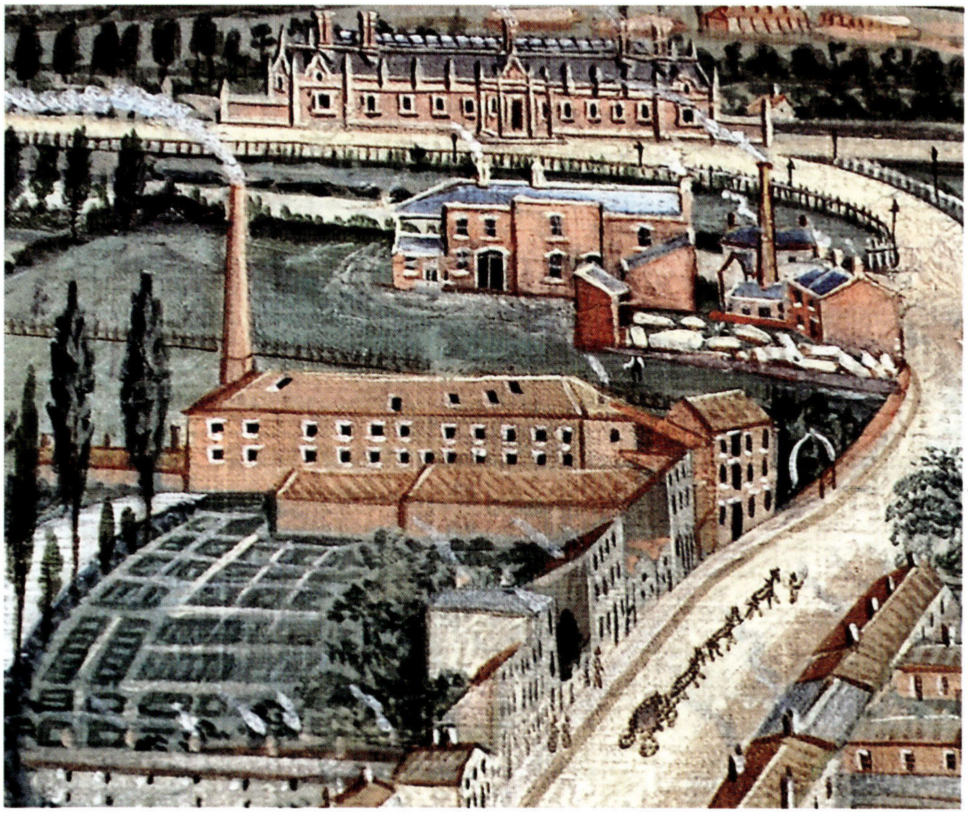

The workplace: the Carpet Factory and Wool Warehouse as seen from the top of the spire of St James's church and depicted on William Brown's Louth Panorama, 1847

Charles Paddison employed a clerk, Thomas Preston (53) who lived on Newmarket. The homes of the workers were in James Street (9), Ramsgate and Newbridge Hill (11), Eve Street (8), Long Lane (3), Vickers Lane, Bridge Street, Spital Hill, Westgate, and Yards off Northgate (3). An indication of the poverty level of workers at the factory is evidenced by the fact that in 1861 Charles Cooper (68), born in Saltfleetby and giving his occupation as carpet weaver, was in the Union Workhouse.

Charles Paddison did not marry, although he had an illegitimate daughter, but one has the impression of a family factory, by that time lit by gas, where workers knew each other socially and attended the same chapels. One can imagine them converging on the factory before dawn and not returning home until after sunset, although some weavers may have worked irregular hours to complete orders.

Part of a carpet design by John Burdett, 1863

Louth carpet factory under Paddison's management reached its peak of production in the 1850s and just into the 1860s, but change and decline were around the corner. Charles Paddison was 44 and, as we saw in the last chapter, was contemplating early retirement. By 1863 the factory was being run by Edward Hoff (44) and his son Robert William (23) from Holbeach. Weaver John Burdett became foreman, and he created new designs in 1863 (3), 1864 (4) and 1865 (2) which were made and exhibited at the 1867 Paris Exhibition: they were highly commended. But could they compete with the increasingly affordable and popular Turkish carpets and the innovative Tapestry carpets which were cheaper imitations of pile carpets? There was the effect of wars in Europe, such as the Franco-Prussian War 1870, and in the United States manufacturers concentrated on the mass market for flat-weave carpets. Together also with the agricultural depression and its effect on the home market, big centres of production such as Kidderminster and Barnard Castle began to feel the pinch – as shown by the immigrant workers in the 1881 Louth census. And the Factory Act applied to the Louth factory after 1867 restricted working hours to 60 hours a week until 1874 and thereafter to 56½hours.

It is no surprise therefore to find that the number of carpet weavers at Louth in **1871** had shrunk by more than a half:

Francis Blanchard (49)	
Matthew Buckley (64)	
Daniel Buckley (28)	
Richard Burdett (45)	
John Burdett (40)	Foreman and carpet designer
John Elvin (28)	son of wool sorter
Joseph Fieldhouse (57)	
James Gardner (44)	
Richard Harrison (43)	from Kendal
William Linthwaite (52)	from Darlington
Thomas Morton (54)	
William Morton (36)	Thomas's son
Walter Parrish (29)	
Thomas Sleight (44)	
William Smurnthwaite (52)	from Darlington
John Smurnthwaite (25)	William's son
Jacob Spivey (66)	
William Swingler (45)	
Joseph Watson (18)	

There was a spinner, Job Beamont (31) from Kidderminster, and a dyer, Joseph Smith (17).

A national survey in 1874 of the number of firms with hand looms making flat-weave or similar carpeting ranged from Kelley of Heckmondwike with 303 to J & S Smith of Glasgow with five. Hoff & Son of Louth was 25th in the list with 34 looms. This seems in line with the number of employees at the peak of production. If it is correct, then there were a considerable number idle and silent in 1871.

The picture at the **1881** census was equally gloomy, when Edward Hoff (66) was Manager and the Louth Carpet & Woollen Factory Company struggled to save the business (as described in the previous chapter). Some stalwarts were still weaving and a few immigrants (average age 40) had arrived from other failing centres, but there were only six men 25 or younger. The final list was:

Robert Aitken (25)	from York
Arthur Ainsworth (38)	from Ashton under Lyne
Herbert Ainsworth (38)	from Liversedge
John Anderton (40)	from Barnard Castle
Samuel Arkell (54)	from Kidderminster
Francis Blanchard (59)	40 years' service; also market gardener
James Dicks Bould (38)	from Dewsbury
George Brumpton (17)	apprentice
Matthew Buckley (74)	30+ years' service
John Buckley (33)	Matthew's son
Richard Burdett (55)	25 years' service
Henry Burdett (17)	Richard's son
Susannah Dickinson (58)	
Joseph Fieldhouse (67)	30+ years' service
James Gardner (54)	20+ years' service
James Gardner (25) Thomas Gardner (22)	James's sons
Richard Harrison (53)	10+ years' service
Walter Parrish (39)	20+ years' service
William Swingler (55)	30+ years' service
John Swingler (30)	William's son
Thomas White (48)	from Barnard Castle
Joseph Wilman (31)	last of five Wilmans to have worked in the factory since the 1830s

There was a spinner, William Wright (17), dyer Joseph Smith (27) had been joined by Edward Elmore (33) from Boston and Henry Sharpe (26) from Binbrook, and a factory girl was Fanny Freeman (25). The total of 27 employees was a few more than in 1871, but the end was in sight. John Burdett had left to set up his carpet warehouse, and Daniel Buckley to deal in antique furniture (at 7 Eastgate), and the longest serving weaver, Francis Blanchard, was already dividing his time between weaving and market gardening.

Part of a carpet design by John Burdett, 1864

What did other workers do when the factory finally closed in 1883? The Burdetts stayed in Louth, as did Samuel Arkell, William Smurnthwaite and Thomas White, and John Buckley became a hawker. Other weavers left to try to find work elsewhere, but makers of flat-weave carpets in Yorkshire and Scotland closed down soon after the Louth factory. Edward Hoff and his family moved to a smaller house on Eastgate, where he died the year after the factory closed.

There is an interesting postscript: the 1891 census lists three independent carpet makers (not weavers) – widow Lucy Monkester (30 Northgate, in business until the Great War), Betty Brumby (25 Charles Street) and Elizabeth Cole (43 Northgate). None of them had worked in the factory, and the private enterprise of the latter two was short-lived, being aged 52 and 73 respectively. In 1892 Walter Lee Needler at 5 Newmarket was listed as tailor and carpet maker, but as tailor only four years later. A trawl of county directories reveals three other carpet makers: Mrs Caroline North in Bourne (1892/96), John Thomas Bowman in Boston (1896 – 1905) and Thomas Towers in Grantham (1900). Output was small, in size and quantity, probably tufted carpets made on a hand loom for local consumption.

In Lincoln, John Aram & Sons advertised themselves as carpet makers as well as upholsterers and house furnishers, but appeared only once, in 1889. The same directory also lists the Lincoln Carpet Co, and the name appears again in 1892, but were they makers or dealers? Neither were specialised manufactories like Louth, which provided employment for weavers skilled in making flat-weave carpets until they were no longer in demand.

Part of a carpet design by John Burdett, 1865
(see The Carpets chapter)

A fragment of a Louth-made carpet was used to make a replica stair carpet, manufactured on Jacquard looms in Bulgaria, and fitted in Danson House, Sidcup. The same replica is also laid on the staircase in Kenwood House, Hampstead Heath.

Chapter 5

The Carpets

A carpet should have something to say for itself

Lewis F Day, 1899

THUS FAR in the story of Louth carpets they have been simply described as flat weave. The full name is ingrain flat weave, where ingrain (a common name in the USA) means that the woollen yarn was dyed with fast colours before weaving. However the generic name is 'Kidderminster' as it was there the ingrain flat weave double cloth/ply method started from 1735. By the 1870s Kidderminster was the leading centre of manufacture, which had also spread to South Yorkshire, Durham, Kendal and Central Scotland. During the 19th century the terms 'Kidderminster' (or 'Kidder') and 'Scotch' were synonymous for ingrain flat weave carpets. When the replica Louth carpet was made (see front and back endpapers) and laid in two country houses in 2007 it was described in the literature as 'Kidderminster'.

In flat weaving the pattern is formed by the intersection of two webs of yarn which results in the design on the front being repeated on the back but with the colours exactly reversed. It was therefore a non-pile reversible and relatively inexpensive floor covering. However, because of its quality and versatility, and suitability for living rooms as well as stairs, it commanded a higher price than Brussels (see below). The long narrow strips, usually 37 ins wide, could be sewn together to make large carpets, sometimes with a contrasting border. Art Square carpets complete with border were made on a broader loom.

The most expensive carpets were those imported from Turkey and Persia. Next came the hand-made Axminster, superseded when the factory there closed in 1835 by Wilton where the loops were cut to form a soft pile with luxurious appearance. Some houses might have a variety of styles for different living areas: for example the 1837 sale of contents of Somersby Rectory (birthplace of Alfred Tennyson) listed, Turkey, Brussels and 'other' carpets. Ingrain flat weave carpets, such as those made in Louth, therefore filled a niche in the market. According to the *Industries of the Eastern Counties* (1890) 'Louth carpets enjoyed a very high reputation throughout the country for their excellent wearing qualities'.

What evidence there is suggests that carpets made in Louth were known by that name and not the generic name. As we have seen, when John Campbell made an inventory of the shop stock in 1830-31, he listed Louth Superfine carpet (2s 9d a yard), together with Brussels (2s 6d a yard) and Venetian (2s) carpets. Brussels is a carpet of uncut loop pile, described as hard wearing and resistant to dirt. Venetian was flat woven, generally striped, with design on the warp, and the weft threads not visible; it was generally used for corridors and stairs.

In the 1870s the shop sold Louth carpet at 2s 10d a yard, Dutch carpet at 2s a yard, and Union carpet at 2s 3d. Dutch carpet was the simplest, cheapest and least durable, woven in single ply and was little more than a thick woollen cloth; it was used for stairs and passages.

A.D. 1825 . . . . N° 5254.

Manufacture of Carpets.

EVE'S SPECIFICATION.

The name Union carpet would appear to refer to the Patent Adam Eve took out in 1825. It was for the invention of 'Certain Improvements in Manufacturing Carpets', denominated as 'Prince's Patent Union Carpet', and communicated to Adam by William Augustus Prince 'living aboard' (America?). It describes the double cloth or two-ply technique as 'in the manner in which Kidderminster, Yorkshire, or Scotch carpeting have always been woven or made'.

That method was described as 'The warp or yarn running lengthways of the piece is divided into four parts, to each part of which a treaddle [sic] is attached. Two parts of the said warp is operated upon by means of the treaddles to receive the shute [shuttle] which formed the ground and two parts of the said warp is operated by means of the other treaddles to receive the shute which forms the figure. Were there no figure in the carpet the manner of weaving would form two separate and distinct pieces of cloth. ... it is only the formation of the figure... which forms the union throughout the carpet...' (In plain ground areas the two-ply cloth forms pockets which are joined by a spotted motif or figure in the weave. One Louth carpet shows this particularly well – see pages 106-107.)

It then goes on to describe the improvement: 'In the weaving ... of the improved carpeting ... one half part of the ground warp and one half part of the figure warp is made to rise or cross the other half parts by means of two treaddles being pressed down at the same time, and a binding shute ... is then introduced ... between the ... warps in that crossed position ... The binding thread causes a combination or union of the ground and figure together, the binding thread not being visible on either side of the carpet does not destroy the beauty of the figure'. The date of 1825 was about the time that Adam Eve introduced the Jacquard mechanism to operate the looms, which would have been needed to weave the improved Union carpet.

We know the origin of the woollen yarn used in Louth carpet making – from local Lincoln Longwool sheep, but where did the dyes come from and who supplied them? A clue may lie with the Bowmars of Goltho. The marriage there in 1815 of Anne Bowmar to our Adam's nephew Adam and their resulting large family has been recorded in The Eve Dynasty chapter. Anne's eldest brother Thomas (born 1792) moved to Leicester and became a dyer, as did his son William (born 1820), who would marry (1846) our Adam's great neice Ann. Could the Bowmars of Leicester have supplied dyes to the Louth carpet factory? The range of dyes required included woad and indigo for blue and weld for yellow, and combined for green; madder for scarlet, brick-red and salmon; weld and madder combined for ochre or orange; cochineal for crimson; and cochineal or madder for pink; and walnut tree roots and walnut husks for brown.

No written records exist of carpets made in Louth, but the carpet collection in Louth Museum – runners, staircarpet, Art Squares and fragments – has a range of patterns which have been donated or acquired from local sources. The first record in the then Louth Antiquarian and Naturalists' Society Minute Book of a gift of Louth carpets (two lengths) was in 1896. The donor was Mrs Colbridge, wife of Isaac John Colbridge, grocer and tea merchant of 14 Mercer Row. He had been a shareholder in the Louth Carpet and Woollen Factory Ltd, 1881-83. (See page 64).

No duplicate patterns have ever turned up. In fact, was more than one carpet made of a particular pattern?

The pages that follow include patterns from the Registered Designs and Trade Marks registers at the Public Record Office, Kew, but no examples of them as carpets have been found. Registered designs are dated, but there is difficulty in dating the carpets in the museum from the patterns – except that simpler patterns are likely to be earlier. Also, bearing in mind the status of buyers of ingrain flat weave carpets and the houses in which they lived, it seems likely that most surviving examples are from the later period of the factory.

All sizable pieces of carpet in the Louth Museum collection are illustrated to full page size to show the repeating pattern. The reverse, in most cases, is shown with a smaller illustration, so there is no standard scale. This applies equally to the registered designs which have been achieved by using four mirror images and four originals to show the full repeating pattern, except that the original point paper (graph paper) design of each is reproduced actual size.

A studio portrait on a lantern slide by photographer Joseph Willey (1829-1893) at 7 Aswell Street. The carpet on the floor is believed to be one made in Louth. Date not known.

Accession No:	LOUTN: T1 On display in Louth Museum
Size:	6ft 9ins x 2ft 10ins (205.7 x 86.4cm)
Colours:	Brown, beige and orange.
Description	Alternate leaf and flower pattern. Ends turned under and stitched with 1½ins brown tape.
Source/provenance:	Donated by Mrs Colbridge, 1896. (See previous page).
Date:	Not known.

Reverse of opposite

Accession No: LOUTN: T2 On display in Louth Museum

Size: 8ft 1ins x 8ft 8ins (206.4 x 264.2cm)

Colours: Green, greeny blue, pale orange/peach and burnt orange.

Description: Art Square with tulips, leaves and small daisy-like flowers, and border of tulips, hop seeds and flowers. Arts and crafts design after William Morris.

Ends turned under and stitched with 1½ins camel-colour tape. Also small red tape label marked 5PP 4981. One corner of carpet has been cut out.

The striped effect on the image opposite shows it to be what would normally be regarded as the back of the carpet. The stripes show where the weft colours for the flowers were introduced. The owner preferred that to the green background and two shades – beige and pale orange – for the tulips. The location of the tape shows it to have been used as the back. An interesting example of reversibility of two-ply flat weave carpeting.

Source/provenance: Donated by Mrs Colbridge, 1896. (See page 87).

Date: 1870s.

Additional note: The tulip was used in a number of Morris designs (see also page 104).

Reverse of opposite

Accession No:	LOUTN: T3 On display in Louth Museum
Size:	13ft 5ins x 10ft 6ins (408.9 x 320.1cm)
Colours:	Dark camel, turquoise, green, pale orange, beige and black.
Description:	Art Square – Turkish style geometric pattern with border and fringed ends.
Source/provenance:	Donated by Louth Toc H.
Date:	c. 1850s.

Reverse of opposite

Accession No:	LOUTN: T6 On display in Louth Museum
Size:	3ft 4½ins x 2ft 11ins (102.9 x 88.9cm)
Colours:	Fawn, green and rusty brown.
Description:	Stylised flower and leaf frond design on ground of hexagons. Runner bound each end with matching woven tape.
Source/provenance:	Donated by Michael Gibson, Louth, 1991.
Date:	Not known.

Reverse of opposite

Accession No:	LOUTN: T10 On display in Louth Museum
Size:	4ft 10ins x 3ft (147.4 x 91.5cm)
Colours:	Oat meal, dark brown, beetroot red, tobacco, yellow ochre.
Description:	Trellis pattern in brown on light ground with stylised flower heads, and red and brown striped pattern on crosses of trellis. Runner cut down from larger carpet, stitched at both sides with worn fringed end.
Source/provenance:	Donated by Miss Muriel Robinson, Covenham St Mary, 1991. Had been used in farmhouse at Covenham, built 1846.
Date:	Design suggests an earlier date, possibly 1820s.

Reverse of underside opposite

Accession No:	LOUTN: T41 Reserve collection at Louth Museum
Size:	5ft 8ins x 4ft 2ins (172.7 x 127cm)
Colours:	Green, light and dark brown and red on spotted light grey ground.
Description:	Greek key pattern with stylised rosettes between on grey ground with spots which are the thread to hold together the double ply of the carpet. Striped effect on Greek key and rosettes show as ground on the reverse (see below). Edges bound with striped tape on both sides. A line of stitching can be seen near the right edge of the image opposite. This shows that two strips of carpet of standard woven width were sewn together to make the required width.
Source/provenance:	Donated by Mrs Joyce Greenfield, Fotherby in 1993. It had been in her grandmother's house at Saltfleetby.
Date:	Possibly 1820s.

Reverse of opposite

Accession No:	LOUTN: T141 Reserve collection at Louth Museum
Size:	11ft (three strips 3ft and one 2ft) x 9ft 3½ins (335.3 x 283.3cm)
Colours:	Cream, gold, black, pale brown and wine.
Description:	Complex of quatrefoil, octagon, roundels and banding, with flowers, lilies and wreaths of leaves. The strips of carpet are hand-stitched together with jute twine using a type of feather stitch which gives a flat seam.
Source/provenance:	Donated by Sue Banks, Alvingham, 2007. Bought from an antiques shop in Brigg, 1950s.
Date:	c. 1850s.

Jute stitching on reverse

Reverse of opposite

Accession No:	LOUTN: T71 On display in Louth Museum
Size:	24ft 3ins x 8ft 10ins (739.2 x 269.2cm)
Colours:	Maroon, dark green and gold.
Description:	Art square – geometric pattern of Persian derivation. Edges and corners bound underneath with 1½ins striped tape; small fringe at ends.
Source/provenance:	Loan from Louth Town Council. Originally in Mayor's Parlour, later Town Clerk's office. Likely to have been made for the Parlour when the Town Hall was built 1853.
Date:	1853.

Reverse of opposite

Accession No:	LOUTN: T154 Reserve collection at Louth Museum
Size:	9ft x 5ft (274.3 x 149.9cm); border 18ins (45.7cm)
Colours:	Turquoise, light blue, green, graded brown, yellow ochre.
Description:	Leaves, flowers and tendrils on ochre ground. Border of large sycamore-style leaves, yellow tendrils and outer contour pattern. Crudely cut and fringed both ends. May have been cut out of an oblong Art Square. Arts and Crafts design after William Morris.
Source/provenance:	On loan from Stuart Barton, Louth. Found in a property in Alford.
Date:	Late 1870s.
Additional note:	Morris produced several designs in the mid-1870s for 'Kidderminster' carpets which were machine-woven in Heckmondwike. Perhaps this may be a near identical copy. (See also page 90).

Reverse of opposite

Accession No:	LOUTN: T155 Reserve collection at Louth Museum
Size:	11ft 10ins x 34ins (360.7 x 86.3cm)
Colours:	Red, black and natural.
Description:	Large and small banded squares with motif on corners, and red and black motifs within. Where part of a white square occurs at the margin, a pocket effect between the two sides of the carpet can be seen: the purpose of the small motifs is to bind together the double ply.
Source/provenance:	Donated by Sally Wildsmith, Thorpe le Vale. Acquired at a sale in Louth mid-1990s.
Date:	Not known.

Reverse of opposite

Accession No: LOUTN: T7 Reserve collection at Louth Museum

Size: 35ins x 12ins (58.4 x 30.5cm)

Colours: Olive green, dark green, biscuit and beige.

Description: Leaf pattern alternately with small sycamore leaf in diamonds banded with Greek key. Probably the fringed end of a runner with the cut end turned and bound with black tape. Had been folded for use as a draught excluder.

Source/provenance: Donated by Miss J Larder, Louth, 1990.

Date: Not known.

Reverse side

Accession No:	LOUTN: T118 Reserve collection at Louth Museum
Size:	21ins x 3ins (53.3 x 7.6cm); 29ins x 3-5ins (73.7 x 7.6-12.7cm); 5ins x 2½ins (12.7 x 6.4cm)
Colours:	Bottle green, two shades of red, beige and yellow.
Description:	Geometric pattern with right angles and crosses to give overall trellis effect. Only example known where the same pattern was used with a slightly different colour mix. These scraps were found wrapped round cords on a drying frame in the laundry of South Elkington Hall (built 1841).
Source/provenance:	Donated by G & B Dobson, South Elkington, 1997.
Date:	Coarse weave suggests a date earlier than 1840.

Which side would you prefer as a floor covering?

Accession No:	–
Size:	9ins x 27ins (22.8 x 68.6cm)
Colours:	Red, pink, ochre, olive green and natural ground.
Description:	Florets on striped three-colour ground, with hexagons of natural ground linked in a trellis form. Long sides turned over and stitched. Fragment of a room carpet made from 27 inches wide strips.
Source/provenance:	Property of Cynthia Winder, Willingham by Stow, originally from grandfather's house in Ramsgate, Louth. It had been bought at a local sale in the late 1940s.
Date:	Not known.

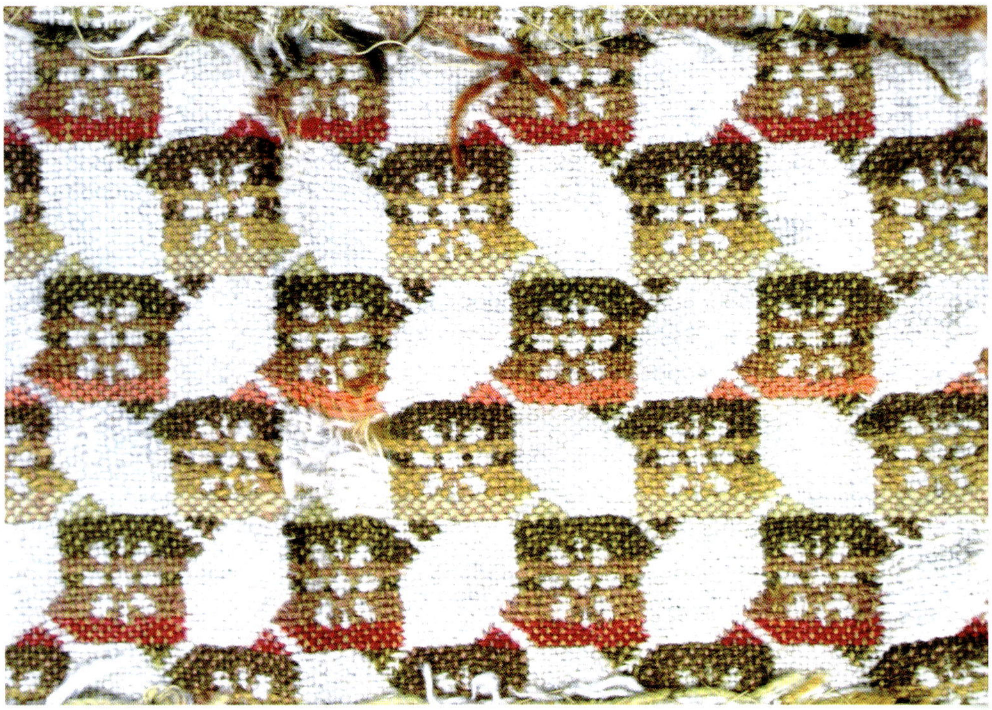

Worn area of ground (lower left) shows the other ply behind

Reverse side

Accession No:	–
Size:	18½ins x 8½ins (47 x 21.6cm)
Colours:	Red, orange, brown, two shades of green and natural ground.
Description:	Alternate rows of leaves and motifs, with foliage borders on each side – the only example seen of this arrangement. Network of colour single warp and weft 'buttons' in natural ground to hold together the double ply in those areas. The striped effect of colours, particularly on the borders, show that this was the underside of a narrow runner or staircarpet. Now a cushion cover.
Source/provenance:	Property of Sally Wildsmith, Thorpe le Vale. Acquired at a sale in Louth in mid-1990s.
Date:	Not known.

Display cabinet of some Louth carpets in the Town Gallery of Louth Museum

They are best viewed from the mezzanine.

A strip of the replica carpet (featured actual size on the endpapers of this book) hangs on the rail for visitors to handle and inspect the method of weaving.

Accession No:	LOUTN: T156 Reserve collection at Louth Museum
Size:	8ft 11ins x 6ft 11ins (210.8 x 248.9cm)
Colours:	Scarlet (rosettes) against ground of green and yellow.
Description:	Bed rug of more open weave than carpets. Ends turned over and stitched.
Source/provenance:	Donated by Mrs Eileen Borrill, Saltfleetby. Originally used by great grandmother.
Date:	1840s/1850s.

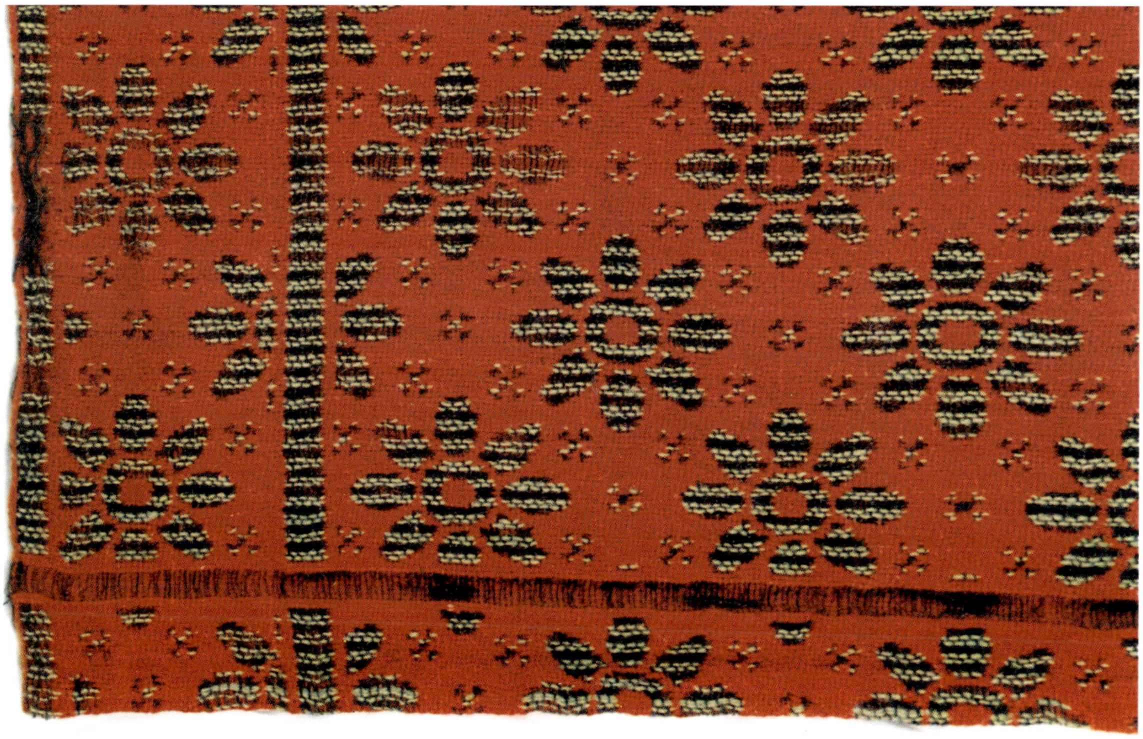

Registered Designs and Trade Marks: Public Record Office, Kew

Class 6: Carpets

Ref: BT 43/107 *Design No:* 24156

Charles Paddison, Louth 7 January 1845

Point paper design (squared paper 16 to one inch) below and repeated pattern opposite.

Registered Designs and Trade Marks: Public Record Office, Kew

Class 6: Carpets

Ref: BT 43/108 *Design No:* 31605

Charles Paddison, Louth 29 November 1845

Point paper design (squared paper 16 to one inch) below and repeated pattern opposite.

Registered Designs and Trade Marks: Public Record Office, Kew

Class 6: Carpets

Ref: BT 43/108 *Design No:* 32336

Charles Paddison, Louth 15 December 1845

Point paper design (squared paper 16 to one inch) below and repeated pattern opposite.

Registered Designs and Trade Marks: Public Record Office, Kew

Class 6: Carpets

Ref: BT 43/113 *Design No:* 74242

Charles Paddison, Louth 10 December 1850

Point paper design (squared paper 16 to one inch) below and repeated pattern opposite.

Registered Designs and Trade Marks: Public Record Office, Kew

Class 6: Carpets

Ref: BT 43/131 *Design No:* 165370.

Hoff & Son, Louth 4 September 1863

Point paper design (squared paper 16 to one inch) below and repeated pattern opposite.

PARIS

UNIVERSAL EXHIBITION

1867.

Class XVIII.—CARPETS, TAPESTRY, &c.

GREAT BRITAIN.

1 BOYLE & SMITH, 9, *Great Marlborough-street, London.*—Carpets.

2 BRINTON & LEWIS, *Kidderminster.*—Brussels carpets, moquettes, chenille carpets and rugs.

3 GREGORY & Co. 212, *Regent-street, London.*—Brussels and velvet-pile carpets.

4 HARRISON, C. *Stourport.*—Brussels and velvet-pile carpets.

5 HENDERSON & Co. *Durham.*—Royal moquette.

6 HOFF & Son, *James-street, Louth, Lincolnshire.*—Carpets.

7 HUMPHRIES, J. & Son, *Mill-street, Kidderminster, and* 3, *King Edward-street, Newgate-street, London.*—Carpets and rugs.

8 JACKSON & GRAHAM, 35, *Oxford-street, London.*—Carpets.

9 LAPWORTH, Brothers, 22, *Old Bond-street, London.*—Carpets.

10 MORTON & Son, *Kidderminster.*—Brussels and velvet pile carpets.

Registered Designs and Trade Marks: Public Record Office, Kew

Class 6: Carpets

Ref: BT 43/131 *Design No:* 166158

Hoff & Son, Louth 17 September 1863

Point paper design (squared paper 16 to one inch) below and repeated pattern opposite.

Registered Designs and Trade Marks: Public Record Office, Kew

Class 6: Carpets

Ref: BT 43/132 *Design No:* 170575

Hoff & Son, Louth 3 December 1863

Point paper design (squared paper 16 to one inch) below and repeated pattern opposite.

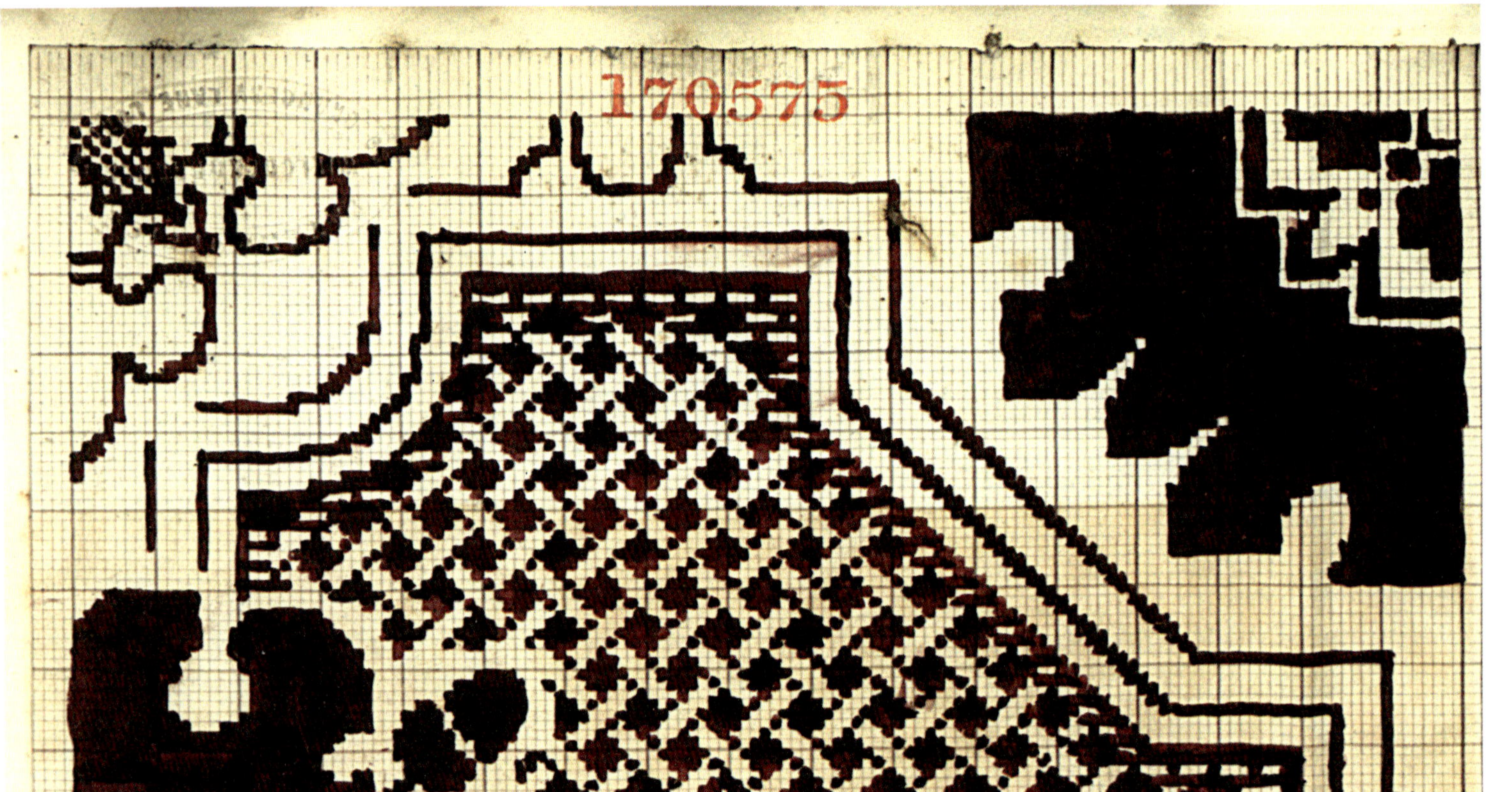

Registered Designs and Trade Marks: Public Record Office, Kew

Class 6: Carpets

Ref: BT 43/132 *Design No:* 172246

Hoff & Son, Louth 4 March 1864

Point paper design (squared paper 16 to one inch) below and repeated pattern opposite.

Registered Designs and Trade Marks: Public Record Office, Kew

Class 6: Carpets

Ref: BT 43/133 *Design No:* 174459

Hoff & Son, Louth 16 May 1864

Point paper design (squared paper 16 to one inch) below and repeated pattern opposite.

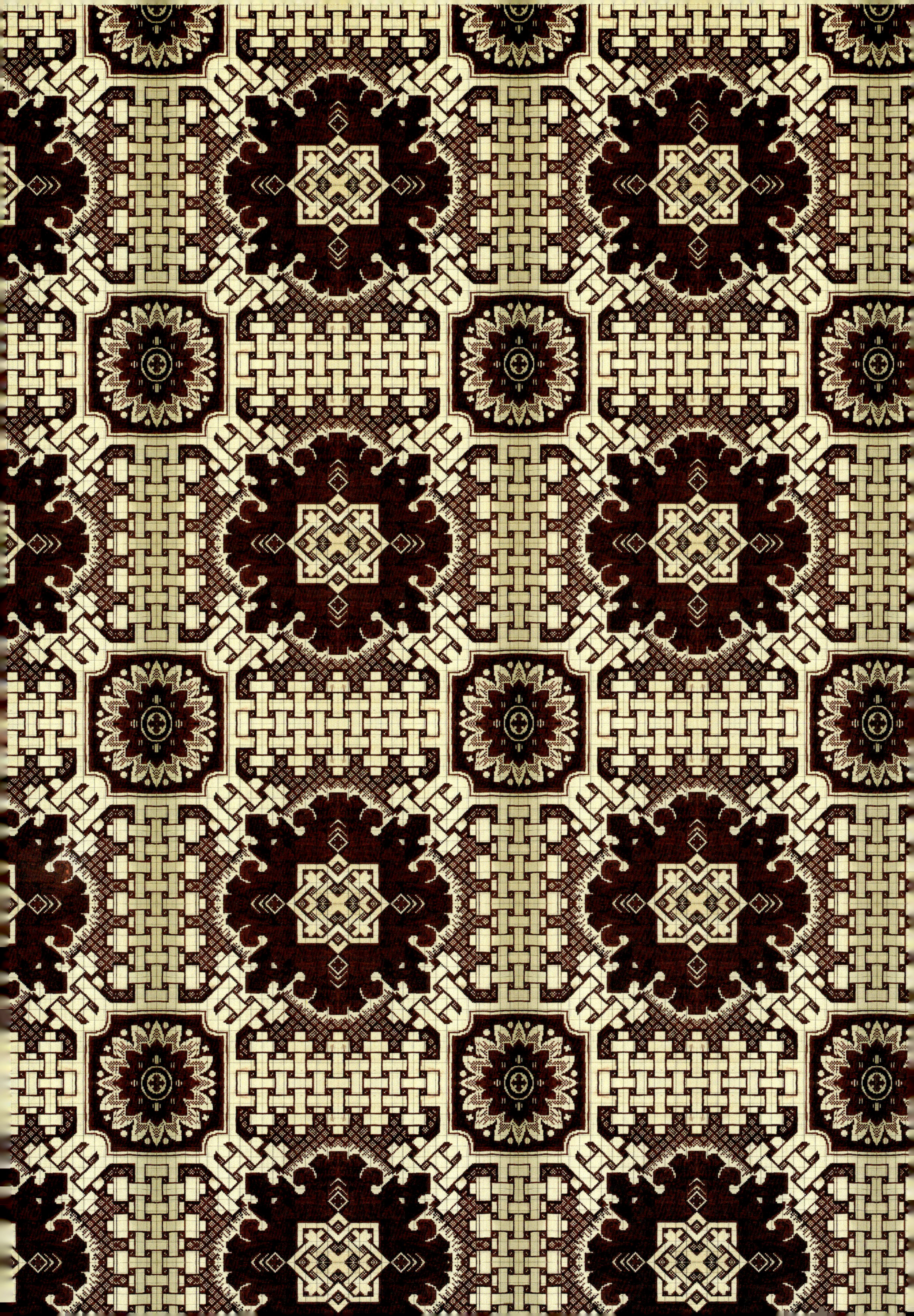

Registered Designs and Trade Marks: Public Record Office, Kew

Class 6: Carpets

Ref: BT 43/134 *Design No:* 178692

Hoff & Son, Louth 20 September 1864

Point paper design (squared paper 16 to one inch) below and repeated pattern opposite.

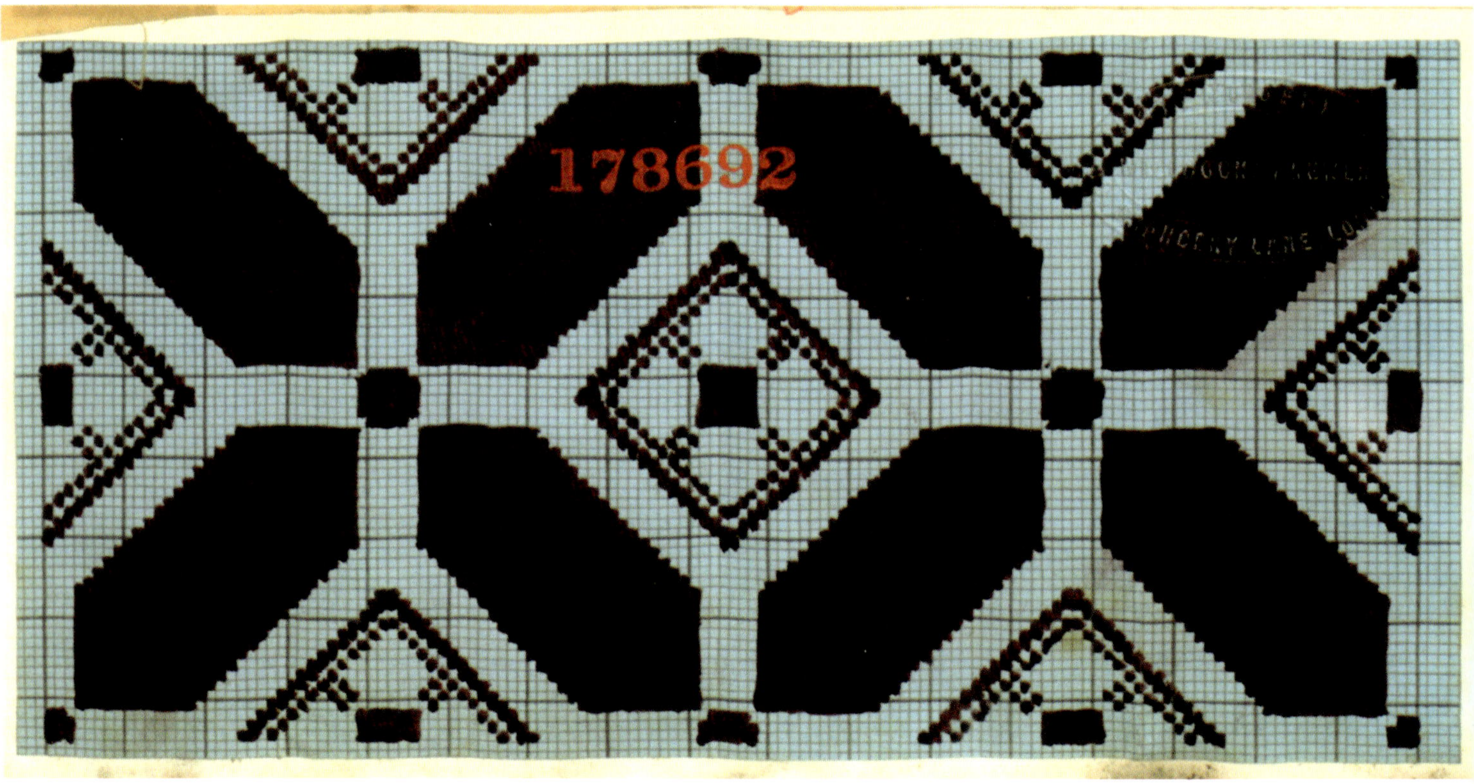

Registered Designs and Trade Marks: Public Record Office, Kew

Class 6: Carpets

Ref: BT 43/135 *Design No:* 187832

Hoff & Son, Louth 28 June 1865

Point paper design (squared paper 16 to one inch) below and repeated pattern opposite.

Registered Designs and Trade Marks: Public Record Office, Kew

Class 6: Carpets

Ref: BT 43/136 *Design No:* 189430

Hoff & Son, Louth 29 August 1865

Point paper design (squared paper 16 to one inch) below and repeated pattern opposite.

The earliest image of Adam Eve's shop, No 1 Market Place

Part of the image of the Market Place
engraved on stone by T W Wallis in 1857

Four of the Georgian bow windows survived into the mid 1880s, this photograph taken just before the change to flat bays with plate glass

Chapter 6

The Shop

JUST OVER a century before Adam Eve went into business as a mercer, an inventory was made of the stock of town-centre mercer Judith Hardy, a widow who died in 1672. It shows a reasonably high class establishment, the type of stock not dissimilar to that which would have been found later in Adam's shop. Fabrics included bombazine (twilled silk and worsted), camblet (thin stuff of wool or goat's hair mixed with silk), cambric (fine white linen), dimity (stout cotton cloth, ribbed and figured, for bed hangings and window curtains), drugget (coarse woollen cloth for floor covering, or if of fine wool for clothing), fustian (coarse thick twilled cotton cloth), prunella (smooth woollen stuff for clergymen's gowns), say (thin woollen stuff or serge), serge (twilled woollen cloth dyed in the piece), shalloon (light woollen fabric), taffeta (fine smooth stuff of silk, wool or cotton with wavy lustre from hot pressing), tammy (fine worsted cloth of high quality, hot pressed to give glazed finish) and woolsey (dress material of cotton and wool).

Haberdashery included varieties of thread including gold and silver, tapes such as ferret (a narrow woollen tape), laces, ribbons, whipcord, buttons, hooks and eyes, whalebone, pins and thimbles. Among ready-made wear were fustian drawers, stomachers, bodices (some with whalebone, and leather for children), capes, oilskins, hosiery, gloves in buck, kid, lamb, sheep and chamois, caps and hats (some of straw, felt and beaver).

Also on sale were groceries, such as spices (pepper, cayenne, aniseed, caraway seed, cloves, cinnamon, ginger and liquorice), sugar (East Indian, brown and loaf), rice, prunes, currants and raisins, honey and treacle, candy and vinegar; hardware: quicksilver (mercury), red lead and pitch, curtain rings, powder horns, powder and shot; and other items including beeswax and sealing wax, horn and ivory combs, leather brushes, brimstone, starch, tobacco and pipes, and writing paper.

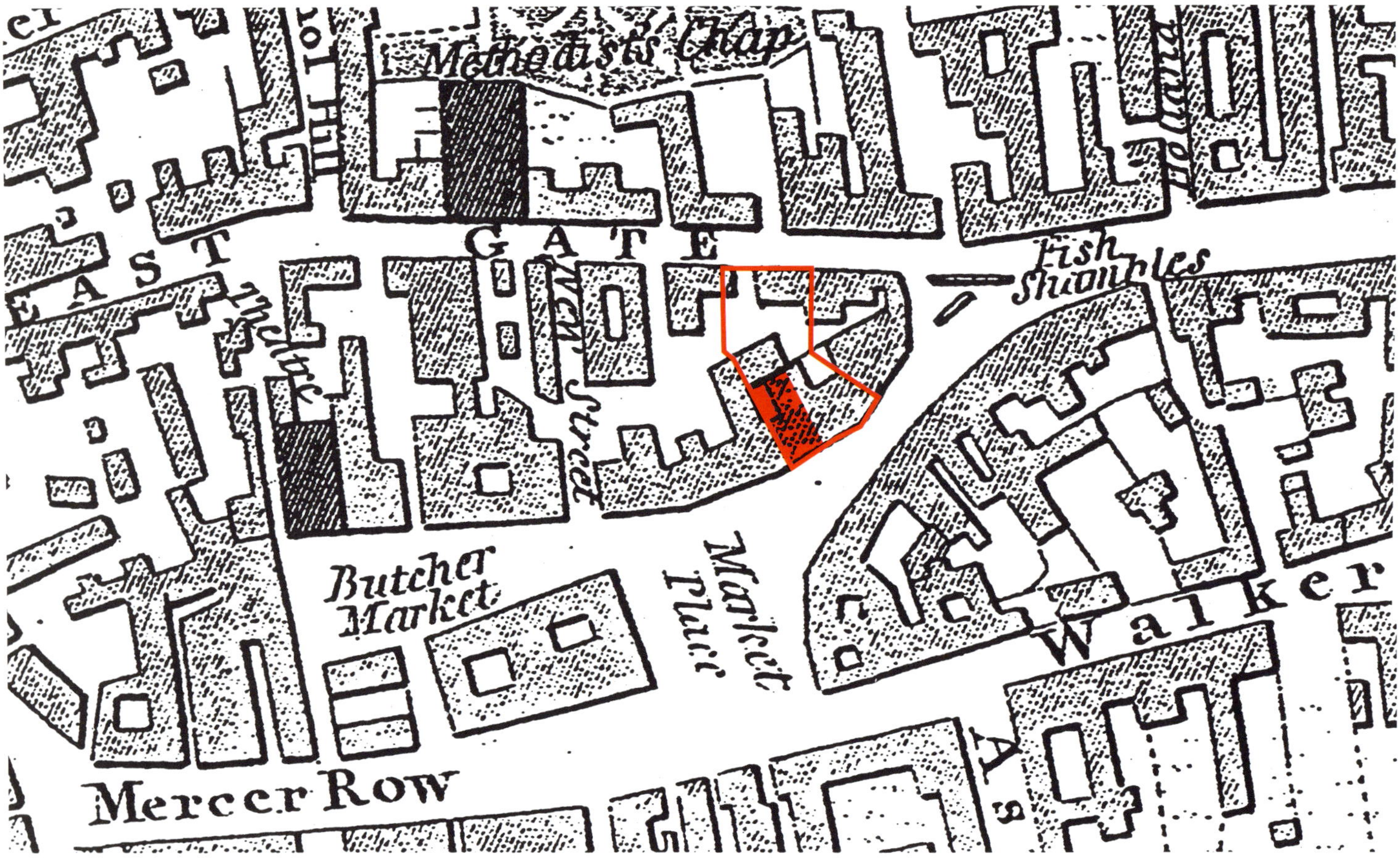

The town centre in 1808 from Thomas Espin's plan. The building in red is Adam's original shop, and the red line marks the boundary of the Eve & Ranshaw shop today.

Any or all of these were very probably part of the stock in the shop at No. 1 Market Place when Adam took it on from Frederick L'Oste by lease dated 26 October 1781. It also seems quite probable (as suggested on page 17) that Adam was already working as an assistant in the shop, which at the date of the Indenture was in the tenure of Frederick's son Charles. Moreover the Indenture states that Adam Eve was 'to have and to hold' the property 'from the twelfth day of May next', that is 1782, with the first rent payment due on 22 November 1782. It would appear therefore that technically Adam's establishment of himself as proprietor of the shop was May 1782! The rent was £15 (£900 today), payable in half yearly instalments. L'Oste paid taxes and rates on the property and was responsible for structural maintenance. He also agreed to fit a new shop floor of deals (Baltic pinewood). Adam was responsible for upkeep of doors, windows and window shutters. By 1785 he had negotiated with Frederick L'Oste to purchase the shop, and taken out a mortgage of £700 for 1,000 years from L'Oste!

The shop was two storeys, with double-bay shop windows and a central entrance; there was one (little) room and kitchen behind and two rooms (chamber and garret) above. As was normal then, Adam lived above the shop. Whether or not he had an assistant or assistants we don't know, but it is certain that his youngest brother William started to learn the trade when he left school in 1789. It is also clear that Adam set out to create a high class establishment to serve the gentry, specialising in good quality Lincolnshire stuff suitable for wearing at the Stuff Ball when it started in 1785 (see The Stuff Ball chapter). His success is evidenced by the description of him at the time of his marriage in 1786 as an 'eminent mercer and draper' – achieved within the space of only five years. Adam continued to live with his wife Sarah above the shop until they moved into the new-built Ivy House in James Street in 1794.

By that time Adam had taken the lease of the factory (1790), which increasingly took his attention and finances. When his brother William was 19 (in 1795) Adam took him into a partnership in running the shop. At the same time they were joined by young apprentice John Campbell (1782-1852) from Howden in Yorkshire. By 1798 (he was then 16) John was well enough established to be asked to witness the Indenture for Adam's deals with Lord Yarborough, Robert Vyner and William Marshall (as described in The Factory chapter). Campbell went on to play a significant part in the development of the shop, as we shall see. Why he came or was sent to Louth, it has not been possible to discover; was it another Adam connection with south Yorkshire? Interestingly he never severed his connection with his home town: he retained ownership of a house, inhabited by his brother James, and land in Howden, which meant that he was on the electoral roll there, certainly in 1834.

The mortgage Adam had taken was transferred to Susan Chatterton in 1802. Three years later Adam dissolved the partnership with his brother (as described in The Factory chapter). William (then 29) married Amelia Leech and set up house in Northgate, and formed a partnership with John Campbell (then 23) to trade as Eve & Campbell, Wholesale and Retail Woollen & Linen Drapers, Grocers etc. The partnership would last until William's death in 1829.

During the Napoleonic Wars the Louth Volunteer Cavalry was formed; Adam was gazetted Cornet in 1803 and Lieutenant in 1810. Also formed was the Louth Volunteer Infantry, both for local defence in the event of an invasion. Among related documents in Louth Museum archives is a list for 1804 of Sergeants, Corporals, Drummers and Privates, the Privates including two workers in Adam's carpet factory – Benjamin Furnish (40; weaver) and Thomas Spivey (36; wool sorter). An Account of February 1805 listed receipts, claims and payments (including items for swords, belts and sashes for Sergeants, to Drill Sergeants for instructing the Corps upon its first formation, musical instruments for the Band, and carriage of ammunition) which showed a deficit of £233 15s 2d. A handwritten and printed notice of December 1806 records a resolution to raise subscription to meet the, by then, debt of £245 11s 5d for clothing the infantry. Adam Eve was one of the Committee appointed to 'solicit subscriptions from the Inhabitants of the Town and Neighbourhood of Louth'. The full list published in May 1808 was headed by the Corporation with £30, followed by local gentry (including ladies), clergy and businessmen. Collections were also made at the Rein Deer, New King's Head and Wool Pack inns. John Campbell subscribed two guineas. The total raised was £743, which enabled the debt to be paid and clothing for 229 men to be bought for £481 as the main items. Eve & Campbell was one of the chief suppliers.

A
LIST
OF
SUBSCRIBERS,
TOWARDS
CLOTHING
THE
Louth Volunteer Infantry,
WITH THE AMOUNT OF EACH PERSON'S
Subscription.

(Jackson, Printer, Louth.)

In the Eve & Ranshaw archive there is a twenty year record (1808 – 1828) of the William Eve and John Campbell finances with details of annual March stocktaking and balance/profit, showing the fluctuations of fortune. It included a time of expansion of the shop and post Napoleonic Wars depression. In 1808 the stock was valued at £7,342 14s 1d (nearly £300,000 today); Income Tax and Town Charges were £60 and the rent (to Adam Eve) was £145. Working capital was £3,000 on which £150 interest was payable. The balance/profit of £1,396 0s 7d (£56,000 today) was divided two-thirds to Eve and one third to Campbell, the financial arrangement of their partnership. Eve was 32 and Campbell 26. Two years later the figures were similar: stock £7,450 and profit £1,407, after allowing for rent of an adjoining tailor's shop.

John Campbell's tax return for 1810 makes interesting reading: £12 1s window tax (21 windows), duty on an inhabited house £4 1s, employing a domestic servant £3 18s, use of a horse carriage £2 13s 6d, tax on his dog 11s 6d, and for hair powder £1 3s 6d, total £24 8s 6d (£634 today).

The renting of the tailor's shop was the first stage in expanding the shop, towards the Fish Shambles and later northwards to give a second frontage to Eastgate. This involved purchase of adjoining property from Stephen Holmes and John Robinson for £400, and investment in more stock, resulting in a balance/profit in 1811 of only £455. However, the following year that figure had risen to £2,305, and the next year (1813) Eve & Campbell bought the original shop from Adam for £300 and took on his mortgage of £750. The working capital was increased to £4, 000. 1814 saw a sharp increase of stock to £11,323, with Campbell allowed £300 for housekeeping: he lived on the premises and accommodated shop assistants and apprentices in the five attic rooms overlooking the Market Place and Fish Shambles. The allocation of profit was changed to an equal division. The same year Eve & Campbell bought a 390 square yards plot of land on a new street being staked out – Cannon Street, from John Bellamy for £130. A warehouse and showroom, joiners' and upholsterers' workshop were eventually built on the site. On the plot immediately to the south an Independent (later Congregational) chapel was built in 1821 – now the Playhouse Cinema. All this activity was an indication of the new impetus which Campbell brought to the business.

In November 1815, 13-years old Charles Bowmar started a seven year apprenticeship and would stay in the business for the whole of his working life. In January that year, then 12, he had been at the wedding of his sister Anne to grazier Adam Eve [4] (see page 15). It is quite possible that William Eve, uncle of the groom, and John Campbell were at the wedding and had agreed to take on Charles as an apprentice when he had finished school at Wragby. His eldest brother Thomas (born 1792) would move to Leicester and become a dyer, and two of his children would marry into the Eve dynasty – William to Ann in 1846 (first daughter of the marriage at Goltho) and Elizabeth to Adam [5] in 1855 (fourth child and first son of that marriage).

In 1817, 13-years old Thomas Ranshaw from Lincoln entered into an apprenticeship. His brother Robert went to farm at Little Missenden (Bucks), married Elizabeth Cortis and had five children: daughter Elizabeth Cortis (1838-1929) married John Bowmar Eve (1821-1887), another offspring of the Goltho marriage, and one of their children, John Frederic (1862-1902) would become a partner in the shop: and son George Ranshaw (1852-1929) who would also manage the shop. (See the Eve family tree).

In 1817-18 Eve & Campbell purchased for £1,000 more property adjoining the shop including five cottages on Eastgate from the estate of Frederick L'Oste (he died in 1807, age 84) which had passed to his sons Charles and Revd Joseph and daughters Mary (who married Revd R Leeke) and Sarah (widow of Thomas Froggatt). The Market Place-Fish Shambles frontage was completely rebuilt with five small-pane bow-shaped display windows (two larger on either side of the shop entrance) on the ground floor, which were unchanged for many years and depicted in T W Wallis's engraving on stone of the Market Place in 1857. Business was good, carrying stock valued at £10,411 in 1818, with a profit balance of £2,971 (£113,000 today).

In 1823 a 2,000 year mortgage at 4½% was taken out for £2,000 (£100,000 today). The lenders were Thomas Skipworth (Cabourne), Philip Skipworth (Tetney) and John Nicholson (Laceby). (Philip Skipworth had his portrait painted which was later in the possession of Charles Paddison.) Stock levels in the 1820s were £8-9,000, Campbell's housekeeper was paid £400 to look after the assistants and apprentices, and profit levels fluctuated slightly: £1,835 in 1824, £1,128 (1825), £1,575 (1826), £1,631 (1827) and £1,308 in 1828.

Charles Bowmar had become an assistant in 1822 and Thomas Ranshaw in 1824. Thomas appears to have had a particular interest in the grocery side of the business as he also became a partner in Cockburn Ranshaw & Co, Tea Dealers and Wine Merchants of Edinburgh until the partnership was dissolved in January 1830. The same year Charles Bowmar became a buyer, making journeys by coach to London, leaving the King's Head at noon and arriving in London at 8pm the following day.

When William Eve died in January 1829, age 53, John Campbell became the sole proprietor. In March he issued an advertisement card, announcing that the business of Wholesale & Retail Woollen & Linen Draper & Grocer would be carried on by himself and 'begs leave to solicit from the Friends of the late Establishment, and from the Public in general, a continuance of that liberal patronage the Firm so long enjoyed, and which it will always be his study to deserve.' There was a NB: 'A considerable portion of the Old Stock will be sold off at very reduced prices.'

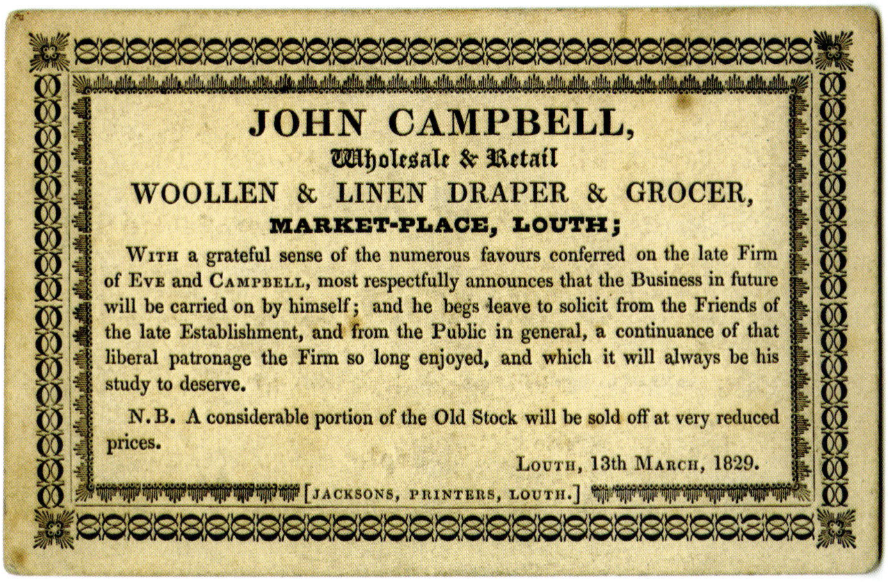
JOHN CAMPBELL,
Wholesale & Retail
WOOLLEN & LINEN DRAPER & GROCER,
MARKET-PLACE, LOUTH;

With a grateful sense of the numerous favours conferred on the late Firm of Eve and Campbell, most respectfully announces that the Business in future will be carried on by himself; and he begs leave to solicit from the Friends of the late Establishment, and from the Public in general, a continuance of that liberal patronage the Firm so long enjoyed, and which it will always be his study to deserve.

N.B. A considerable portion of the Old Stock will be sold off at very reduced prices.

Louth, 13th March, 1829.

[Jacksons, Printers, Louth.]

Eve had left instructions about the disposal of stock in trade and fixtures which were part of his partnership with Campbell. Fixtures were valued at £161 3s 7d. At the same time the shop premises were valued at £3,180 and the Cannon Street property at £130. It was found that there was a default in mortgage interest payment, and Eve's trustees (Thomas Grant, nephew, William Grant Allison, solicitor and Eve's eldest son William Henry) together with Campbell paid off the mortgage of £2,000 in full.

Campbell made a detailed inventory of stock at March 1830 and 1831, recorded in a small ledger now in the Eve & Ranshaw archive. It gives a comprehensive view of what was on sale in the shop: paper (wrapping and writing); groceries, locks, feathers etc in warehouses and shop; over 22,000 yards of fustians and checks at prices ranging from 4d to 3s a yard; nearly 950 silk handkerchiefs (9d to 7s each); 2,800 pairs of hose (4d to 2s 6d); 64,000 yards of crapes [sic] etc (8d to 4s a yard); gloves; cloaks (including silk); muffs and tippets; parasols; pins and needles; damask table linen; silk and woollen shawls; counterpanes; silk hose; damask and green cloths; muslin dresses; hats; twist; silk thread; dyes; ribbons; black and white veils; velvet; scarlet and fine worsteds; print cloth; Irish linen lawns; large numbers of 'sundries' in ware rooms; fringes; tapes; cotton balls; reel cotton; calicoes; ducks (trousers); flannels; knitting cotton; whalebone; umbrellas (including silk); blankets; 2,800 yards of woollen cloth (1s 6d to 24s a yard); 900 yards of Louth Superfine carpet at 2s 9d a yard and 210 yards of Superfine remnants; 376 yards of Brussels (tufted) carpet (2s 2d to 3s 3d a yard); hearth rugs; 830 yards of Venetian carpet (8d to 2s a yard); rugs and coverlets; oilcloth; buttons; Irish linens; wool sheets.

It is noticeable that although hats (for gentlemen) were listed, bonnets for ladies were not; perhaps this was because there were 18 milliners in the town in 1826 and still a dozen in 1834.

The inventory also included the following: gas pillars (the business had been quick to install lighting when the Gas Works opened in 1826); funeral bier, cloth and palls; scales and weights; iron chests; brewing utensils; stamps; crane and rope; truck and barrow; looking glass; coffee and sugar mills; wrappers and boxes. Total: £6,932 10s 4d. The content of the 1831 inventory was similar, total £7,807 16s 9d.

In January 1831, Campbell issued another card announcing that 'the engagement between himself and Mr Walmesley, his Cutter, having terminated, he has employed as his successor Mr [John] Freeston (late with Messrs [James] Grubb & Co, [Mercer Row] Louth) who has had many years' experience in some of the first houses of London….it is his [Campbell's] determination to furnish the very best articles of Clothing at the lowest possible price'. (Freeston became a good friend of carpet maker Charles Paddison.)

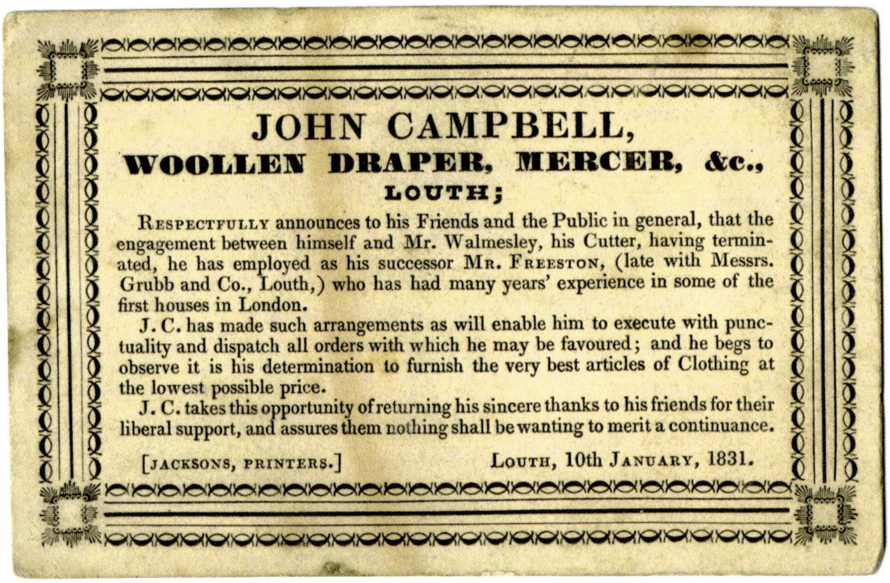
JOHN CAMPBELL,
WOOLLEN DRAPER, MERCER, &c.,
LOUTH;

RESPECTFULLY announces to his Friends and the Public in general, that the engagement between himself and Mr. Walmesley, his Cutter, having terminated, he has employed as his successor MR. FREESTON, (late with Messrs. Grubb and Co., Louth,) who has had many years' experience in some of the first houses in London.

J. C. has made such arrangements as will enable him to execute with punctuality and dispatch all orders with which he may be favoured; and he begs to observe it is his determination to furnish the very best articles of Clothing at the lowest possible price.

J. C. takes this opportunity of returning his sincere thanks to his friends for their liberal support, and assures them nothing shall be wanting to merit a continuance.

[JACKSONS, PRINTERS.] LOUTH, 10th JANUARY, 1831.

A month later Adam died. Campbell was one of his executors and trustees along with Thomas Oldham of Saltfleetby, but it was Campbell who did most of the work in carrying out the terms of Adam's Will. Clearing up the affairs took six years and surviving in the Eve & Ranshaw archive is a ledger with detail of the cash account. It is interesting to note that the account was opened on 7 February, four days before Adam died. He had signed a codicil to his Will on 4 February, and clearly he was expected to die. The physician who attended him was Dr Banks, who charged three guineas. Because of Campbell's work as an executor, at the same time as managing his shop business, it is convenient to record here the main entries and their implication.

Robert Hubbard was paid 2s 6d to shave Adam after death, Henry Coulam made the coffin, £15 10s, and Pearson Bellamy the lead lining, £15 10s, and there were payments to the gravediggers at Scartho. Funeral costs were £97 2s 6d, with an additional item charged to the 'grocery account' of £4 8s 1d. (In today's money the funeral arrangements were about £5,700; nothing but the best it would seem). Proceeds of a sale in June 1831 are recorded at £671 6s 6d (£30,500 today). There were outstanding bills for wool supplied to the factory: William Fell 47½ tods at 21s a tod - £49 17s 6d, and Hodgson £146 12s and Foster £200 8s. Campbell paid the wages of the factory workers and reclaimed from the estate. Journeys were made to deal with Adam's business connections, for example Campbell to Hull, and Charles Bowmar to London and to Gainsborough, Retford and Worksop (three days), each charged at two guineas.

There were accounts for the education of Henry and Charles Paddison – from William Espin for the last quarter's schooling of Charles £1 9s (which confirms the conjecture on page 27 about the boys' education), but an item of £29 18s 11d for Henry's schooling was from another source which suggests that Henry (then 16) was receiving private tuition. Two years later, in 1833, William Fridlington of Brackenborough was paid £70 (£3,500 today) for one years' board and a further £22 19s for Henry Paddison who was learning farming (see page 29), followed by Henry's mother being paid £8 7s for five months' board; and Henry was allowed £21 (£1,000 today) to buy a horse. In 1834 William Duckett was paid £68 8s 9d to board Charles for a year.

We have already met William Paddison the shoemaker (see page 26) who it appears made shoes for Adam: the accounts record a late payment in 1833 of Adam's shoe bill for £11 6s 8d (£570 today). The following year Henry Paddison was still using the same maker for his shoes, £5 10s (£270 today), which the executors paid.

Routine matters were collecting rents from Adam's houses on James Street and Eve Street, paying rates including those on a granary on Padehole (Northgate), and fire insurance on the factory. Eleanor Paddison was paid her half-yearly annuity of £20, usually dealt with by her eldest son John. There were also advances on the legacies to John, Henry and Charles; the maximum they could each receive was £500. The payment of one other legacy is recorded, that of £100 to Robert Anderson Storr of Boston, paid as stipulated in the Will two years after Adam's death.

In 1834, when Adam's financial affairs were still being cleared up, William Espin had already taken on the factory and was spending money on improvements including installation of steam power (see page 61). He had the facility to borrow to achieve that, and the account ledger has an entry of payment of half-yearly interest of £56 5s on a mortgage of £2,500 (the equivalent of £130,000 today) which had been provided by – Campbell & Co. The link between shop and factory was being continued.

During the 1830s Charles Bowmar was lodging on Upgate with Mrs Jane Pell, widow of James Pell, surgeon of Alford. They married in the mid-1840s and lived first in James Street and then at 175 Eastgate (Trinity Terrace). They did not have any children. They employed a cook and a housemaid; in 1861 the cook was Mary Brant (25) from Theddlethorpe, and the housemaid was Fanny Spivey (26), daughter of carpet weaver Isaac Spivey.

Charles Bowmar and Thomas Ranshaw were taken into partnership with Campbell in 1834, styled as Campbell, Bowmar & Co, Mercers, Drapers, Grocers, Haberdashers and Merchant Tailors. Soon afterwards the firm was Campbell, Bowmar & Ranshaw under a seven-year copartnership (renewed in 1847). Also in 1834 John Bowmar Eve (sixth child and second son of Adam Eve [4] and Anne (Bowmar) and born at Ivy House, Haugham, and nephew of Charles Bowmar) began his apprenticeship.

Thomas Willey (1805-1901)
A 'valued assistant and friend' of the firm for 60 years from the time of the ownership of Campbell and Bowmar. 'His services were rewarded by the grant of a pension!'
(see pages 153 and 155)

The shop, living chambers, warehouse, fixtures and stock were insured for £3,600 (£190,000 today), and the brick and tile wool and grocery warehouse with fixtures and stock facing Eastgate for £200. A clause in the policy required that gunpowder in canisters not exceeding 25 pounds in weight should be in the first warehouse on the floor of a chamber open to the tiles.

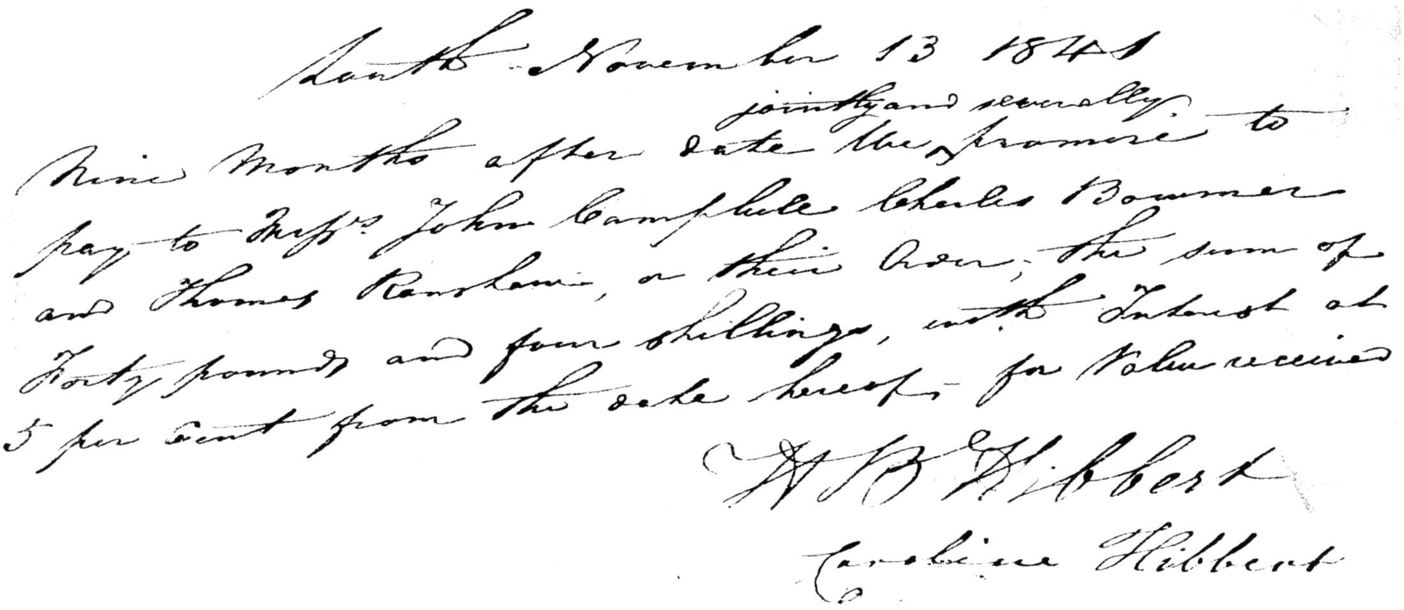
Louth November 13 1841
Nine Months after date we jointly and severally promise to pay to Messrs John Campbell Charles Bowmer and Thomas Ranshaw, or their Order, the sum of Forty pounds and four shillings, with Interest at 5 per Cent from the date hereof for Value received
W H Hibbert
Caroline Hibbert

A problem in managing the shop was bad debts. In March 1832, labourer Edward Graves of Gayton was convicted of issuing a forged bank note to John Campbell; the death sentence was commuted to 'transportation beyond the seas' and he was sent Parmelia in New South Wales. Customers who could not pay issued promissory notes: John Hewson (1835) for £150 (£7,800 today); W H Hibbert (1841) two notes totalling £86 8s (£3,900); Godfrey Egremont, Westgate (1842) for £102 11s 7d (£4,600); W H Hibbert (1848) for £15 16s 10d (£750). Langley Gace, Westgate provided a handwritten note that 'I not being provided with the means to discharge' the debt of £19 5s 9d (£850) 'at present' and agreed to pay by instalments - £10 in March, £5 in May and the balance of £4 5s 9d in June (1847). The firm's solicitor was W Grant Allison, later Allison & Sons. Their account for 1853-55 lists over thirty customers with outstanding debts, including well-known local people, for example J W Yorke Esq. of Walmsgate Hall who owed £10 8s 2d (£540), and Revd George Ayscough Chaplin, Rector of Raithby and Vicar of Haugham. A letter demanding payment was charged at 3s 6d. In extreme cases, such as Benjamin Harrison in 1853, taking action in the County Court was necessary, where Court fees were £2 8s 8d (£123). Such revealing documents are in the Eve & Ranshaw archive.

Were the partners too easy on some customers in allowing them to build up debts, or was it perhaps more likely the case of wives buying more than their husbands could afford? The fact that signatures on two of the promissory notes were witnessed by wives seems to bear out the latter suggestion.

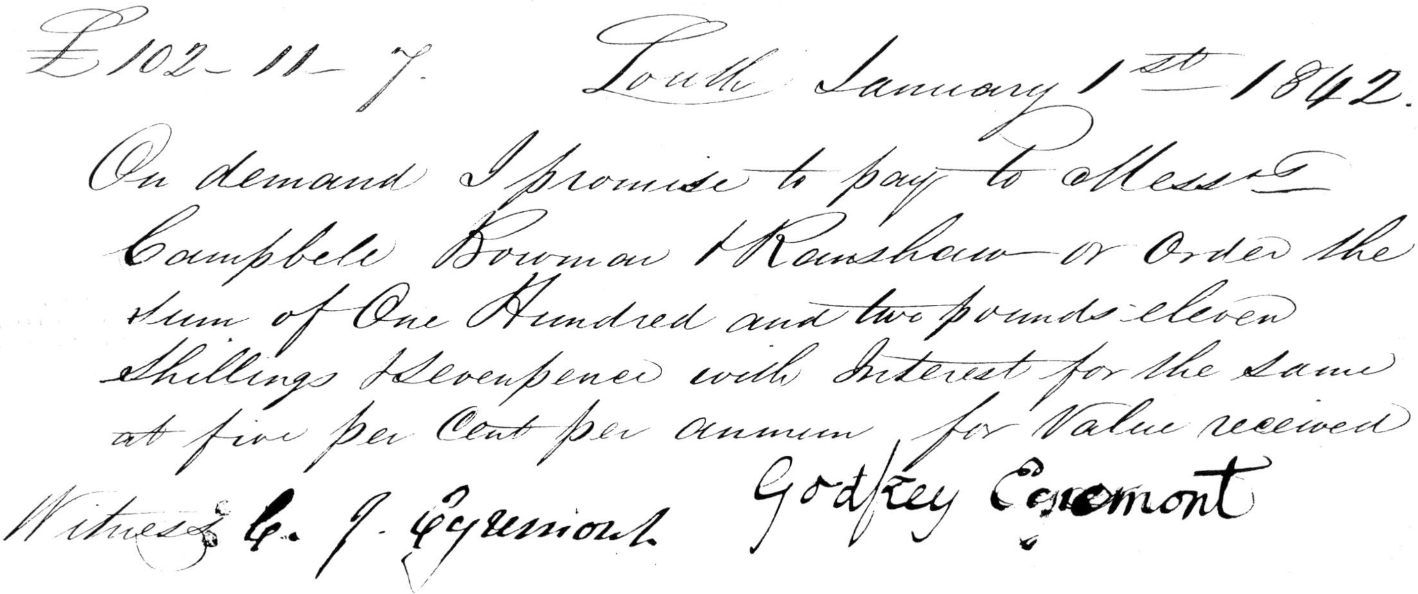
£102-11-7. Louth January 1st 1842.
On demand I promise to pay to Messrs Campbell Bowman & Ranshaw or Order the sum of One Hundred and two pounds eleven Shillings & Sevenpence with Interest for the same at five per Cent per annum for Value received
Witness C. J. Egremont Godfrey Egremont

The **1841** census shows that there were sixteen assistants, apprentices and servants (most of them Lincolnshire born) living above the shop with John Campbell (his wife having died some time in the 1830s).

Edmund Brotherton (25)	Assistant
James Searby (19)	Assistant
John Bowmar Eve (20)	Assistant from Haugham
Joseph Holmes (22)	Assistant from South Ormsby
George Plummer (24)	Assistant, not from Lincolnshire
Charles Harris (21)	Apprentice
Herbert Gilbert (15)	Apprentice
Robert Betts (14)	Apprentice
J C Ludbury (23)	Assistant
J W Cunnington (23)	Assistant from Spalding
Richard Bartram (17)	Apprentice, not from Lincolnshire
John Richard Howard (15)	Apprentice
Edward Manders (17)	Servant
Jane Trevor (35)	Housekeeper from Ingham
Ann Trevor (18)	Servant; daughter of Jane
Ellen Robinson (36)	Servant from Market Rasen

Around 1842/43 the grocery side of the business was discontinued, except for tea and coffee, and the description of the firm was shortened to Linen & Woollen Drapers & Tailors. Thomas Ranshaw had married Elizabeth from Horncastle (1835/36) and their son Robert was born in 1837, followed by five girls – Susanna 1839, Elizabeth 1842, Jessie 1844, Maria 1846 and Emily 1850. The family lived in Eastgate and moved to 3 Temple Terrace in the 1850s.

It is worth noting that the East Lincolnshire Railway opened in 1848, giving Louth better connections, particularly to London and to centres manufacturing the kinds of cloth and other goods to sell in the shop. In the **1851** census Assistants were described as Journeymen, and Jane Trevor was still housekeeping for John Campbell.

John Bowmar Eve (30)	Journeyman Draper
Joseph Holmes (32)	Journeyman Draper
Samuel Harvey (37)	Journeyman Draper, from Tuxford, Notts
James Eve (25)	Journeyman Draper; younger brother of John Bowmar
Emmanuel Mountain (21)	Journeyman Draper from Saleby
John Gildow (23)	Journeyman Draper from Saltfleetby
William Cunnington (21)	Journeyman Draper (younger brother of JW; see 1841)
Michael Hewson (22)	Journeyman Draper from Harrington
Charles Calvert (19)	Apprentice from Withern
Jane Trevor (45)	Housekeeper
Ellen Robinson (46)	House servant
Ann Trevor (29)	House servant
Charles Pinning (23)	House servant from Harpswell

Gentlemen's fashions in the 1850s

James Eve was at school in Grantham until he was 16 (in 1842; see page 17), and served his apprenticeship in the 1840s. He married Leonora Rainey of Spilsby about 1856 and opened his own shop on the High Street there as Linen and Woollen Draper, Silk Mercer and Milliner, doubtless with the help of the legacy of £300 (£135,000 today) left to him when he was five by his great uncle Adam. They had three children, including Allan James who wrote the historical note about his great great great uncle James (see pages 13 and 16). Leonora died in 1866 and James in 1903.

John Campbell had his portrait painted by Bennett Hubbard in 1851. It shows a man with a kindly face and his faithful dog (he always had a dog), and through the window Howden church as a reminder of his origin. The portrait found its way into the collection of Louth Mechanics' Institute and was neglected until it passed to Louth Museum. It was restored and framed by Dian Hall Conservation in 2009 with a grant from the Association of Independent Museums/The Pilgrim Trust Conservation Scheme. Campbell died in 1852, aged 70, after 57 years in the business, 47 of them as co-partner, senior partner or sole proprietor. The success of the business today owes much to his guiding hand in the first half of the 19th century. Adam had made a sound choice when he took him on as a teenage apprentice.

John Campbell (1782-1852). A key figure in the history of the shop and in the business for 57 years
Reserve collection at Louth Museum

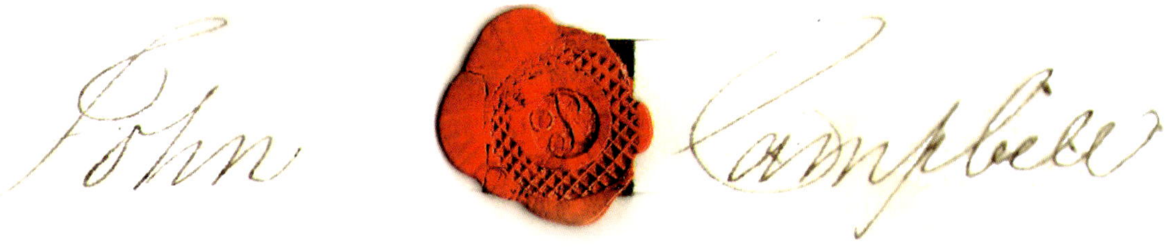

The firm became Bowmar & Ranshaw. Robert Ranshaw, Master Draper Thomas's son had joined as an apprentice in 1850; he became an assistant in 1857, and shortly afterwards was taken into partnership (as a Master Draper) together with John Bowmar Eve – so that in 1860 the firm's name was Bowmar, Ranshaws & Eve. That year John Bowmar Eve married Elizabeth Cortis Ranshaw (1838-1929), niece of Thomas Ranshaw, and lived above the shop before setting up house at 3 Temple Terrace, and then with their family of six surviving children occupied the former home of Adam the carpet maker, Ivy House on James Street. J B Eve was a Borough Councillor in the early 1870s.

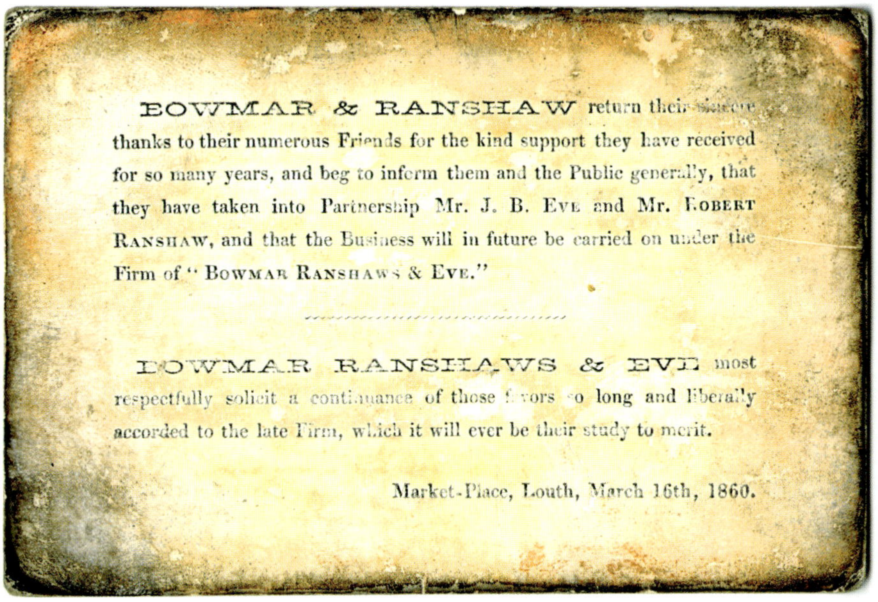

BOWMAR & RANSHAW return their sincere thanks to their numerous Friends for the kind support they have received for so many years, and beg to inform them and the Public generally, that they have taken into Partnership Mr. J. B. Eve and Mr. Robert Ranshaw, and that the Business will in future be carried on under the Firm of "Bowmar Ranshaws & Eve."

BOWMAR RANSHAWS & EVE most respectfully solicit a continuance of those favors so long and liberally accorded to the late Firm, which it will ever be their study to merit.

Market-Place, Louth, March 16th, 1860.

Business card issued in March 1860 to announce the change of the name of the firm to BOWMAR RANSHAWS & EVE

Between the change of name of the firm, John Freeston, the cutter who had been taken on by Campbell in 1831, decided it was time to strike out on his own. In March 1857 (the end of a financial year) he presented to Bowmar & Ranshaw an account due (presumably for wages) of £635 13s (about £30,000 today). It would be interesting to know how this was calculated. Freeston set up as Tailor, Woollen Draper and Hatter at 6 Mercer Row, where he traded about ten years.

John Bowmar Eve's wife was not present at the shop on the day of the **1861** census, but his younger sister Matilda (27) was in charge of the domestic arrangements along with housemaid Mary Anne Bentley (17) from Spilsby and footman Henry White (17) from West Ashby. The live-in assistants and apprentices were:

Joseph Smith (30)	Assistant from Grantham
William Clemment (25)	Assistant, from Whittlesea, Cambs
Joseph Gresswell (20)	Assistant from Great Steeping
John Goodhand (25)	Assistant from North Thoresby
Charles Billyard (28)	Assistant from Frampton; he would spend his working life in the shop
Richard Wingad (35)	Assistant from Helpringham
John Ellwood Sutton (18)	Apprentice from Louth
Thomas Mantle Rickard (16)	Apprentice from Waltham

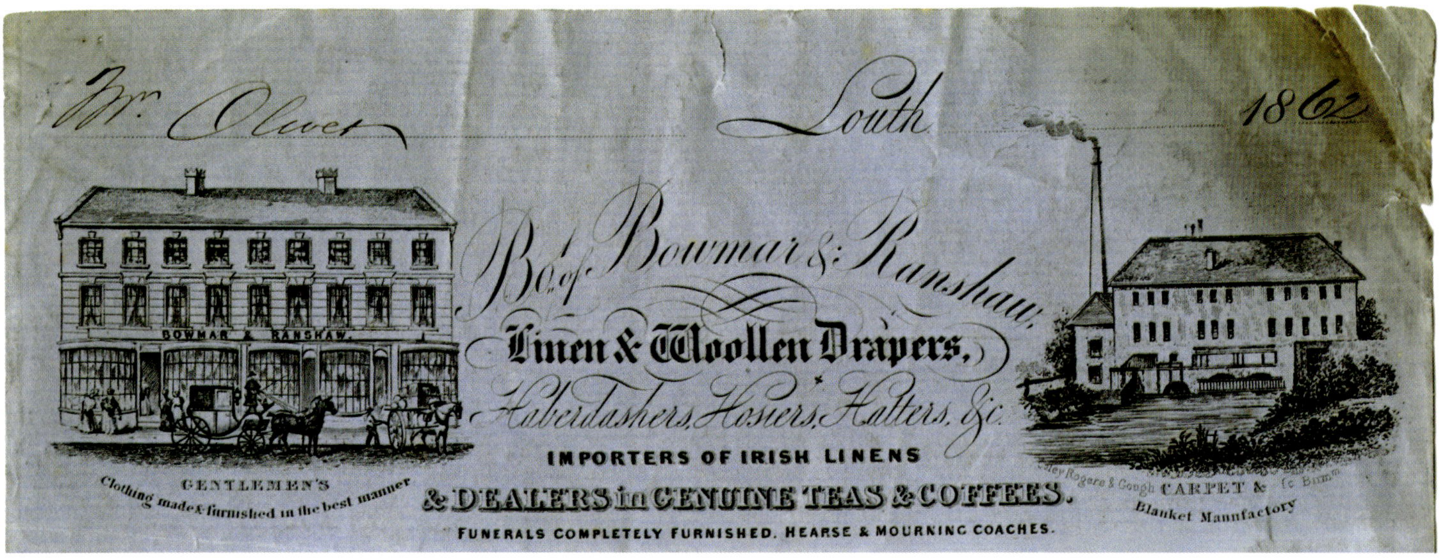

Mr. Oliver   Louth   1862

Bo.t of Bowmar & Ranshaw,

BOWMAR & RANSHAW

Linen & Woollen Drapers,

Haberdashers, Hosiers, Hatters, &c.

IMPORTERS OF IRISH LINENS

GENTLEMEN'S Clothing made & furnished in the best manner

& DEALERS in GENUINE TEAS & COFFEES.

CARPET & Blanket Manufactory

FUNERALS COMPLETELY FURNISHED. HEARSE & MOURNING COACHES.

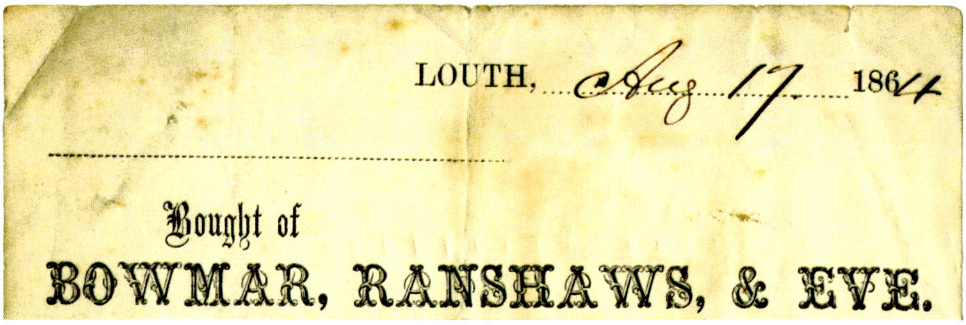

LOUTH, Aug 17 1864

Bought of

BOWMAR, RANSHAWS, & EVE.

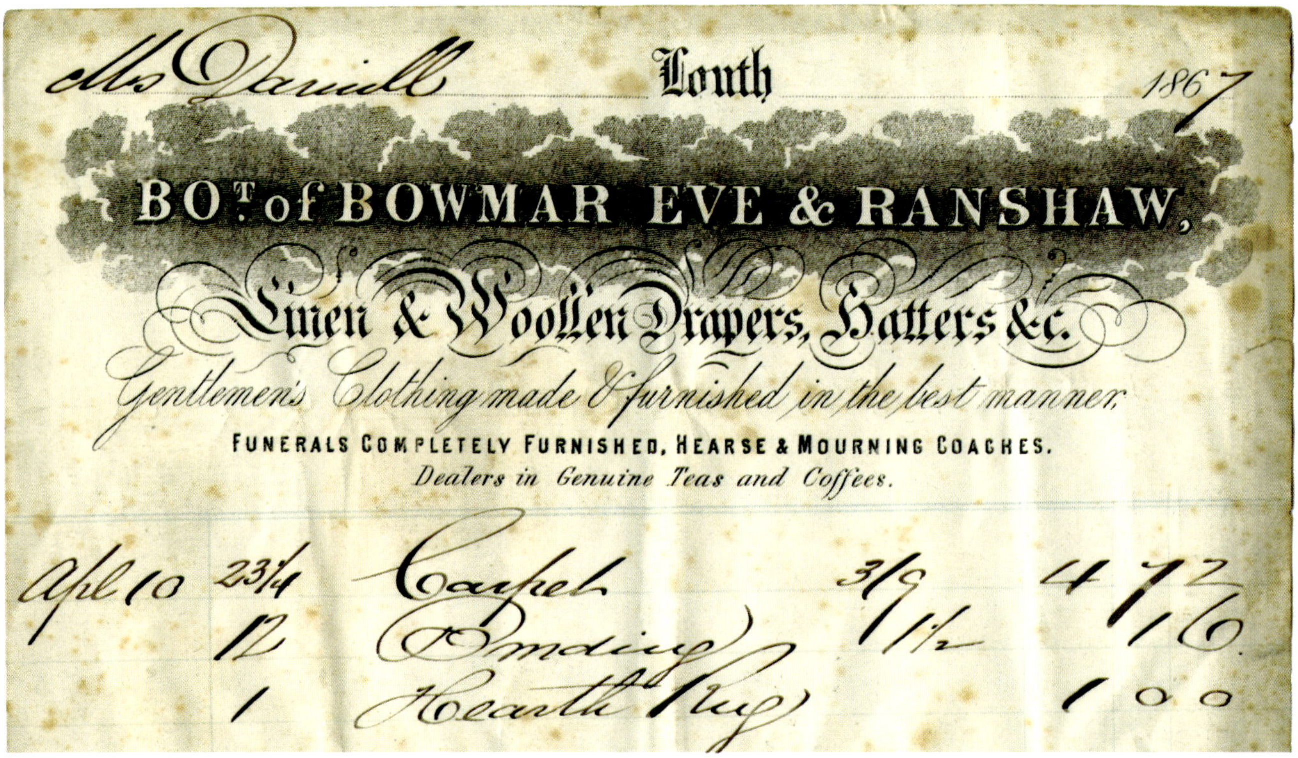

Ms Darnill   Louth   1867

BO.T of BOWMAR EVE & RANSHAW,

Linen & Woollen Drapers, Hatters &c.

Gentlemen's Clothing made & furnished in the best manner.

FUNERALS COMPLETELY FURNISHED. HEARSE & MOURNING COACHES.

Dealers in Genuine Teas and Coffees.

Apl 10	23¼	Carpet	3/9	4 7 2
	12	Binding	1½	1 6
	1	Hearth Rug		1 0 0

Changing billheads in the 1860s

In the 1850s Charles Bowmar and Thomas Ranshaw had expended £916 (about £37,000 today) on improving the property. Further extensive alterations were made in 1861 which involved internal changes and a new frontage to Eastgate. (The Market Hall and shops adjoining to the west were built in 1866-67). Thomas Ranshaw died suddenly in September 1864, aged 60, and the firm became Bowmar, Ranshaw & Eve. Charles Bowmar's wife died in the mid 1860s and in 1869 he retired, aged 67, due to poor health. He had been 53 years in the business. However, his retirement led to an active part in public affairs: he was appointed a Borough Magistrate and a Poor Law Guardian for Louth, and was elected Chairman of Directors of the Louth Gas Co and Chairman of the Management Committee of the Cottage Hospital on Crowtree Lane (designed by James Fowler and built 1873) to which he made donations. He had played a prominent part in the rebuilding of Holy Trinity church in 1866. When he died in February 1887, aged 85, his obituary described him as a sound and practical businessman and noted his friendly hospitality and benevolence to the poor.

The billhead of the firm in the 1860s announced them as Linen & Woollen Drapers, Haberdashers, Hosiers, Hatters etc. Importers of Irish Linens and Dealers in Genuine Teas and Coffees. Gentlemen's Clothing made and furnished in the best manner. Funerals Completely Furnished. Hearse and Mourning Coaches. The billhead also carried an illustration of the Carpet & Blanket Manufactory, although at the time it was being run by Hoff & Son. However the shop did store and sell carpets and blankets.

A crinoline could be bought for 11d (5p), gloves for 1s (5p), hose for 1s 6d (7½p), handkerchiefs for 9½d (3½p), a necktie for 2s (10p), a black silk apron trimmed with crape for 7s (35p), a chamois leather Swiss vest (waistcoat) covered with silk for 8s 6d (42½p), a waterproof mantle for £1 11s 6d (£1.57), a hearthrug for £1 and a 23ft by 4ft carpet for £4 7s 2d (£4.35). To calculate the price of these items today, multiply by 50.

At the **1871** census the domestic arrangements for live-in staff at the shop were in the hands of two of the late Thomas Ranshaw's daughters – Elizabeth (29) and Maria (25), assisted by a cook (Ann Ringrose, 28), housemaid (Fanny Robinson, 29), kitchen maid (Jane Rowe, 18) and a page (Stephen Wilkinson, 17). Also living in was draper's clerk Edwin Dunn, (23 from Nottinghamshire), together with nine shop assistants (below) that made a total of 16 people living over the shop.

Richard Wingad (45)	
Charles Billyard (38)	
Thomas Hollingsworth (23)	
George Senescall (22)	
William Smith (27)	from Huntingdonshire
Upton Harrison (21)	
Richard Cammack (21)	
Dan Goy (22)	from Nottinghamshire
William Harris (32)	from Nottinghamshire

A tour of the shop is detailed below and it is possible to envisage polished mahogany counters with shelves or drawers below, and shelves, drawers and cupboards on the wall behind. And one or two Bentwood chairs in front of each counter, customers for the use of. (Such chairs were still in use into the 1930s). With crowded living conditions on the top floor, it seems likely that younger employees, such as the page boy, slept under one of the counters (not unusual in Victorian shops at that time).

A Paris hat

Surviving in private hands is a small customer's annual account book, embossed in gold BOWMAR EVE & RANSHAW LOUTH, covering the period 1867-1876. The partners then were Charles Bowmar, John Bowmar Eve (Charles's nephew) and Robert Ranshaw. The customer was Mr Phillipson. A scour of Lincolnshire directories for the period reveal him as William Phillipson, ironmonger at 98 Eastgate, who became Canal Inspector (for the Louth Navigation) in 1871 when he moved to Ramsgate, and his son John ran the hardware business.

The account book shows what he and his wife wore, what household and other goods he bought, how his lifestyle changed when he became Canal Inspector, and includes details of funeral costs. The account starts in February 1867, and figures in brackets below are the equivalent sum today (not including VAT). A Cashmere mantle cost £1 5s (£60), a shawl £1 2s (£53), a silk jacket £1 9s (£70) and a silk dress £2 10s (£120). He bought a Napoleon cravat for 3s 9d (£8.50) and five more in the next four years. Small items included collars, buttons, binding, linen cuffs, cotton, needles, lace, flannel, velvet, Alpaca, and hairnets, for example. Yards of calico may have been for lining shelves in his ironmonger's shop. An umbrella cost 8s (£19). The total for 1867 was £25 18s 2d (£1,217) paid in February 1868.

The account for 1868 included 1lb coffee 1s 4d (£3.30), ½lb black tea 1s 9d (£4) and ½lb green tea 2s (£4.70), kid gloves 2s 10d (£6.50), Tweed skirting, a petticoat 10s (£23.50) and another mantle for £1 4s 6d (£58). In 1869 his wife had a dress 19s (£48), a crinoline 5s 6d (£13), a Paris hat 12s (£30) and a parasol 10s 6d (£25), whereas he had two velveteen jackets at £1 (£48) and £1 2s 6d (£50). Household items included nine yards of Dutch carpet at 2s a yard (£470), oilcloth and more calico, window muslin, teacloths and a cotton counterpane 7s 3d (£17.30). The total for 1869 was £16 2s 4d (£790).

The 1870 account contains an interesting item in the purchase of 13½ yards of Louth carpet at 2s 10d (£7.30) a yard, compared with 12½ yards of staircarpet at 2s (£4.80) a yard, plus 23 yards of carpet binding at 1½d (or 28p) a yard. Personal items were a cloth jacket 10s 6d (£26.50) and two other better quality silk jackets at £1 2s (£52.80) each and a shirt at 11s 6d (£27). 1871 must have been the year Phillipson was appointed Canal Inspector: in March he bought a double breasted frock coat for three guineas (£154) and a vest (waistcoat) for 10s (£39), with an Alpaca skirt 13s 6d (£33) and a mantle with cape £1 6s (£64) for his wife. Two months later he bought two silk jackets at 25s (£61) each and three best shirts with fine linen fronts and wristbands at 8s (£19.50) each. And for the house he bought a remnant of Louth Super carpet for £3 (£147) and a pair of blankets for £1 (£49). It was an expensive year at £25 3s 4½d (£1,232).

1872 was even more expensive: £31 9s 10d (£1,480) because it included a presumably family funeral – a black Napoleon and a black silk tie, a hat with two extra bands 15s 3d (£38), three pairs of black kid gloves, elastic braces 3s (£7), 60 yards of black silk £8 3s 8d (£383), black Doeskin trousers £1 5s (£59), silk umbrella 8s 6d (£21), a silk morning coat with vest and trousers £4 10s (£212), fitting out seven men (perhaps assistants at his son's hardware shop) with black crepe, gloves and ties, and funeral services including cloaks and mourning rings.

1873 purchases in February and May were a black cloth jacket with silk trim £1 8s 6d (£68), new velvet collar and buttons and repair of overcoat 8s 6d (£21), a black cloth vest 15s (£35) and a silk hat 14s 6d (£33) for himself, and a crinoline, a grey skirt and Cashmere mantle £1 10s (£70) for his wife; plus a pair of super blankets £1 8s (£66) and a hearthrug for 18s (£42). Most of the purchases in 1874 were for his wife: a black Cashmere mantle £1 17s 6d (£84), a check shawl 7s 6d (£15), two crinolines, two corsets at 5s (£12) and 6s each, two skirts, kid gloves and a new parasol. Mrs Phillipson's husband had an important job, and she needed to dress accordingly. However, it would appear that she did her own sewing as most years accounts included cotton, pins and needles and fabrics such as flannel (scarlet in 1874). The purchase of two aprons at 4½d each and three at 1s (5p or £2.40 today) suggests that they had housemaids.

The last year of the account book was 1875. Phillipson was not listed in the 1876 directory, just his son John and the hardware business at 98 Eastgate. However, the annual account for 1875 was settled in May 1876. Early in 1875 William splashed out on a black Super Doe frock coat, vest and lined trousers for £5 19s (£285) and in July a black silk jacket for £1 10s (£72). He also bought 10½ yards of Dutch carpet at 2s 9d (£6.90) a yard, 14 yards of Union carpet at 2s 3d (£5.50) a yard and 4½ yards of floor oilcloth at 3s (£7.35) a yard. (For explanation of the different quality of carpeting, see The Carpets chapter). Curiously he appears to have returned to Eve & Ranshaw for tea and coffee (the only previous purchase was in 1868): 1lb coffee in May at 1s 4d (same price as 1868) and 1lb in July at 1s 8d, black tea at 3s (3s 6d in 1868) and 1lb of mixed tea at 3s 6d.

Phillipson's total spend at Eve & Ranshaw over nine years was £162 12s 9d, an annual average of £18. The equivalent today would be £7,819 total and £869 annual average. How, one wonders, would that compare with account holders today? With his own account book and settling promptly in full, he would have been regarded as a 'valued' customer.

We can now return to the sequence of owners of the shop. After Charles Bowmar's death in 1869, James Eve was made a partner, as well as running his own shop in Spilsby. So the firm became Eves & Ranshaw. James retired from the partnership in 1875; his Spilsby shop continued into the mid-1880s; he died in 1903. Meanwhile George Ranshaw, the third Ranshaw to join the family firm, had come to Louth as an apprentice in 1866, then spent four years in London for further experience. While there he joined the London Volunteer Corps. He returned to Louth in 1877. George was the nephew of Thomas Ranshaw and cousin to Robert, brother in law of John Bowmar Eve and uncle to John Frederic Eve. It was in the late 1870s that the name of the business became established as EVE & RANSHAW.

Also in the same decade John Bowmar Eve's eldest son John Frederic joined the firm after he left school, probably in 1878 when he was 16. After serving his apprenticeship he went to Marshall and Snelgrove at Scarborough for three years to gain further experience, and returned in 1888 to become a partner.

The **1881** census recorded George Ranshaw, 28, Master Draper and still single, living above the shop. The housekeeper was Elizabeth Beslock (63) from Norfolk, with cook Lucy Marshall (26) from Sturton and housemaid Ellen Hales (20) from Rigsby. The seven live-in draper's assistants were:

Thomas Meanwell (31)	from Coningsby
George Ibberson (29)	from Cambridge
William Sargesson (27)	from Burgh (le Marsh)
Fred Evison (23)	from Quadring
John Puckeridge (21)	from Draycott, Wilts
Richard Dyas (20)	Louth
Joseph Ritson (19)	from Malden, Essex

The census returns show a turnover of young assistants gaining experience before moving on, but there were other senior and long-serving assistants who lived at home. Examples were Charles Billyard who moved out of the shop to live on South Street, and Thomas Willey who was an assistant for 46 years. Just how long John Mawer was associated with the firm in uncertain: he was an accountant and his signature was on a bill of 1863, he became a partner in 1881 and retired in 1888. It was during that period that a set of rules for assistants and boarders was drawn up.

Former staff entrance on Eastgate

Rules to be observed by assistants in the employ of Eve, Ranshaw and Mawer

Shop Rules

1. All assistants to be in the shop before the Breakfast Bell rings.
2. One junior to be in the shop by 7.30am.
3. Reading newspapers and books in the shop strictly prohibited.
4. Every assistant is expected to come forward and serve in any department where required, if not busy in his own.
5. Each assistant to stand behind his own counter and avoid standing at the door.
6. No assistant is to leave the premises either on business or otherwise without permission from the Counting House.

House Rules

1. The house will be closed punctually at 10.30pm every night excepting Saturdays when the time for closing will be 11pm and Sundays when it will be 10pm, and all lights to be extinguished in the bedrooms within half an hour of the before mentioned times.
2. Anyone wishing to remain out later must obtain permission from the housekeeper; disregard to this rule will be followed by immediate dismissal.
3. The latch key will only be granted on very special occasions and permission can only be obtained from one of the firm.
4. Washing in the bedrooms will not be allowed after breakfast and no assistant is allowed to go upstairs with boots on their feet; slippers must be provided or the house boy will fetch anything required.
5. Strangers are not permitted to enter the house and assistants not to enter the kitchen.
6. Ten minutes is allowed to each assistant after 10am on Sunday to finish dressing.
7. All arrangements made by the housekeeper must be strictly adhered to.
8. Smoking only allowed after 2pm on Sundays and after the shop is closed on weekdays.
9. The front door not to be used when the back gates are open.

By order

Sunday was the only day off, except Thursday afternoons (half-day closing for town shops), and attendance at church would be expected (the partners were staunch Anglicans). It also appears that the shop was open late on Saturday nights. One assistant penned a poem bemoaning late night customers on a Saturday and pleading for masters to pay wages in time for assistants' wives to go to market in daylight hours.

Saturday Night

Don't wonder if we go to sleep
In sermon time tomorrow,
'Tis vain to try to awake to keep,
We own it to our sorrow.

Yours visits are so late at night
We cannot but be weary;
When Sunday comes we can't be bright
Nor wake up gay and cheery.

We pray you dames and neighbours strive
To come at better hours;
We think these matters you'll contrive
If you put forth your powers.

Ye masters help us wages pay
Early, that wives may carry
Their cash to market while 'tis day,
Not until the night-fall tarry.

Help us to shut up shop betime.
Then, when the Sunday's dawning
With pleasure we shall hear the chimes
That usher in the morning.

All employees, assistants, dressmakers and servants, could however look forward to four Bank Holiday Mondays off. And some of them, long-serving Charles Billyard for example, could remember the days before the Bank Holiday Act of 1871 which established Easter Monday, Whit Monday, August Bank Holiday (then the first Monday in the month) and Boxing Day as statutory days off for employees.

George Ranshaw was made a partner in August 1881, but there is no record of any event to mark the centenary of the business. He married Florence Elizabeth Hulbert of Croydon about 1884; he was 32 and she was nine years younger. They lived first at 3a Hill Terrace, Cemetery Road, where their children Alan George, Dora Eland and Marjorie Edith were born, and then moving to 5 Priory Terrace and to 1 Temple Terrace after Robert Ranshaw left Louth.

John Bowmar Eve died in September 1887, after 53 years in the business (the same number of years as uncle Charles Bowmar). His surviving widow, Elizabeth Cortis, nee Ranshaw, then lived with her daughter Catherine Maud (Kate) at Ormlea on Eastgate; Elizabeth died in 1929. John Bowmar had been a Churchman and Conservative, and served on the Borough Council 1872-75 and 1883-86. His funeral procession was headed by two long-serving shop assistants – Thomas Willey and Charles Billyard, and all the other assistants followed the family mourners. Funeral arrangements were made by business partner John Mawer. The account in the *Louth & North Lincolnshire Advertiser* noted that 'while diligent in business, [John Bowmar Eve] was generous and open-handed to a fault. His hand was constantly in his pocket for religious and philanthropic objects, and also for threepences and sixpences at the solicitations of a host of spongers who besieged him in season and out of season.' He left £10,764 to his brothers Thomas of Tathwell (who died the following year) and James of Haugham, both farmers.

Robert Ranshaw retired from the business in 1888, when he was 53. He had joined the volunteer Louth Artillery Battery when it was formed in 1860 and risen to Lieut. Colonel of the Battery. He was a member of the Louth Naturalists', Antiquarian & Literary Society, publishers of this book, to which he made donations and gave books and a painting of the thatched church at Markby. He left Louth about 1893 and became chairman of Marston's Dolphin Brewery at Poole in Dorset. He died at Bournemouth in 1924, aged 88. When he retired from the Louth business he was replaced as partner (in 1889) by John Frederic Eve, who later became a Lieutenant in the Louth Artillery Battery.

There is some uncertainty as to the date when the Market Place frontage of the shop was changed to the present plate glass windows. A photograph, probably taken in the late 1880s, shows the far right bow had been removed, confirmed on an undated ground floor plan of the shop. However the illustrations in the entry for the business in *Introduction to the Eastern Counties: Business Reviews: A Guide to Leading Commercial Enterprises*, published about 1890, shows both the old bow windows and the five new plate glass display windows. There is a Memorandum of Agreement of 1882/84 in the Eve & Ranshaw archive between the Mayor and Burgesses (the Borough) and Eve & Co (signed by John Bowmar Eve and Robert Ranshaw) relating to the removal of two bay windows on the Eastgate frontage in order to enable the street to be widened. The conclusion is that both changes were made in the mid to late 1880s, effected by George Ranshaw and John Frederic Eve.

It is now worth quoting in full the entry in the *Business Review* which shows, together with earlier evidence, that the business was in fact a Department Store, and had been for nearly two decades. [The first London department store was opened by William Whiteley in 1866.]

continued on page 158

Part of the tiled shop doorway laid in the 1880s

EVE & RANSHAW,

MARKET PLACE, LOUTH,

Linen and Woollen Drapers,

TAILORS, HATTERS, AND OUTFITTERS,

CARPET & BLANKET WAREHOUSEMEN.

Funerals Completely Furnished.

HEARSE AND MOURNING COACHES.

TEA AND COFFEE MERCHANTS.

1879

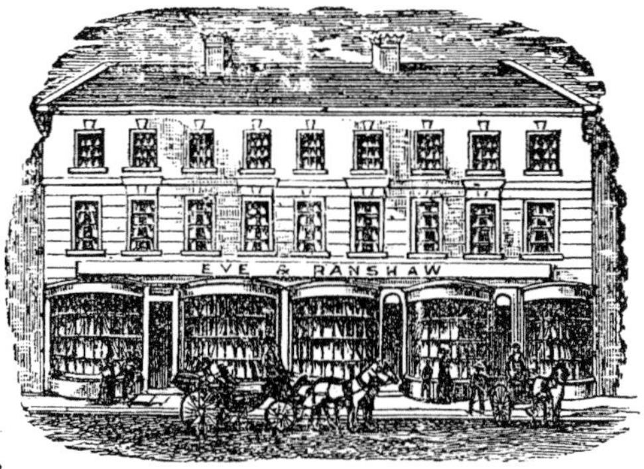

EVE & RANSHAW,

Market-place and Eastgate, Louth,

Linen & Woollen Drapers,

TAILORS, HATTERS, & OUTFITTERS,

CARPET & BLANKET WAREHOUSE.

☞ TEA & COFFEE MERCHANTS.

1884

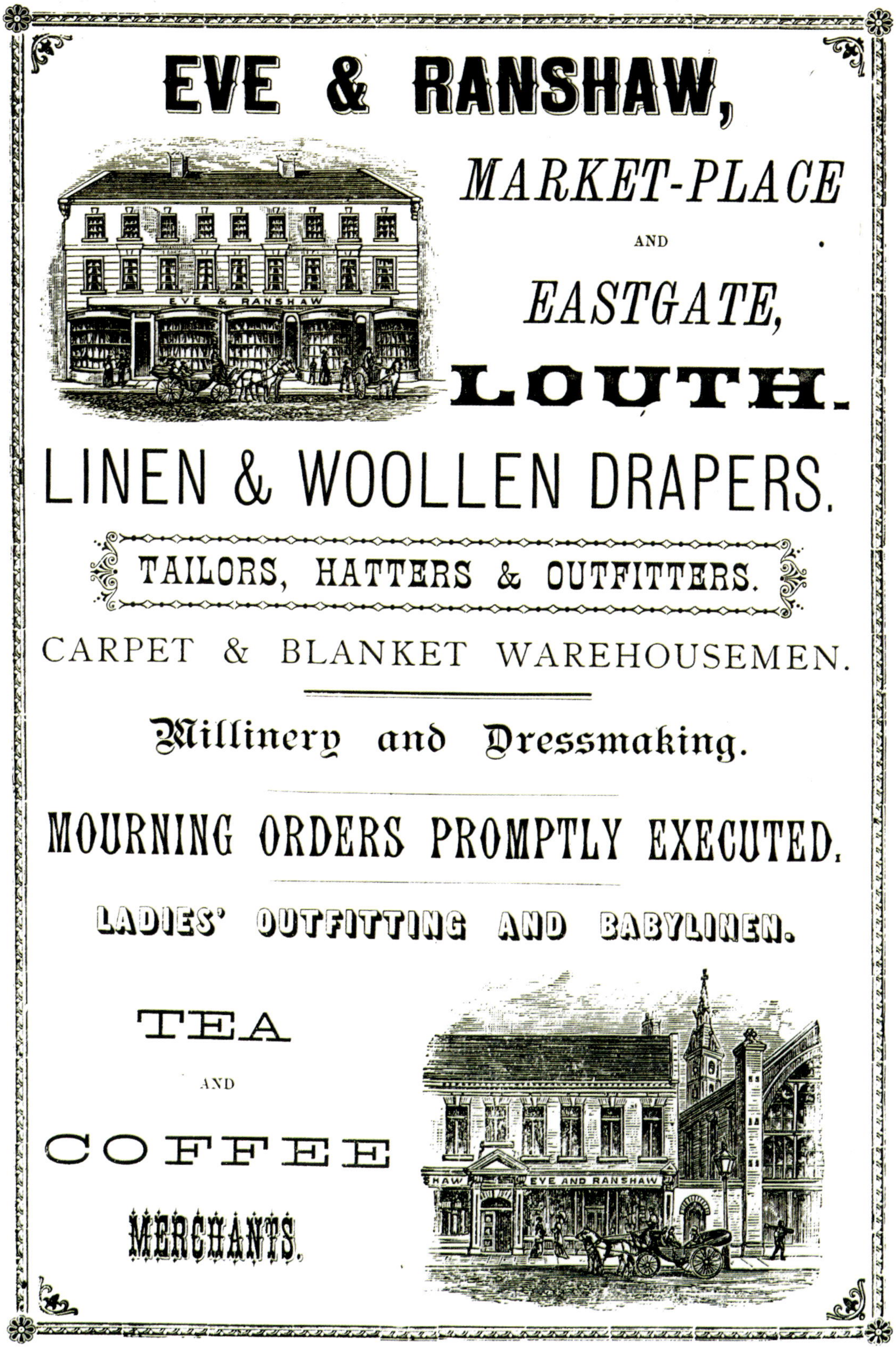
EVE & RANSHAW,
EVE & RANSHAW
MARKET-PLACE
AND
EASTGATE,
LOUTH.
LINEN & WOOLLEN DRAPERS.
TAILORS, HATTERS & OUTFITTERS.
CARPET & BLANKET WAREHOUSEMEN.
Millinery and Dressmaking.
MOURNING ORDERS PROMPTLY EXECUTED.
LADIES' OUTFITTING AND BABYLINEN.
TEA
AND
COFFEE
MERCHANTS.
EVE AND RANSHAW

1885

Eve & Ranshaw. General Drapers, Silk Mercers, Tea & Coffee Merchants

'The premises have a frontage in the Market Place of 75 feet, with five handsome plate glass windows. The interior is the shape of the letter L, the longer portion extending backward from the Market Place in a direct line of 139 feet, terminating in a substantial front with two plate glass windows in Eastgate.

On entering from the Market Place we find on the right the Bradford dress material, hosiery, glove and fancy departments, with counting-house in the rear, and staircase leading to the millinery, dress and mantle showrooms. Almost facing the entrance is the staircase approaching to the tailoring and gents' outfitting departments. The longer portion is devoted to tea and coffee, Irish, Scotch and Barnsley linens, flannels, blankets, calicoes, Manchester goods generally, and furnishing, the latter department occupying a large space at the Eastgate end for the display of the extensive stock of tapestries, damasks, repps, curtains, blinds, mattresses, beddings, linoleums, floorcloths etc, with a staircase communicating with the carpet showrooms above.

'On the upper floor, extending along the whole frontage, are showrooms for the display of silks, dresses, mantles, furs, millinery, and ladies' and children's underclothing. And on this floor, running in the direction of Eastgate, is a handsome room 67 feet long and lighted by five skylights, occupied by the tailoring and gents' outfitting departments, in which is to be found a choice of Scotch, Irish and West of England suitings, trouserings and overcoatings, also macintoshes, dressing-gowns, carriage and horse rugs, hats, flannel and Oxford shirtings and shirts, garments of various textures for underwear etc. Portmanteaus, Gladstone bags, ladies' travelling trunks and bonnet cases are included in this room.

'Passing on, we come to the department for the cheaper kind of carpets, hemp, jute, felt etc, in which are also cocoa mattings and mats. Beyond this is a spacious and lofty room, erected in 1883, and set apart for showing the extensive stock of Brussels, tapestry, Kidderminster and other carpets and squares, and all the art squares so much in use. There are also separate workrooms connected with the tailoring and millinery and dressmaking departments, the latter alone giving employment to more than forty workwomen.'

PERFECTION OF SILK.

TRADE MARK REGISTERED.

EARLY in the Spring, "Perfection of Silk" *(Manufactured by* C. J. BONNET & CO.*) was introduced and recommended by us as being the finest production of the kind ever brought under our notice.*

Since that time this Silk has had the approval and commendation of the leading Silk Mercers in every locality throughout the United Kingdom.

Absolute guarantees were given that it would be free from defects, such as splitting or greasing, common to ordinary makes.

These guarantees have been fully maintained.

Black Silk Costumes *are now in general demand, and* "PERFECTION OF SILK" *will be the most popular.*

EVE, RANSHAW & MAWER,
LOUTH.

AUTUMN, 1886.

At the census of **1891** there were more employees, 19 of them, living above the shop, including for the first time female dressmakers and milliners and one of them a draper's shopwoman. Times were a-changing. It is also noticeable that only the houseboy came from Louth. The list is probably about half of the total number of employees.

Elizabeth Gibbett (50)	Housekeeper	from Little Bowden, Northants
Betsy Jaques (21)	Cook	from Saltfleetby
Charlotte Jaques (18)	Housemaid	Betsy's sister
Arthur Ratcliff (32)	Clerk	from Sedgley, Staffs
James Hodgson (31)	Assistant	from Caunton, Notts
Arthur Titley (24)	Assistant	from Hainton
Tom Potter (29)	Assistant	from Doncaster
Walter Parker (24)	Assistant	from Friskney
Henry Simpson (26)	Assistant	from Worksop
Samuel Hurst (22)	Assistant	from Huddersfield
William Tock (23)	Assistant	from Burringham
Walter Milne (18)	Assistant	from Manchester
Clara Tavenner (24)	Draper's shopwoman	from Cheltenham
Mary - (28)	Milliner	from Lincoln
Susan Griffin (23)	Milliner	from Boston
Julia Hudson (39)	Dressmaker	from Grandborough, Warwicks
Fanny Green (28)	Dressmaker	from Skendleby
Ida Walton (19)	Dressmaker	from Stocksteads, Lancs
Ernest Bywater (15)	Houseboy	Louth

The same year as that census (1891) a new draper's shop opened at 32 & 34 Mercer Row, almost facing Eve & Ranshaw across the Market Place. It was founded by Robert Trousdale Sandwith, who had married Edith Kenyon daughter of Frederick Kenyon, silk mercer in Soho Square, London. The Sandwith family had been in the 'rag trade' from the 17th century when Thomas was a woollen draper in Bury St Edmunds, but with no thought in 1891 of the possibility 86 years into the future of trading as Eve & Ranshaw Ltd. (see page 180)

The last census list available is for **1901**, when all boarders at the shop were from outside the town. It has not been possible to trace the employees who lived in Louth as the record of occupation did not give the name of the shop in which they worked. Note however the presence of a page boy: did he have a uniform (one imagines with a pill-box hat) and what were his duties? To direct customers to the department they required? Also, one of the assistants, Frederick Newland, would rise to become a partner in the business.

R T SANDWITH
Mercer Row

Elizabeth Marshall (55)	Housekeeper	from Northants
Madeline Cooke (21)	Housemaid	from North Somercotes
Thomas Robinson (20)	Assistant	from Hull
Edward Walker (24)	Assistant	from Alford
Thomas Needham (23)	Assistant	from Cumberworth
Frederick Newland (30)	Assistant	from Grantham
Eleanor Oliver (39)	Dressmaker	from Ireland
Alice Nelson (28)	Dressmaker	from Manchester
Rosamund Hardy (34)	Milliner	from Spalding
Louisa Woolley (21)	Milliner	from Bourne
Mary Young (26)	Draper's Assistant	from Belleau
Mabel Young (21)	Draper's Assistant	Mary's sister
Frank Tyler (19)	Clerk	from Billingborough
Herbert Epton (16)	Page boy	from Withcall

continued on page 162

EVE & RANSHAW,

MARKET PLACE and EASTGATE,

LOUTH,

LINEN and WOOLLEN DRAPERS,

Tailors, Hatters & Outfitters.

CARPET & BLANKET WAREHOUSEMEN.

Millinery and Dressmaking.

MOURNING ORDERS PROMPTLY EXECUTED.

LADIES' OUTFITTING AND BABY LINEN.

AGENTS FOR DR. JAEGER'S SANITARY UNDERCLOTHING.

TEA AND COFFEE MERCHANTS.

both 1892

GOULDING'S HOUSEHOLD ALMANACK.

EVE & RANSHAW

Family Drapers,

TAILORS AND OUTFITTERS,

Market-Place and Eastgate,

LOUTH.

DRESSMAKING AND MILLINERY,
LADIES' UNDERCLOTHING.
☞ Special attention to MOURNING ORDERS.

CARPETS, HOUSEHOLD LINENS,
LINOLEUMS AND OILCLOTHS.

LACE, MUSLIN, AND TAPESTRY CURTAINS.
BEDDING AND MATTRESSES.

SUITS MADE TO MEASURE. FIT GUARANTEED.
OVERCOATS AND MACKINTOSHES.
☞ Clerical Collars, Ties, Hats, and College Caps.

UNDER VESTS AND PANTS,
In Merino, Lamb's Wool, and Silk.
☞ SHIRTS AND SHIRTMAKING.

PORTMANTEAUS, GLADSTONE BAGS,
LADIES' WICKER TRAVELLING BASKETS.

AGENTS FOR

Dr. Jaeger's Sanitary Underclothing, &c.

All Parcels of the value of 20/- and upwards sent carriage paid.

DISCOUNT FOR CASH.

TEA AND COFFEE MERCHANTS.

EVE and RANSHAW,

Furnishing Drapers,

LOUTH, Lincolnshire.

High-class Dressmaking & Millinery.

LADIES' & GENTLEMEN'S UNDERCLOTHING.

HIGH-CLASS TAILORING.

First-class Fit and Style Guaranteed.
Hand-sewn Garments.

LOW-PRICED SUITS

Made to Measure from 36s. each.
TROUSERS to Measure, from 10/6 each.

Men's and Boys' Ready-made Overcoats,

AT ALL PRICES.

PORTMANTEAUS, GLADSTONE BAGS,
Ladies' Wicker Travelling Trunks, &c.

CARPETS, LINOLEUMS, OILCLOTHS, CURTAINS, &c.

Iron Bedsteads and Bedding OF EVERY DESCRIPTION.

Noted for Household Linens, Blankets, Calicoes, &c.,

BEST VALUE COMBINED WITH MODERATE PRICES.

Dining Room, Drawing Room, Bedroom Suites.

Occasional Chairs, Bamboo Furniture, &c.

EVE & RANSHAW, LOUTH.

both 1896

EVE & RANSHAW,

FURNISHING ✝ DRAPERS,

LOUTH, Lincolnshire.

High-Class Dressmaking and Millinery.

LADIES' AND GENTLEMEN'S UNDERCLOTHING.

HIGH-CLASS TAILORING.

First-Class Fit and Style Guaranteed. *Hand-Sewn Garments.*

SUITS made to measure from 36/- each. TROUSERS to measure from 10/6 per pair.

MEN'S & BOYS' READY-MADE OVERCOATS AT ALL PRICES.

Portmanteaus, Gladstone Bags, Ladies' Wicker Travelling Trunks, &c.

CARPETS, LINOLEUMS, OILCLOTHS, CURTAINS, &c.

IRON BEDSTEADS AND BEDDING OF EVERY DESCRIPTION.

NOTED FOR HOUSEHOLD LINENS, BLANKETS, CALICOES, &c.

Bedroom Suites, Occasional Chairs, Bamboo Furniture, &c.

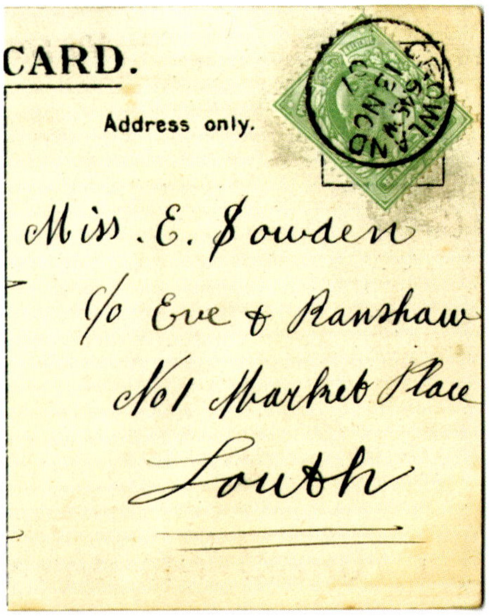

Address on a postcard to a live-in assistant, from her brother Jack in Crowland, 13 November 1907

None of the censuses after 1861 listed live-in apprentices, but it would appear that George Ranshaw was experiencing some difficulty with those living at home. In April 1901 he wrote to Marris Willows & Smith, silk mercers and general drapers in Hull seeking advice. Their reply stated that 'our apprentices do the sweeping at night at the close of business and they come half an hour before the assistants in the morning to take the wrappers down and do the dusting. Our work is all done in sections and we make no difference but keep them at it during the whole of their apprenticeship'. Their approach was more authoritarian than George's fatherly approach.

The last of the Eves to be associated with the firm, John Frederic, died at his home, Ivy House on James Street, in October 1902 at the early age of 40, from typhoid fever, following a holiday in Norway in August. He had not taken an active part in public affairs, but had devoted his time and energy to the development of the business. His obliging manner won for him the respect of all and particularly his employees. He left £13,500 to his cousin William Bowmar Eve, farmer at Theddlethorpe. He was an active Freemason, serving as Worshipful Master of the Lindsey Lodge in 1900, and he was highly esteemed by the Louth Artillery Battery of which he was Lieutenant.

He was accorded a military funeral and shops in the town closed as a mark of respect. The funeral cortege was headed by members of the Louth Artillery Battery with arms reversed, followed by a gun carriage bearing the coffin draped in a Union Jack, his horse, and nine carriages carrying members of the family and eight lady assistants from the shop, and then the page boy, two maids, 12 assistants and four apprentices. Analysis of the mourners listed in the *Louth & North Lincolnshire Advertiser* report reveals names that can be added to those recorded in 1891/1901: lady assistants – Young, Thompson, B Nell, Curtis and Williamson; male assistants – Rutherford, Walters, Cook, Webster, Brown, Storey and Vamplew [Charles]; apprentices – Crowther, Pratt, Sivil and Street [George Percy]; and Miss Southwell, housekeeper and F Riggall, page. (Vamplew, then 28, and Street, then 18, would later become partners with George Ranshaw.)

A remarkable aspect of the burial in Louth Cemetery was the decoration of the grave by Mabel Young, Arthur Titley and Mr Matthews, each representing employees in a department. 'The grave was lined with Virginia leaves and tendrils, relieved with white anemones round the top. Both at the head and at the foot was a bow of broad white merv ribbon, with long streamers, from the centre of which were trails of asparagus fern and Virginia creeper. About twenty inches upwards from the brickwork, the grave was surrounded by white wadding, overshadowed with sprays of asparagus fern. Round the inner ledge was a finish of white dahlias and asters intermixed with foliage and fern, and the bottom of the grave was strewn with autumn leaves'.

continued on page 168

Eve & Ranshaw furniture removals van on Horncastle Road (The Beeches in the background) about 1900

The funeral procession of John Frederic Eve
parading through the Market Place, 7 October 1902

John Frederic Eve

EVE & RANSHAW,
Furnishing ✦ Drapers,
UPHOLSTERERS,
AND CARPET WAREHOUSEMEN,
LOUTH, Lincolnshire.

HIGH-CLASS

Dressmaking, Millinery & Tailoring.

Ladies' and Gentlemen's Underclothing.

HOUSEHOLD LINENS, BLANKETS AND CURTAINS.

Furniture, Bedsteads, Mattresses,
Bedding, Linoleums and Mattings.

1905

GOULDING'S HOUSEHOLD ALMANACK.

EVE & RANSHAW,
Furnishing Drapers,
LOUTH, Lincs.

Dressmaking and Millinery.
Ladies' and Gentlemen's Underclothing.

HIGH-CLASS TAILORING.
BUSINESS SUITS to Measure from 42/-
TROUSERS to Measure from 10/6 per pair.

READY-MADE OVERCOATS.

PORTMANTEAUS, GLADSTONE BAGS, TRAVELLING TRUNKS,
CARPETS, LINOLEUMS, OILCLOTHS,
CURTAINS, &c.

BEDSTEADS & BEDDING
OF EVERY DESCRIPTION.

HOUSEHOLD LINENS, BLANKETS, CALICOES.

Dining Room, Drawing Room, and Bedroom SUITES.

Occasional Chairs, Bamboo Furniture, &c.

EVE & RANSHAW, LOUTH.

1906

Established 1781. *Nat. Telephone 2.* *Telegrams: "Ranshaw Louth."*

Eve & Ranshaw,

FURNISHING DRAPERS and SILK MERCERS.

LOUTH.

High-Class Millinery and Dressmaking. . . .
Ladies' and Gentlemen's Tailoring. . . . . .

Mantles, Costumes, Blouses, Gloves, Laces, etc.

* * *

Noted for . . .

Household Linens and Blankets, Carpets,
Linoleums, Bedsteads and Bedding . . .
Household Furniture, Blinds, etc.

Branch Establishment:

5, Market Place
(late Dalingwater & Co.)

Ladies' and Children's Outfitting, Corsets . . Dressing Gowns, and . Children's Millinery.

Layettes,
Trousseaux, etc.

1908

GOULDING'S HOUSEHOLD ALMANACK.

High-Class MILLINERY, DRESSMAKING, TAILORING.

HOUSEHOLD LINENS,
FURNITURE, BEDSTEADS, BEDDING.

INSIDE AND OUTSIDE BLINDS AND ROLLERS
MADE AND FIXED COMPLETE.

Branch Shop for

LADIES' & CHILDREN'S OUTFITTING,

No. 5, MARKET-PLACE.

1909

ESTABLISHED 1781 BY ADAM EVE.

NATIONAL TELEPHONE No 2. LOUTH. LINCOLNSHIRE. Feb 4 1910

The Representatives of the late Mrs Upton Raithby

BOUGHT OF EVE & RANSHAW, GENERAL DRAPERS & FURNISHERS.

HOUSEHOLD FURNITURE, LINENS, BEDSTEADS, MATTRASSES, BEDDING &c.

HIGH CLASS TAILORING, MILLINERY, AND DRESS MAKING.

ACCOUNTS RENDERED HALF YEARLY NETT. INTEREST CHARGED ON OVERDUE ACCOUNTS.

Billhead 1910

A LARGE ORDER.

"WHAT CAN WE GET FOR YOU, MADAM?" "WINGS!"

(Punch 1893)

A rare 1890s photograph of the staff who worked in the cutting room at Eve & Ranshaw.

Garden features created by nursery man George Moody in the Market Place in July 1909 when the Lincolnshire Show was held in Louth. Eve & Ranshaw, right background, has the sun blinds down with the name on each one. Note the man leaning out of one of the top floor rooms (live-in staff bedrooms) to fix a flag in a socket.

The death of Eve left George Ranshaw as sole proprietor, as John Campbell had been, and it is convenient to diverge for a moment from the chronological story to record stages in the leasing and financing of the property. Earlier in the chapter reference was made to John Campbell's brother James, to whom John appears to have left his rights to part of the shop and to the property on Cannon Street. A study of documents in the Eve & Ranshaw archive (now in Louth Museum) reveals a declaration made in February 1874 by Mary Campbell (84) of Howden, widow of James, that her daughter Mary had married James Bruce and that their surviving three children were Mary Campbell Bruce living at Cubbington, Warwicks, James Campbell Bruce, barrister at Lincolns Inn, Middx, and Joan Campbell Bruce of Cubbington, medical student. The purpose of the declaration was to establish the rights of John Campbell's great nephew and nieces to properties he had bought in 1811 to amalgamate into the shop and the property in Cannon Street he had bought in 1814. John Campbell had died in 1852 and it had taken 22 years to resolve the matter of ownership. The result was the sale in 1874 of the properties to John Bowmar Eve, Robert Ranshaw and James Eve for £5,000.

In order to finance this purchase the partners had to take out a mortgage of £2,500 at 4½%. £100 of the capital was paid off in 1890 and a further £100 in 1892. In November 1895 a valuation of the freehold properties was made by David Briggs of Calthorp & Briggs of Brigg. The shop was described as having office, showrooms and workshops, with a dwelling house adjoining [used as temporary accommodation for staff during major alterations]. The report stated that the property was in an excellent state of repair 'and the sanitary arrangements were good', and that 'within the last few years considerable sums have been spent in additions and alterations'. The property, including land, warehouse and workrooms 'recently built' on Cannon Street, was valued at £5,400 (£349,000 today) and 'a good and safe security for £2,700'.

In December 1895 the remaining mortgage of £2,300 with an additional £200 was transferred to Samuel Hynman Montgomerie of Copthorne Fawley, Southampton (he died in June 1915), and then to Thomas Cheney Garfit of Kenwick Hall and Bartholomew Claypon Garfit of Gunby Hall. The partners then were George Ranshaw and John Frederic Eve. In 1920 the mortgage was transferred again, to Allan Charles Hyman Allanby, (Chief Officer, Union Castle Steamship Co) and Ronald Hinman Allanby (Captain, later Major, Seaforth Highlanders Regiment). A C H Allanby died in February 1938, and Major Allanby, living at Nairn in Scotland, transferred the mortgage to Mrs Florence Muriel Cameron of Nairn. £1,000 was paid off in October 1944 and the balance of £1,500 (of the original mortgage taken out in 1874) in November 1950 by Eric Vamplew (see below).

Meanwhile, following the death of George Ranshaw in 1929 and Charles Vamplew (see below) in 1930, an additional mortgage of £7,000 at 5½% was provided by George's widow, Florence Elizabeth, who had gone to live at Sutton on Sea, and James William Burnett Read, manager of Lloyds Bank in Louth. It was repayable at £1,000 a year, but the final balance of £1,000 was not paid (by Eric Vamplew) until December 1950. Those final payments on the two mortgages were made after the incorporation of Eve & Ranshaw Ltd as a company (see below).

Opposite: A full page advertisement in a guide to Nottinghamshire and Lincolnshire, early 1920s. In the centre pictures note the Bentwood chairs for customers in front of the counters. The photograph bottom right is No 5 Market Place (see page 170).

EVE & RANSHAW

Furnishing Drapers

Removal & Storage Contractors : : : :

Cabinet Makers & Upholsterers : : : :

Complete Funeral Furnishers : : : : :

HIGH-CLASS TAILORING & GENT'S OUTFITTING. *TRAVELLING REQUISITES.*

Tailoring and Gent's Outfitting Department.

Costume and Blouse Department.

DRESSMAKING AND MILLINERY. *LADIES' AND CHILDREN'S OUTFITTING.*

Costumes, Coats, Blouses, Sports Coats, etc. ∴ *Hosiery, Gloves, Fancy Goods.* ∴ *Household Linens, Blankets, etc.*

Carpets. *Linoleums.* *Mattresses.* *Feather Beds.* *Bedsteads.*

Telegrams :
"Ranshaw, Louth."
Telephone : : 2.

MARKET PLACE & EASTGATE

Branch Shop for Millinery and Ladies' Underclothing.

LOUTH

Decorative glass front door 1920s

We can now return to the chronological story from 1902. For the next thirteen years George Ranshaw ran the business on his own, while also taking an active part in public affairs. He was Churchwarden of St James for many years, President of the Louth & District Tradesmen's Association, Commissioner for the Louth Navigation, Director of the Louth Gaslight Co, Committee member of the Louth General Friendly Society, member of the Louth Valuation Board, on the Management Committee of Louth & District Hospital (Crowtree Lane), a manager of Louth Savings Bank (Little Eastgate), a manager of the Lindsey County Council Primary Schools in the town, a member of the Louth Naturalists', Antiquarian & Literary Society, and was on the Executive Committee organising the Palestine Exhibition in Louth in 1908. He had played football and was elected President of the Louth Thursday Football Club when it was formed in 1895. His particular pleasure in later years was playing bowls on summer evenings and on Thursday afternoons (half-day closing for shops), and he was made Chairman of the Louth Bowling Club when it was formed in 1908.

That year (1908) he bought the Wool Mart (built by the Old Corporation in 1825) on Kidgate from farmer Christopher Adlard for £390. Ranshaw was already renting it as a furniture warehouse for the furniture removals side of the business. In the conveyance document he was described as Draper and Furniture Warehouseman. The firm had two entries in the 1909 Lincolnshire Directory: 'Linen & woollen drapers, silk mercers, outfitters, bedstead, furniture and carpet warehousemen, furniture removal & storage contractors' and 'Tea & coffee merchants'. Ranshaw had also opened a branch at 5 Market Place (formerly ladies' outfitters Dalingwater & Co) for 'Ladies' and Childrens Outfitting, Corsets, Dressing Gowns and Children's Millinery, Layettes & Trousseaux'.

There was also the funeral arrangements side of the business. The bill for the funeral of Mrs Upton at Raithby in 1910 totalled £12 15s 10d (£700 today). That included gloves for the bearers, use of the bier, a polished oak coffin with solid brass handles and engraved plate (£8 10s - £468 today), horse hire and the cost of a dog cart from the Masons Arms. The heading on the bill stated that accounts were rendered half-yearly. The business was then on the telephone: NTN (National Telephone Number) Louth 2.

In 1915 Ranshaw took on former assistants Frederick Newland (72 Newmarket) and Charles Vamplew (3 Westgate) as partners. It was probably in the period following the Great War that the system of live-in staff ceased. Newland retired in 1923, at which time the Tea & Coffee Department was closed. In 1922 Ranshaw and his wife had moved from 1 Temple Terrace to Woodville, 160 Eastgate, where this book is now being written. It was here that he died on Sunday 17 March 1929, aged 76, having been in the business 63 years, the longest serving of any. His executors were his widow and J W B Read, manager of Lloyds Bank. The value of his share in the firm was calculated at £10,398, of which £3,398 was paid to his widow in August and the remaining £7,000 formed the mortgage referred to above.

"And what style of hat does madam require?"
"Well, between ourselves, I want something that will shock the vicar's wife!"
(Punch 1929)

Charles Vamplew was the son of Samuel Vamplew who came to Louth about 1880; he was a 'machinist' and later thrashing machine proprietor. Charles's brother Henry took over the thrashing machine business, based at the windmill on Horncastle Road, which passed to his son Frederick Headland (the second Christian name being the maiden name of Henry's wife). Charles was apprenticed to Eve & Ranshaw and became a tailor's cutter. He married Annie Stamper of Louth, and their only son Eric Headland was born in 1904. Eric went to Louth Grammar School and then to London to train in the drapery business before becoming an assistant under his father and George Ranshaw.

George Ranshaw
(1852-1929)
63 years in the business

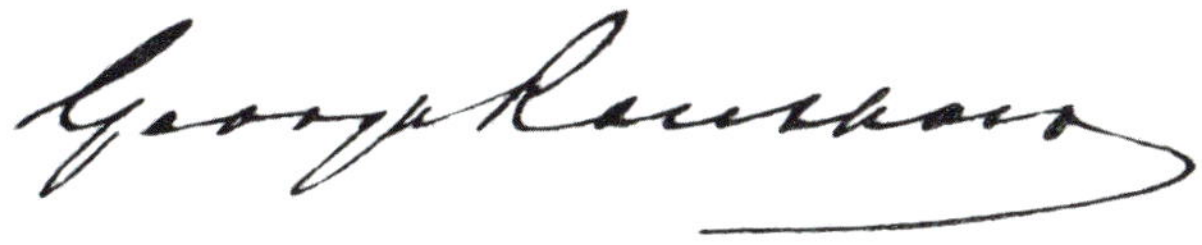

Ranshaw's death in 1929 left Charles Vamplew as sole proprietor, but he died eighteen months later on 4 September 1930, aged 56. His widow Annie was the sole executrix, and action had to be taken to establish a new managing partnership. That was for Charles's son, Eric Headland Vamplew to head a partnership with George Percy Street (son of Walter Charles Street, chemist and druggist, 13 Cornmarket) who, having served an apprenticeship with the firm had gone to be a draper's assistant at a shop in Coney Street, York and then to Sheffield to manage a similar shop. Eric would act on his mother's behalf who, according to the Deed of Partnership of 13th December 1930, was a 'sleeping partner'.

The property was valued at £6,360 (£236,000 today) and stock at £7,229 19s 7d. Book debts were estimated at £3,540 and liabilities at £1,751. An annual rent to Annie Vamplew as owner of the shop was agreed at £330 10s (£12,560 today). Percy Street would put in a share of £500 and be paid an annual salary of £300 (£11,400 today) plus 1¼% commission on gross sales. Eric and Percy would be allowed three weeks annual holiday, to be taken at different times.

Annie Vamplew

Charles Vamplew

They got off to a flying start, realising that 1931 marked the 150th anniversary of the founding of the firm. They produced an advertising and information poster to commemorate the event from Saturday 31 October to Saturday 7 November. It included a brief history based on original dates and claiming that Adam Eve opened his shop of 31 October 1781 (but see the beginning of this chapter). However, the statement that 'The venture was a small one but with untiring energy and business acumen he soon made much progress, that his shop became the rendezvous of the leading gentry of the district' is certainly true. Moreover that with 'the splendid growth and extension of the business… Eve & Ranshaw became a by-word for the quality of their goods and the straightness of their dealing'. 'This', the new partners wrote, 'is the high standard of excellence which it is the determination of the firm to perpetuate'. There was also a brief history of the carpet factory and related deeds were displayed in one of the shop windows. Also on show were several pieces of Louth made carpet; what happened to them?

For the week of commemoration there was a 10% discount on all purchases (except proprietary articles). The proud claim was that your house could be completely furnished by the shop. A particular attraction was the Linen Department where 'a loom has been installed… and during the celebrations customers will be able to watch the actual process of weaving tea-cloths… A dependable yarn has been selected… and the tea-cloths as they are made will be sold for 11d (5p) each. We invite all who are interested in weaving to come and watch'.

The new partners decided that the showroom and warehouse and the upholsterers' and joiners' shop on Cannon Street were surplus to requirements, and in 1931 and 1932 they were sold to the Borough Council. Annie Vamplew retired as 'sleeping partner' in 1936 (she died in 1948, aged 76) and Eric Vamplew and Percy Street continued through the 1930s and the years of World War Two. In 1940 it was possible for a bride to obtain a complete outfit for little more than £12 (£400 today), when the ivory lace wedding dress cost £5 15s 6d (£193 today). And in 1950 a lady's pink suit sold for £7 14s 3d (£225 today), including alterations at 17s 6d.

From 1927 to 1949, first Charles Vamplew and then Eric kept meticulous annual accounts of all items bought from the shop – at retail prices. Discounts to staff did not come in until after 1950. The account books are interesting in showing stability and changes in retail prices. An analysis will be found in Appendix C.

In December 1950 the firm was incorporated under the Companies Act to become Eve & Ranshaw Ltd, with Eric Vamplew as Managing Director and Percy Street as the other Director. The shop and the Wool Mart were leased by Eric as owner to the Company for 21 years at an annual rent of £523. That was raised to £750 in 1957, of which £50 was for the Wool Mart. However, in July 1960 the lease of the Wool Mart was relinquished as the Company no longer had a use for it.

Eric Vamplew

Percy Street

Painting by W. L. Rodgerson, 1944

What was it like to work as a shop assistant in the 1950s? Janet Pratt (now Stevenson) left Monks' Dyke School in 1952 to work in the ladies' underwear department and recorded her experiences in her memoirs. She was interviewed by Eric Vamplew and met for the first time the fearsome Miss Bushell. She did have a Christian name, Ethel, but it was never used; she lived in a flat over the adjoining shop, 2 Market Place. It was she who kept an eagle eye on the lady assistants, quick to find fault, almost never praised them and seldom smiled. Janet's weekly wage was £1 10s 1d (£1 12s 6d less 2s 5d for the insurance stamp): that would be £39 today.

Jean Blanchard was the senior assistant in the underwear department. Throughout the shop surnames were always used – so it was Mrs Blanchard and Miss Pratt. Juniors had to arrive by 8.45am, through the staff entrance on Eastgate with a passage where bicycles could be left, through a door into the shop, sign in with the time of arrival in Mr Miller's book, and then up the front staircase and left to the underwear department. The floor was carpeted in green with a central beige runner to direct customers to the counters, behind which assistants stood on linoleum. The underwear department had a wooden armchair with padded seat for the use of customers.

Underwear was displayed against a backdrop of black cloth and in the glass-fronted knitting wool counter, on top of which were knitting patterns, monthly *Stitchcraft* magazines and knitting needles. Behind the counter was a shelved fixture for skeins of knitting wool, always difficult to keep tidy, and cupboards for brands (Hosene, Southall and Mene) of sanitary pads. Near the counter was a headless and armless model to display a nightdress or dressing gown. Once when it was placed in a shop window ready for making up a display, Janet was asked to cover it up pending being properly dressed!

Opposite the counter was a narrow cream table for underwear display and a cupboard for Chilprufe combinations, and vests and knickers of wool and shiny celanese (a synthetic fibre). Chilprufe underwear of pure wool in cream included combinations with legs down to the ankles, and knickers were also available with long legs. The celanese long legged knickers ranged from small to extra, extra outsize. A special unit of drawers accessed by up and over glass doors contained nightdresses and bedjackets, underslips, panties, brassieres and suspender belts. Brands included Kayser Bondor, Berlei, Kestos and Gossard. Corsets and corselets, some boned back and front were kept in individual boxes. However there was also a popular boneless roll-on, the Gossard Silkskin.

Effecting a sale involved writing out a bill and using that wonderful device the compressed air chute. Place bill and money in a cylinder, put it in the chute, press a button and off it whizzed to the office where Nancy Glentworth (later Adlard) receipted the bill, put it and any change in the cylinder and back it whizzed to the department. Most items sold were put in paper bags, but larger ones were wrapped in brown paper and tied with string. Staff got a discount on goods bought in the shop.

Monday was the day for changing displays, including shop windows, vacuuming the floor and cleaning counters and fixtures. Window dressing units were kept in the top floor attics facing the Market Place, once bedrooms for apprentices and assistants, but not yet fitted with electric light in the 1950s. Juniors had to take turns in daily hoovering and dusting the stairs. A ten minute break was allowed in the morning and an hour for lunch. Miss Bushell made her rounds of her departments to make sure that everything was being done to her exacting standards. At about four o'clock the counter books were changed, black and red alternate days. At a few minutes to 5pm displays were covered with paper and cloth, and at 5pm the routine was to say goodnight to Miss Bushell, and sign out.

Janet Pratt at 16 when she started at Eve & Ranshaw

Nancy Glentworth

Pam Castledine (later Clapp) Officer Manager who became a Director and served 29 years **(see page 180)**

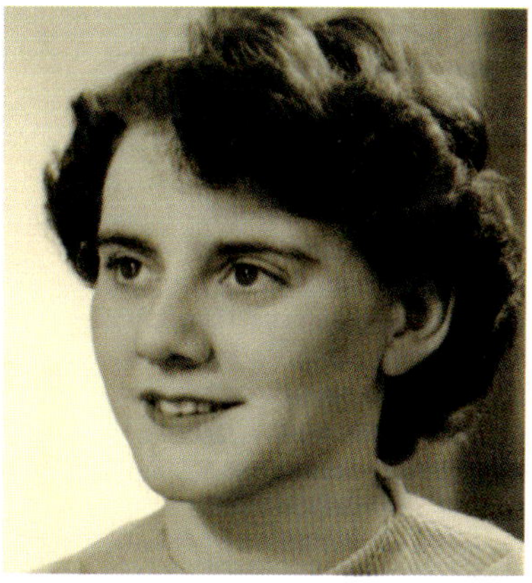

Brenda Stephenson Dress material and accessories

Reg Charles
Upholsterer and cabinet maker

Miss Ethel Bushell

Other departments in the shop included haberdashery, gowns and fabrics (with a fitting room), furniture and soft furnishings run by Mr Botting with Reg Charles as upholsterer and cabinet maker who also made coffins (Eve & Ranshaw were also funeral directors), and baby and children's wear (including Grammar School uniforms).

There were the January sales, and the summer sale was in July when old stock was displayed at reduced prices. The Chilprufe combinations were always reduced but never sold! For the Coronation in 1953 there were special window displays, and the company placed related adverts in local newspapers, and the shop closed on Coronation Day, June 2nd. At Christmas staff received a box of chocolates. Holiday entitlement was two weeks, usually taken in the summer.

In 1954 Miss Bushell moved the children's department in order to display a range of glassware she had bought as a new line. Dusting these every morning was a nightmare. Janet recalls having the job and breaking a wine glass, one of a set of six. She decided to confess to Miss Bushell, but when knocking on her office door and asking to have a word was told 'Go away girl'. After weeks of trying and getting the same response, Janet put the five glasses at the back of the shelf and hoped for the best. In fact she had left by stocktaking time.

continued on page 180

21 November 1953

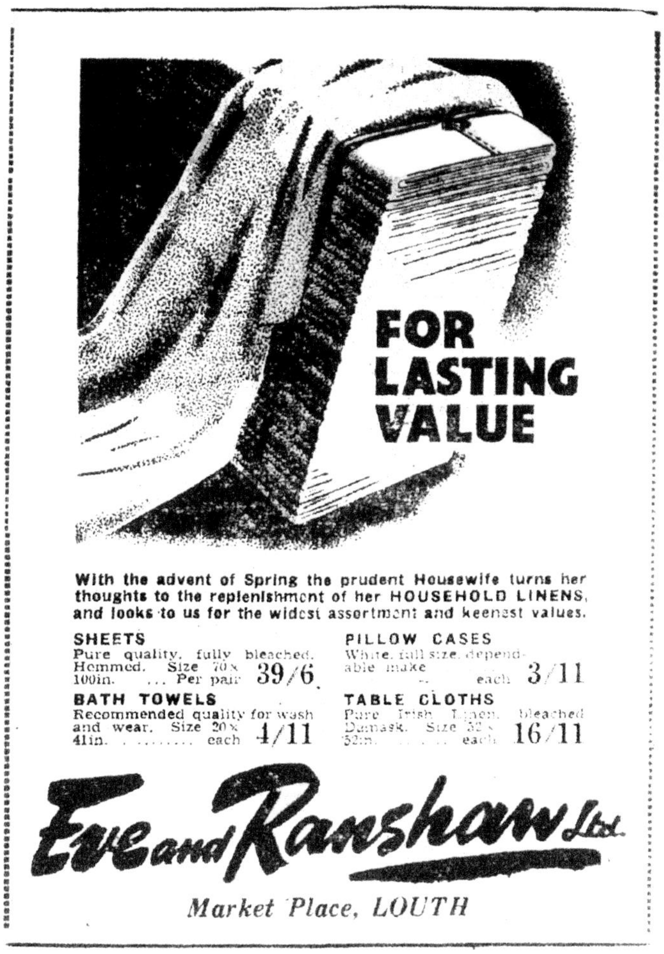

14 March 1953

21 March 1953

28 March 1953

4 April 1953

11 April 1953

25 April 1953

9 May 1953

16 May 1953

27 June 1953

15 August 1953

3 October 1953

10 October 1953

The Furniture Department closed in the late 1960s, and in January 1971 the rent of the shop to the Company was raised to £2,500 for three years. At that time Eric Vamplew was Chairman of the Directors and the other Directors were his wife Dora, Percy Street (with particular responsibility for the Furniture Department) and his wife Nesta, Joan Kenny (Head of the Ladies' Outfitting Department) and Mrs Pamela Clapp (Accounts) nee Castledine who had joined the firm when she left Louth Girls' Grammar School in 1951. The management of the business was essentially in the hands of Eric and Percy, where Eric was the real driving force, while Percy preferred to spend part of some working days playing snooker.

Percy Street died in Northampton in 1974, aged 90, leaving three Directors: Eric Vamplew (Chairman), Joan Kenny and Pamela Clapp. Three years later there was a major change in the management of the firm. We have noted earlier in the chapter (page 159) the drapers R T Sandwith at 32 & 34 Mercer Row. Robert Trousdale Sandwith's son Robert Christopher was educated at King Edward VI Grammar School and apprenticed in York before taking over the business when his father died. He served in RAF Coastal Command and Combined Operations in World War Two. He was a founder member of Louth Rotary Club and of Louth Golf Club, and served as President of Louth Chamber of Trade & Commerce. In 1977 he took a controlling interest in the Limited Company, of which he became Chairman, with his son Robert David (born 1944) as Managing Director. The Eve & Ranshaw property was transferred later. David brought to the firm a wealth of business experience in a sportswear company and in a London company importing textiles and garments including four years in Hong Kong. Other Directors were Olive Mary Sandwith (Christopher's wife), Eric Vamplew (he retired two years later at the age of 75 after 52 years with Eve & Ranshaw; he died in 1995, aged 91) and Pamela Clapp as Company Secretary (she retired in 1996 after 45 years with the firm).

Robert Christopher Sandwith (1910-1986)

200 years
Eve and Ranshaw LTD.
1781 to 1981
Double Century Celebration

Four years later in 1981, Eve & Ranshaw celebrated its Double Century with the publication of the booklet *Double Century 1781-1981* (see Introduction to this book), and the *Louth Standard* published an eight-page supplement. The Fashion Buyer then was Mrs Joan Bentley who had been trained and worked with Christopher Sandwith. Her work entailed searching the market for current trends and attending shows to meet representatives of fashion houses. For example, the bridal section of the shop had dresses from the exclusive range of Hillary Morgan of Grantham. Mrs Bentley had to buy for both city life and the county scene, and popular then was the reversible skirt.

The Workroom overlooking Eastgate was where the coffins were once made, with a glue-pot always on the bubble, and great difficulty they had in getting the coffins down the narrow back stairs. In 1981 there were sewing machines with Mrs Connie Parrish in charge. The work included soft furnishings and accessories for home, hotels and offices – curtains, linings, pelmets, drapes, swags, cones, valances, dressing table covers, stool covers, cushions and loose covers. There were also fashion alterations.

Joan Bentley

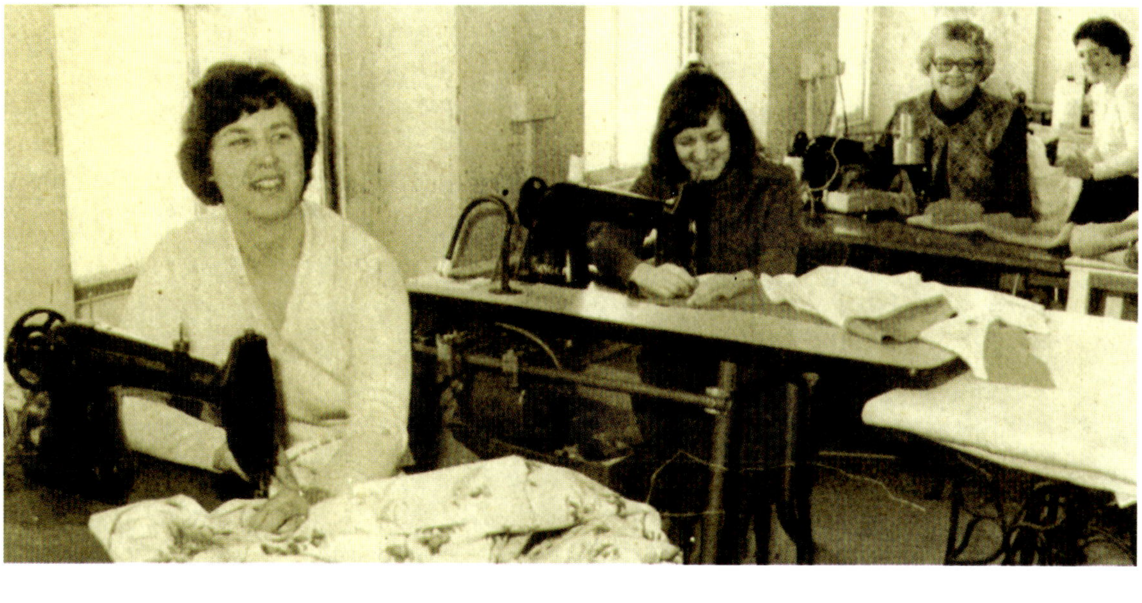
The Workroom, Connie Parrish third from left

Buying for the Lingerie Department were Denise Campbell and Mrs Christine Hitchman, who had seen a transition from rigid, hookside, bush-front, lace-up corset to the elastic roll-on girdle and then to lightweight non-rubberised fabric glamour girdles. The main factors, they said, were lightness of fabric and maximum comfort. They also saw the change in nightdresses from Winceyette for winter and cotton lawn for summer to non-iron brushed nylon for winter and double nylon with frills for summer. By the 1980s polyester had replaced nylon, but customers were reverting to the 'undeniable comfort' of pure cotton.

In the Fabrics Department Wendy Rainthorpe and Mrs Sandra White found that demand for materials for home dressmaking was on the increase, and they were there to advise on both material and thread. As part of the 200th anniversary a dressmaking competition was organised, with marks for suitable fabric, basic skills, neat zips and hems, and finish.

Celebration teatowel

Another member of staff who came over with Christopher Sandwith was Ruby Garbutt, the Furnishing Fabric buyer. She had started as an apprentice in the late 1930s when her weekly wage was 7s 10d (37½p), equivalent to £14.25 today. The day then started at 9am and closing times were 6pm on Monday and Tuesday, 7pm on Wednesday and Friday (market days) and 1pm on Thursday (half-day closing); Saturday normally meant a 12-hour day to 9pm or 'as long as there were customers to be served'. She had seen changes from blankets to duvets (the original natural filled Scandinavian quilt 'fnug') and sheets which once varied in weight and types of cotton and linen became standardised with easy-to-care-for material for the housewife to launder.

Ruby Garbutt

Accessories ranged from tights, gloves, scarves (long ones were in vogue then), costume jewellery, belts and handbags to kitchenware, glass and crystal, paintings and 'knick-knacks'. Here the skill of the assistants, Veronica Gladding and Sandra Goodley, was to judge the changes in fashion when buying for the next season.

Looking back, what is noticeable about the newspaper supplement is that the firm was run by men and the selling was by women – for women. No mention of menswear – that department having ceased some years earlier. Garments and hats for men were always part of Adam's original stock in trade. Discounted items in the Winter Sale in January 1982 were for the ladies and the home – sweaters and cardigans, skirts and dresses, Candlewick housecoats, duvets, sheets and Fogarty pillows, new curtains, tea towels and place mats. Gentlemen, don't despair: the Menswear Department was revived in the late 1980s and is now near the Eastgate entrance. And today there is also a section for shoes (nothing like that in Adam's day – he had his own shoemaker).

2009

Eve & Ranshaw has never been a shop to stay still. There has always been change, expansion and change to keep up with fashion and the needs of customers – including a clientele beyond Louth. That's what the Eves and the Ranshaws and others did – and so it is today. Early in 2009 there was refitting of departments at the Eastgate entrance to the shop.

To bring the story to 2010, let it be recorded that David Sandwith is Chairman and Managing Director, with fellow Directors his brother Peter Rodney and A C J (Charlie) Hickman (son in law of Eric Vamplew), and that the full-time and part-time staff are:

Robert David Sandwith, Managing Director

Non-Executive Directors: Charles Hickman & Peter Sandwith   Company Secretary: Marcus Sandwith

Fashion

Full Time: Joan Maltby – Fashion Buyer, Dianne Parrott – Fashion/Gifts/Accessories Buyer, Melanie Harries – Window Displays
Part Time: Jean Middup – Alterations
Part Time Sales: Jayne Egan, Malvina Willis, Ann Beck, Sandra Willerton, Lesley Wilkinson

Gifts, Hosiery, Accessories

Full Time: Anne Rothwell
Part Time Sales: Leyla Johnson, Maxine Storr, Rebecca Kettle

Soft Furnishings & Linens

Full Time: Jacqueline Limm – Soft Furnishing/Bedding Buyer, Janet Fowler – Machinist
Part Time: Helen Kennedy – Machinest, Michael Phidas– Curtain Estimator/Fitter
Part Time Sales: Diane Reeson, Anne Barton, Katrina Boswell

Menswear

Full Time: Sandra Patchett – Menswear Buyer
Part Time Sales: Angela Simpson, Dorothy Holmes

Lingerie

Full Time: Denise Swift – Lingerie Buyer
Part Time Sales: Jean Bird

Office

Full Time: Janette Arnold – Office Manager
Part Time: Allison Cox – Purchase Accounts, Carol Williams – Sales Accounts

Maintenance

Part Time: Kenneth Arnold, Margaret Desforges

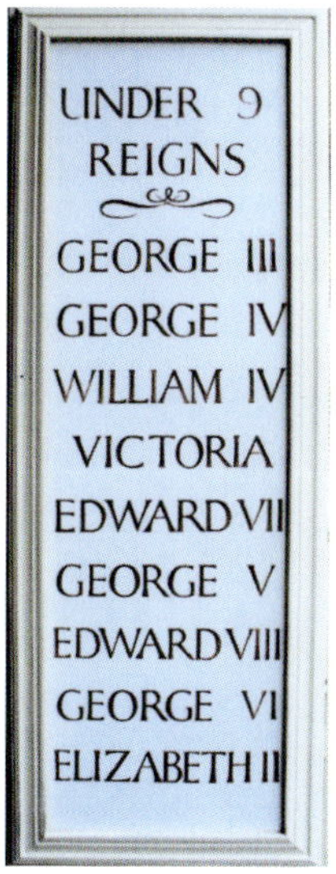

From a painting by Sarah Batey, 2007

The first Stuff Ball in the Windmill Inn, Alford in November 1785
Painting by Tom Brooker

MARKET PLACE, ALFORD.

The Windmill Hotel in Alford about 1900. The first floor bay window lights the room where the first four Stuff Balls were held.

Chapter 7

The Lincolnshire Stuff Ball

ONE OF THE bright ideas of the Revd Gideon Bouyer to promote and publicise the spinning of wool and the weaving and wearing of woollen garments was to hold a Stuff Ball (stuff was worsted). This he achieved through the Society for the Promotion of Industry in the Southern District of Lindsey, formed in 1783, and it quickly became a highlight in the social calendar of the county.

In August 1785, a number of gentlemen, friends of the Society who had entered into a Subscription to encourage plans for the employment of the poor, placed an announcement in the *Lincoln, Rutland & Stamford Mercury* signifying that they would give a BALL and CARD ASSEMBLY on 17 November at the Windmill Inn, Alford. Ladies and gentlemen would be admitted gratis if the ladies wore orange-coloured stuff gowns and petticoats spun and woven in Lincolnshire; ladies who had spun their own gown to wear a white ribbon, others blue. Gentlemen needed to obtain a ticket from a Subscriber and to appear without any cotton or silk in their dress except stockings, that is woollen waistcoat, coat and breeches – but what about the shirt?

A list of the Subscribers was at the Windmill Inn, the Bluestone Inn, Louth, the Bull Inn, Horncastle and the White Hart Inn, Spilsby. Gentlemen were also invited to be a Subscriber on or before the last day of September. Stewards for the Ball and Card Assembly were Thomas Chaplin Esq of Tathwell, John Popple Esq, Revd Henry Colston, Vicar of Bilsby and Rector of Ulceby with Fordington, and Revd Gideon Bouyer. The Patroness of the Ball was Gideon's wife Elizabeth.

Ladies who wished to bespeak a dress for the Ball were requested to place their order as soon as possible. With each gown and petticoat would be given a ticket with the name of the weaver, seller and buyer or of the weaver and employer. Production of the ticket was required to gain admission to the Ball. Ladies who spun their own wool would need to get it dyed – lichen dyes were the easiest to produce orange (fast and fadeless) and then to find a local weaver. One such was Richard Allison of Theddlethorpe, who had a simple four-shafted loom, the warp of about 24 strands to the inch raised by four pedals. With a light beat and throwing the shuttle across the warp threads he would produce a fine twill for the dressmaker.

It took time. Would it not be easier to visit the shop of Adam Eve, woollen draper in Louth, or a similar establishment in another market town, to place an order for a dress? Adam would have to find a dyer, a weaver and a dressmaker. It was all part of the Society's scheme to boost the local wool economy, and doubtless Adam took advantage as part of building up his business.

It was reckoned that some three hundred people from many parts of Lincolnshire attended the first Stuff Ball. The room at the Windmill Inn was crowded, dancing through to dawn in clothes made of wool would undoubtedly be warm and John Griffiths the proprietor of the inn would do well out of it in providing the refreshments. The Ball was a success, but the demand for worsted of a standard colour – the shades of orange had ranged from pale orange to russet, suggested the need for one good dyehouse.

According to the *Lincoln, Rutland & Stamford Mercury* 'the hazard, expense and delay in dyeing and finishing goods at a considerable distance was a discouragement to able and industrious weavers whose work was beneficial to the training of spinners and employment of the poor under the auspices of the Society of Industry'. Establishment of a central dyehouse would also improve the quality of worsted yarn. At a meeting of the Society (41 gentlemen present) at the Bull Inn, Horncastle in October 1786 a subscription was opened for the purchase of a hot-press and other utensils for a dyer, hot-presser and finisher of Wildbore tammies, durants and other goods made of worsted, 'to be applied to the improvement of manufactured goods made of longwool and the employment of the poor in general and the infant poor in particular'. The estimated cost of the hot-press and utensils was £400 (£24,000 today). A committee of 17 trustees were charged with managing the undertaking, and subscription lists were opened in Louth, Alford, Spilsby, Horncastle, Lincoln, Grantham, Boston, Caistor, Gainsborough and London which raised £320, the balance being met from the general funds of the Society.

Wildbore was the name of a firm in Grantham. Tammy was a fine worsted cloth of high quality, hot-pressed to give a glazed finish. Durant was woollen stuff, called by some 'everlasting', also hot-pressed and glazed but with creases (pleated). At around two shillings (20p) a yard, the material for a worsted gown ranged in price from £2 4s to £3 7s (£150 to £270 today).

It had been the intention to lend the hot-press and utensils to a dyer who would find suitable premises in Louth. The search for premises proved fruitless and Charles Chaplin of Tathwell assigned a plot of land near the Navigation for the remaining 83 years of his lease. To meet the additional cost of building the dyehouse the Society had to take out a mortgage of £300. A detailed account of costs in *An Account of the Origins, Proceedings and Intentions of the Society for the Promotion of Industry* (1789) shows William Dunn as the builder (£184), Salt & Gothard, Lindsey & Berwick and Wigglesworth & Eyers as iron founders (total £282), William Cooper for pewter and lead vessels (£48) and transport costs totalling £35, together with work by whitesmiths (including Bartholomew Howlett, father of Bartholomew the engraver), plumber, ironmonger, millwright and supply of press-paper. Total cost including carriage of materials was £650 (£39,000 today). James Ibbetson was appointed as dyer, and he also built a fulling mill with the aid of a loan of £50 from the Society.

The subscription list for the hot-press and dyehouse indicated who was at the meeting in Horncastle: it included Sir Joseph Banks of Revesby, Sir Peter Burrell (later Lord Gwydir) £20 each (£1,200 today), Robert Vyner of Gautby Hall and Ayscough Boucherett of Willingham Hall £15 each as the leading subscribers, together with later subscribers the Earl of Exeter of Burghley House 20 guineas, Charles Pelham of Brocklesby and Sir John Thorold of Weelsby £20 each, and George Heneage of Hainton Hall £15.

Revd Gideon Bouyer contributed 3 guineas (£150 today) and his wife one guinea. There were thirteen other clergy subscribing (from a total of 80), all in South Lindsey, and there were fifteen ladies. The total raised by the Society was £700, leaving £50 cash in hand. It is noticeable that Adam Eve contributed 3 guineas, the same amount as Thomas Chaplin, an indication of the progress of Adam in commercial as well as social status (he had married an heiress earlier in the year), and clearly he must have seen it as a form of investment in an establishment to provide quality dyed worsted for his shop and potential purchasers of ball gowns.

Sir Joseph Banks

The name of Sir Joseph Banks at the top of the list is a reminder of his keen interest and active involvement in the problems of the Lincolnshire wool growers, particularly following the renewed embargo laws on wool export in 1781. He was on his annual autumn visit to Revesby when the Society met in Horncastle in October 1786, having arrived from Spring Grove, Heston at the beginning of September. His somewhat eccentric sister Sarah Sophia supported his interest in wool and had three dresses made from the finest fleeces: Scrub for everyday wear about the house, Titum as second best, and Hightum for great occasions.

The 1787 Stuff Ball at the Windmill Inn, on 25 October, was specifically advertised as 'for the encouragement of the Lincolnshire Stuff Manufactory', built in Louth earlier that year. 'Too much cannot be said', reads the entry in the *Lincoln Date Book,* 'in praise of the Lincolnshire ladies, who appeared in gowns and petticoats made of stuff grown, spun, woven, dyed and finished in Lincolnshire, as displayed the most laudable zeal in support of their infant manufactory'. The Patroness was the Rt Hon Lady Willoughby, of the highest family in the county, who chose the colour. Every lady 'intending to honour the Ball with her presence' was requested to place an early order with a manufacturer who would, with the dyer and hot-presser or finisher James Ibbetson, sign the admission ticket. Subscription entrance for gentlemen was half a guinea (10s 6d or about £33 today). No gentleman living in South Lindsey could be admitted as a non-subscriber, but the Committee had power to issue five shilling tickets for the 'admission of strangers'. Subscriptions could be entered at the Windmill Inn, the Bluestone Inn, Louth, the White Hart, Spilsby and the Bull Inn, Horncastle. The Stewards were Willoughby Wood of South Thoresby and John Popple.

In June 1788 Robert Vyner jnr (1762-1810) of Gautby Hall married Lady Theodosia Maria daughter of the Earl of Ashburnham. When they took over the Hall in 1799 they had it enlarged and for a period it was a place of glittering social activity. They had nine children. Lady Theodosia was Patroness for the last Stuff Ball at the Windmill Inn on 13 November 1788. She chose brown olive for the ladies' gowns and light blue for petticoats. The gentlemen were reminded that they should appear without silk or cotton in their dress, except stockings. One enterprising woollen draper at Alford placed an advertisement in the *Lincoln, Rutland & Stamford Mercury*: George White 'begs leave to acquaint those Ladies who please to honour him with their commands, that they may be supplied with STUFFS of the Lincolnshire Manufactory, and of the colour fixed for the Ball'. He also noted that he had 'A suitable STUFF of the Long-Wool Manufactory for Gentlemen'.

Subscriptions could be entered at the usual inns, or the office of Richard Lucas, the treasurer, in Alford. The Stewards were Charles Burrell Massingberd of South Ormsby Hall and Charles Chaplin of Tathwell. Doors opened at 8pm and dancing commenced at 9 o'clock, with minuets and country dances until six in the morning. The event was reported as 'a most brilliant attendance from various parts of the county'.

Such was the popularity and excitement of the Ball for the nobility and gentry – and for those of 'trade' who could afford the entrance subscription (did Adam and Sarah Eve go?), that a fourteen-verse poem appeared a fortnight later in the *Lincoln, Rutland & Stamford Mercury*. Much of it was typically verbose, but contained such lines as: 'Let our Lincolnshire wool ball your patronage claim', 'Reviv'd at the tidings new industry smiles', 'Tis joy to see beauty move gracefully round', and ends with 'That industry works what benevolence plann'd'.

Earlier that month – on Tuesday 4 November 1788 – Adam and Sarah would surely have been at the Ball in the Mansion House in Louth, the focus of the social life of the town. The Warden, Robert Neve, a merchant and the same age as Adam, was authorized by the Corporation to give a Ball to mark the Secular Anniversary of the Glorious Revolution – the landing at Torbay in 1688 of William of Orange and his declaration to defend the liberties of England and the Protestant religion. The invitation was to all ladies and gentlemen of the town and neighbourhood, the expense thereof being 'paid out of the Corporation purse'. Undoubtedly present on that occasion, by virtue of his office, was Charles Chaplin of Tathwell, High Steward of Louth (on his own because his wife Elizabeth had died two years earlier); he held the position from 1782 to his death in 1795, and was followed by his eldest son Thomas from 1795 to 1804. Charles's fifth son, George, who never married, became a good friend of Adam.

The novel as well as social status of the Stuff Ball required a larger venue more convenient for travel, and from 1789 it was held in the County Assembly Rooms (built 1744-45) on Bailgate in Lincoln. *The Lincoln, Rutland & Stamford Mercury* reported that there was 'a most numerous and respectable attendance of the nobility and gentry resident in the county. The Assembly Room was scarce ever known to be fuller than on the present laudable occasion: a circumstance which cannot fail of affording pleasure to our numerous readers, as it indicated, in the strongest manner, that a cause thus publicly countenanced and supported must ultimately be productive of the most solid and lasting advantage to this extensive county'.

The Patroness was Lady Dorothea Banks, travelling from Revesby. An added significance of the event in Lincoln was the failure of the 1788 Wool Bill to remove export restrictions, despite efforts of Sir Joseph Banks and other Lincolnshire landowners. It was a protectionist Bill which favoured merchants and manufacturers against the interest of growers.

The Patroness in 1790 was Lady Elizabeth Monson, then in following years the Duchess of Ancaster, Lady Brownlow, Lady Thorold, Lady Mary Milsington, Lady Charlotte Beauclerk – the list as it continued reading like a roll-call of the leading families of Lincolnshire. The advertisement for the Ball in the Assembly Rooms, above Hill, Lincoln on Friday 18 November 1796 'for the encouragement of the stuff manufacturing' stated the usual conditions: 'ladies to be admitted gratis on their appearing in a Stuff gown and petticoat of the colour appointed by the Patroness [brown and blue] spun, woven and finished within the County, and producing a ticket signed by the Weaver and Dyer at Louth, one of which tickets will be delivered with every twelve yards of stuff; gentlemen to appear without silk or cotton in their dress, stockings excepted. Tickets delivered for gentlemen 10s 6d each at the White Hart and Rein Deer Inns, Lincoln, also at Mrs Camms, Keeper of the Assembly Rooms, above Hill and at Mr Steel's, Draper, below Hill.' There was also a special note: 'By particular desire of the Lady Patroness and Stewards, some front seats, distinguished by crimson covering, will be reserved for ladies intending to dance minuets, upon which it is requested that they will have the goodness to place themselves, and that other ladies will permit these seats to be wholly appropriated to that use' – nothing so vulgar as a printed notice on the seats.

A meeting of wool growers at the Talbot Inn, Caistor in July 1802 agreed that the reduction in the value of wool was the general preference for cotton 'by all ranks of society'. They saw it as their duty, as well as in their own interest, to encourage the use of woollen cloth and more especially 'the wearing of stuffs in our own families'.

The Stuff was plain in 1805 and could be obtained at a moderate price from Mr Bustin of Louth (the son of William Bustin who had come from Durham to manufacture ball stuffs). By the time Gideon Bouyer left Lincolnshire in 1810, the original purpose of the Stuff Ball was half-forgotten, although stuff was still being worn in 1815 when 'the meeting was not so large as on some previous years, nor was the stuff so universally worn'. In 1823 Mrs Turner of the Stonebow, Lincoln advertised 'a most extensive assortment of Millinery and Dresses for the occasion [of the Ball], bought especially in London'. However, stuff was still being made: in 1825 Mrs Turner advertised that she had been 'appointed by the Lady Patroness [Hon Mrs Hobart] as sole agent for the Ball stuffs [dark blue]'.

In 1825, when restrictions on the export of wool were removed, there was also a ball at Sleaford with a similar purpose to the original Stuff Ball. *The Lincoln, Rutland & Stamford Mercury* reported: 'The perfection to which manufacturing of British long wool has arrived was agreeably shown by the handsome, modest and useful dresses which were displayed by both sexes [!] at the fancy stuff ball at Sleaford on 14 February which was most respectably and numerously attended; and the laudable spirit of establishing an annual meeting to encourage the growth and consumption of British wool universally prevailed in the party'.

The previous year John Parkinson (his father John had been Steward of the Lincolnshire estates of Sir Joseph Banks) had started a factory in his new created 'industrial township' of New Bolingbroke for weaving crepes and bombazines (twilled dress material of worsted with silk or cotton added), styling himself as stuff manufacturer, dealer and chapman. New Bolingbroke was an isolated place in the middle of the recently drained West Fen, and within two years Parkinson was bankrupt.

There was no Stuff Ball in 1826 because of building work on the Assembly Rooms, and the following year the requirement to wear garments of stuff was lifted, the Patroness, Lady Ingilby (of Kettlethorpe) having requested that ladies should adopt blue as the colour in any material, either for dresses or trimmings, and the event became known as the Colour Ball, to maintain the tradition of a different colour or colours each year.

In 1828 the event was advertised as the Annual Ball and Supper, under the patronage of Mrs Boucherett (of Willingham Hall) with Stewards Charles Winn, High Sheriff (of Appleby Hall) and Sir Edward Ffrench Bromhead (Lincoln). Ladies were not expected to appear in stuff but were requested to adopt Pouceu (poppy) as the prevailing colour, 'a specimen of the exact colour to be seen at Mrs Turner's, milliner on the High Street, Lincoln'.

After some forty years, the Stuff Ball was a fixture in the social calendar. The lifting of the embargo on the export of wool in 1825 had no effect. Family parties and friends travelled by coach from all parts of the county, perhaps putting up for the night in Lincoln, or returning home at dawn. According to the list of leading parties at the 1833 Ball, Alfred Tennyson was with the Edens from Harrington Hall.

By that time it was probably not obligatory to wear 'stuff', but to obtain a ticket it was necessary to purchase so many yards of stuff and be able to produce a receipt for it.

Attendances through the 19th century were regularly over two hundred, and advertised as the Stuff Ball, the Colour Ball or the Stuff and Colour Ball – as it was in 1862 when held on 5 November. The Patroness on that occasion was Mrs Sherwin Gregory of Harlaxton Hall, the colour was scarlet, and the Stewards were the Duke of St Albans (Redbourne Hall) and Henry Chaplin who had just achieved his majority and inherited the Blankney and Tathwell estates from his uncle Charles who had died three years earlier. The following night there was also the Dispensary Ball in the County Assembly Rooms.

In 1891 the (Stuff) Ball was held in January and ticket prices raised to fifteen shillings for gentlemen and ten shillings for ladies. Lady Sophia Allenby was the Patroness and the colours blue and silver.

1904

The event continued into the 20th century, no Ball during the Great War, and in 1920 was known again as the Stuff Ball, held on Tuesday 28 December, Patroness Lady Sheffield (of Normanby Hall), colour yellow. The last annual Stuff Ball was held in November 1938 when the colour was turquoise, its original purpose probably long forgotten. However it was revived periodically, including one to mark the 200th anniversary in 1985.

Today the memory is recalled by an annual Stuff Lunch in the autumn.

Postscripts

Baa, baa, black sheep,
  Have you any wool?
Yes, sir, yes, sir,
  Three bags full;
One for the master,
  And one for the dame,
And one for the little boy
  Who lives down the lane.

The origin of this nursery rhyme is not known, and Lincoln Longwools are white, but Adam Eve was once a little boy living down a lane.

The question which our Adam's grandfather Adam never solved was: who were the mother and the biological father of the baby found in Scartho churchyard in 1725 and named James? Our Adam became a good friend of George Chaplin (1760-1835) of Tathwell; George was the fifth son of Charles (1730-1795). Charles's father Thomas (1684-1747) had inherited Tathwell from his father John (1642-1714) who had married Elizabeth Hamby, daughter of Sir John Hamby of Tathwell.

John Chaplin was Sheriff of Lincoln in 1690, and MP, Recorder and High Steward of Grimsby. His younger brother Sir Robert (c1680-1728) was made a Baronet in 1715, the year he became MP for Grimsby. However, Sir Robert was apparently the black sheep of the Chaplin family: he was a director of the South Sea Company and when the bubble burst in 1720 (the directors having taken over three-fifths of the National Debt) he was expelled from the House of Commons the following year for 'insider dealing'. He died intestate. Could he have been the Baronet whose coronet was embroidered on the clothes left with the foundling? And one wonders if Adam's friend George Chaplin knew about the downfall of his great uncle Sir Robert.

Appendix A – **Shop Lease to Adam Eve, 1781**

This Indenture made the Twenty sixth day of October in the Twenty second year of the reign of his Majesty King George the third And in the year of our Lord one thousand seven Hundred and Eighty one between Frederick L'Oste of Louth in the County of Lincoln Gentleman of the one part and Adam Eve of Louth aforesaid Mercer and Grocer of the other part Witnesseth that for and in consideration of the Rent Covenant and agreement hereinafter reserved and contained on the part and behalf of the said Adam Eve his Executors Administrators and Assigns to be paid done and performed He the said Frederick L'Oste Hath Demised Leased and to farm letten And by these presents Doth Demise Lease and to farm let unto the said Adam Eve his Executors Administrators and Assigns All that Shop and fixtures thereunto belonging and a little Room on the North side of the said Shop, Also a Chamber and Garratt over a kitching fronting a yard belonging to the said Frederick L'Oste situate in Louth aforesaid and now in the tenure of Charles L'Oste Mercer and Grocer Together with all and singular the Ways Easements paths and passages Water Watercourses Lights profits Comodities and advantages and Appurtenances whatsoever to the said Shop, little room, Chamber Garratt and premises belonging or in any wise appertaining To have and to hold the said Shop, fixtures, little room, Chamber and Garratt and all and singular other the premises hereby demised with their and every of their appurtenances unto the said Adam Eve his Executors Administrators and Assigns from the Twelfth day of May next for during and unto the full term of seven years from thence ... ensuing and fully to be compleat and ended yielding and paying therefore yearly and every year unto the said Frederick L'Oste his Heirs and Assigns during the continuance of the said term the Rent or Sum of fifteen Pounds of lawful money of Great Britain on the Twenty second day of November and Twelfth day of May by even and equal portion the first payment thereof to begin and be made on the twenty second day of November one thousand seven Hundred and Eighty two Provided always that if it shall happen that the said yearly sum of fifteen Pounds or any part thereof shall be behind and unpaid by the space of thirtyone days next after either of the said days in which the same ought to be paid as aforesaid (being lawfully demanded) Or if the said Adam Eve his Executors Administrators or Assigns shall not do and perform all the singular the Covenants and agreements herein contained or his of their parts and behalf to be done and performed Then in any of the said Cases it shall and may be lawful to and for the said Frederick L'Oste his Heirs and Assigns into and upon the said Demised premises or part thereof in the name of the whole wholly to enter and the same to have again reclaim possess and enjoy as in his and their first and former Estate and the said Adam Eve his Executors Administrators and Assigns thenceforth utterly to expell move and put out these presents or any hereinbefore contained to the contrary Thereof in any wise notwithstanding And the said Adam Eve for himself his Heirs Executors and Administrators doth Covenant promise and agree to and with the said Frederick L'Oste his Heirs Executors Administrators and Assigns shall and will during the continuance of the said term hereby Demised will and truly pay or cause to be paid unto the said Frederick L'Oste his Heirs or Assigns the said yearly rent or sum of fifteen Pounds on the days and times and in the manner and form above mentioned for payment thereof according to the reservation thereof as aforesaid And also that the said Adam Eve his Heirs Executors Administrators or Assigns shall and will at all times hereafter during the continuance of the term hereby Demised at his or their own proper Costs and Charges well and sufficiently repair amend and support uphold maintain preserve and keep the Doors, Windows, Window Shutters fixtures of the said Demised premises in by and with all and all manner of needful and necessary reparation and amendment whatsoever from time to time and at all times during the continuance of the said term hereby Demised premises so often as need or occasion shall be and require and the same premises being so well and sufficiently repaired upheld maintained and kept in repair at the end of the said term or other sooner determination thereof shall and will peaceably and quietly leave surrender and yield up unto the said Frederick L'Oste and his Heirs or Assigns (Casualties by fire Storms Tempests Hurricanes and other inevitable accidents always excepted) and also that the said Adam Eve his Heirs Executors and Administrators shall not at any time or times during the said term assign or otherwise depart with this Indenture or the premises hereby Demised or any part thereof to any person or persons whatsoever Except to a person or persons in the trade and business of a Mercer, Draper or Grocer or to the said Frederick L'Oste his Heirs or Assigns But if the said Adam Eve his Heirs Executors and Administrators cannot let or assign the said Demised premises to a Mercer, Draper or Grocer or the said Frederick L'Oste his Heirs or Assigns will not accept of such assignment that then and in such case the said Adam Eve his Heirs, Executors and Administrators shall and may assign or let the said Demised premises to any person or persons whatsoever for the remainder of the said term And the said Frederick L'Oste for himself his Heirs Executors and Administrators doth hereby Covenant promise and agree with the said Adam Eve his Heirs Executors and Administrators doth hereby Covenant promise and agree with the Executors Administrators and Assigns by these presents That he the said Frederick L'Oste his Heirs Executors and Administrators shall and will at all times hereafter during the continuance of the term hereby Demised bear pay and discharge all taxes Charges Impositions and Parish rates which shall be Taxed Charged Imposed Assessed upon the said Demised premises or any part thereof And also shall and will at his or their own proper Costs and Charges make and lay a new floor in the said shop with deals And also keep all the said Demised premises in good and sufficient repair (Save and Except the Doors, Windows and Window Shutters and fixtures of the said Demised premises) in by and with all manner of needful and necessary Reparations and amendments whatsoever from time to time and at all times during the continuance of the said term hereby Demised when and so often as need or occasion shall be and require And that the said Adam Eve his Executors Administrators and Assigns paying the said yearly rent of Fifteen Pounds and performing all and every the Costs rents and agreements herein contained which on his or their parts and behalf and or ought to be done and performed shall and may peaceably and quietly have hold and enjoy the said Shop, little Room, Chamber Garratt, fixtures and premises mentioned or intended to be hereby Demised as aforesaid with the appurtenances for and during the said term hereby Granted without any lawful... trouble or interruption of or by the said Frederick L'Oste his Heirs or Assigns of or by any other person or persons claiming or who shall or may thereafter claim by from or under their or any of them or thro' his their or any of their acts means or pronouncement In Witness whereof the parties to these presents have hereunto set their hands and Seals this day and year above written.

Sealed and Delivered (being
first duly stamped) in the
presence of
Eliz Robinson
Jn Robinson

... Adam Eve and
L'Oste signatures
torn out ...

Appendix B

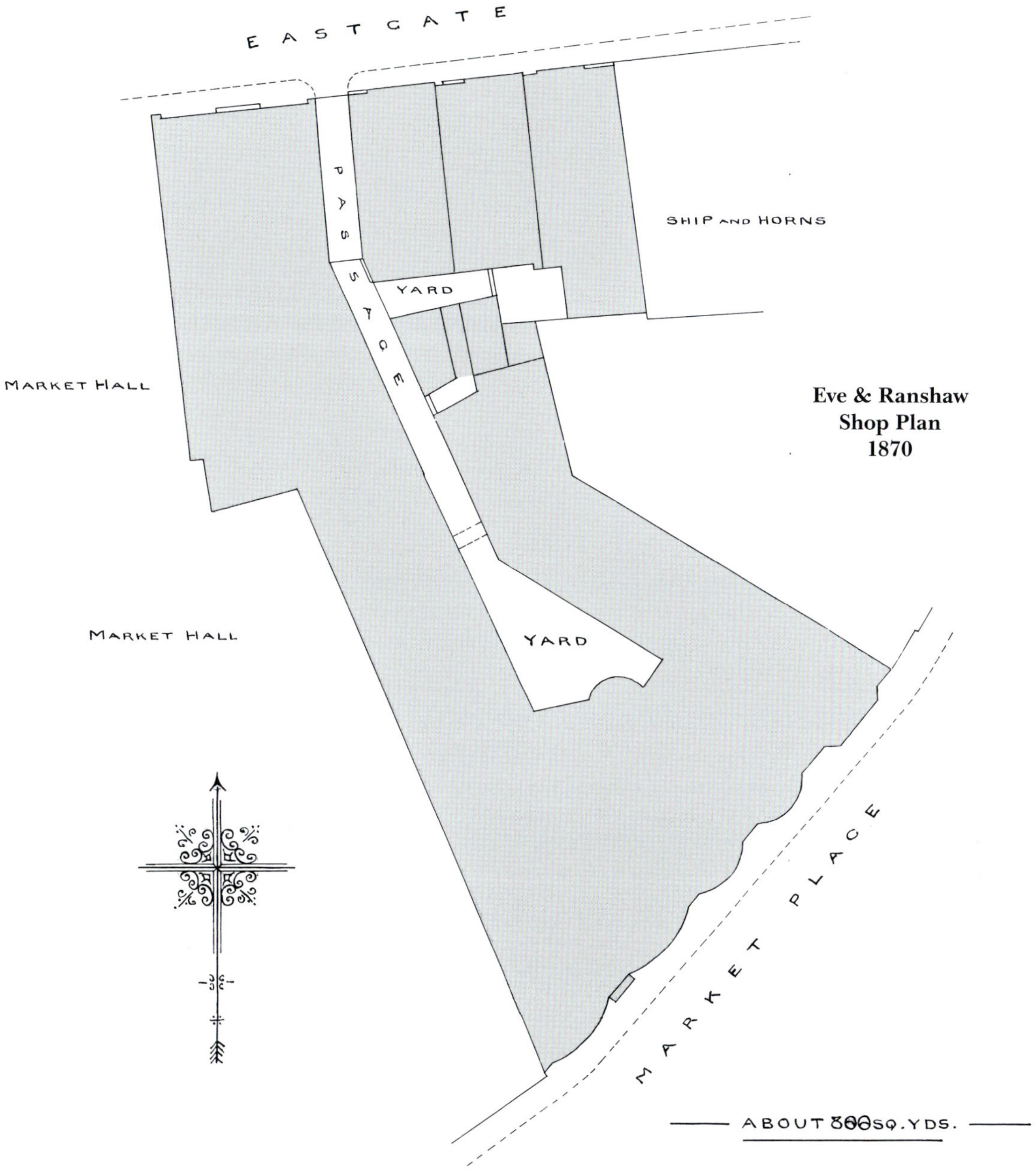

**Eve & Ranshaw
Shop Plan
1870**

Shop roofs from Market Hall scaffolding. Original shop just out of picture bottom right

Appendix C – **Charles and Eric Vamplew Personal Account Books 1927-1949**

Mention was made on page 172 of these books, red and gold embossed EVE & RANSHAW, LOUTH. The first, 1927 to 1936 was for Charles, and then his widow Annie from September 1930 (she retired as 'sleeping partner' in 1936). That for their son Eric ran from 1933 (he had taken over the running of the shop in December 1930) to 1949 (Eve & Ranshaw became a Limited Company in December 1950). Every item they bought from the shop was recorded – from a single button to an expensive suit or dress, at full retail price. This analysis reviews major items, including furniture, but does not include socks and stockings, collars, handkerchiefs, knitting wool, patterns and thread, soap and cosmetics, or alterations, repairs and cleaning of clothes. However, the total yearly spend does include the costs of occasional repair or fitting works at their houses. Figures in brackets are the equivalent price today.

In **1927** and **1928** Charles bought himself four suits: worsted double breasted £5 8s 9d (£195) – interesting to note worsted still being stocked, grey tweed £4 10s (£162), blue serge £5 (£180) and a fancy Cheviot £5 8s 6d (£195), and two hats – soft felt 14s (£25) and hard felt (bowler) 11s 9d (£21), while his wife Annie had two fawn silk dresses £2 7s 9d (£84) and a navy pleated skirt 8s 11d (£15.40). They also had items of furniture including an Axminster rug 13s 6d (£23), camp bed £1 7s 10d (£48), deck chair 4s (£7.20), upholstered wicker chair £1 7s 9d (£60), and a miniature billiard table £2 4s (£79). Total spend in the shop for the two years, including minor items, repairs etc, was £94 10s (£3,400).

Total of items purchased in **1929** was £80 16s 2d (£2,909) including two more suits for Charles, grey worsted £4 17s 9d (£175) and grey flannel £3 5s (£117) – a shop owner needed to be smartly dressed, a frock coat £1 9s 11d (£54), a grey double-breasted overcoat £3 14s 3d (£133) and another bowler, while Annie had a black and white crepe dress £2 9s 11d (£90), a Jaeger cardigan 12s 4d (£22) and two hats, black trimmed with ribbon and gardenias 15s 11d (£28) and navy felt trimmed with fancy leaves 11s 6d (£19.80). For the house an oak combination bedstead cost £1 6s 6d (£48), a loose cover for a Divan chair £1 17s 6d (£67), a down quilt 12s 9d (£23) and a carpet sweeper £1 5s 6d (£45).

Other items of comparative interest in **1929** and **1930** were a black Henry Heath hat £1 1s (£38), two more soft felt hats, a fawn straw hat 8s 11d (£16.60), a black hat trimmed black and green 11s 9d (£21), Vantella shirt 7s (£13), flannel day shirt 8s (£14.40), pair of boots £1 10s 5d (£55), choker fur tie £2 9s 6d (£106), black suede gloves 5s 9d (£10.80), grey gloves 8s (£14.40), raincoat £1 5s 9d (£46), fancy tweed suit £3 5s 6d (£120), grey tweed suit £5 10s 7d (£205), tweed jacket £1 2s 6d (£42.50), brown check overcoat £2 11s (£94.30), black fur trimmed coat £2 8s (£89), pair of sheets 9s 11d (£16.90), bedspread 8s 11d (£10.60), two pyjama suits 7s 6d (£13) and 10s 6d (£19), and Chilprufe combs (combinations) 9s 6d (£16.50).

Charles Vamplew died in September 1930 and the accounts record the funeral and mourning costs of £36 10s 8d (£1,425). The following year Annie invested about £60 (£2,350) in household items including a settee and two divan chairs £25 6s 9d (£988), Axminster carpet £6 17s 10d (£265), 13¼ yards stair carpet £4 8s 4d (£171), walnut bedstead £8 (£312), oak hallstand £3 19s 6d (£155.50), easy chair £3 19s 6d (£149.30), four dining chairs £3 17s 6d (£140) and better quality bedspread £1 9s 6d (£57.70) and sheets 16s 2d (£31.20), a hassock 4s 9d (£8.90) and a fancy cushion 6s 9d (£13.60). Personal items included two more pairs of Chilprufe combs for a guinea (£49.90). Items for Eric included two worsted suits, brown £4 12s 9d (£180) and grey £4 16s (£187) and a soft felt hat 11s 6d (£20).

Annie's spend on herself in **1932** included a blue/pink dressing gown £1 3s 6d (£46.80), blue silk nightdress 18s 6d (£30) and a pink dressing jacket trimmed with swansdown 4s (£8), from which, together with other items such as a purple princess skirt and matching knickers 19s 5d (£37.60), one may deduce that her favourite colours were shades of blue and pink. She also bought a helio skirt 11s 9d (£22.80) and a helio white scarf 7s 11d (£14.30), blue and white dress and grey blouse 12s 11d (£24.60) each, white blouse 9s 11d (£20.50), black skirt 8s 11d (£18.40), black and grey hat £1 11s 9d (£43.80), grey gloves 9s 4d (£20.40) and a grey bag 9s 11d (£20.50). Note how many items were one penny less than the full shilling, then, as now, a psychological selling point. The saving of one penny then would be the equivalent of about 42p today.

Items bought by Eric through this account show his need to keep up appearances: grey worsted suit £4 12s 6d (£185), grey tweed overcoat £3 15s (£150), sports jacket £1 7s 6d (£54.80) and four soft felt hats, 10s 4d (£20), grey 10s 6d (£21), and two black 17s 10d (£32). Then in **1933** he added three more suits, a blue worsted £4 11s 3d (£183.20), fancy brown worsted £3 19s 11d (£164) and grey flannel £3 12s (£147.60), an overcoat £3 3s (£129), a Dexter raincoat £2 2s (£86.10) and another soft felt hat 10s 6d (£20.50).

Annie's spending in **1934** included a black and white dress £2 2s 9d (£85), two princess skirts, a necklace 8s (£16), a pink bedjacket 4s (£8), a blue locknit set 7s 11d (£16) and four blue cushions, two silk covered and one down filled £2 15s 8d (£110), and three more pairs of Chilprufe combs. In **1935** there was another blue silk cushion 14s (£28), a navy and white spot silk dress including making £1 15s 8d (£71.20), a black and white dress £1 5s 11d (£52) and navy georgette coat £4 5s (£170). Household items included a pouffe hassock 7s 5d (£14.80), an oval mirror 16s 6d (£32.20) and a down quilt bedspread £2 19s 6d (£120). Total spend for all items in 1935 was £30 2s (£1,204) compared with £21 19s 6d (£868) in **1936** when she retired. Among the last items recorded were an oak dressing chest and tallboy £6 7s 6d (£254.08), a 4ft oak bedstead £2 7s 6d (£94.80) and fireside chair £1 8s (£56); and a necklace £1 1s 3d (£49), ear-rings and a bracelet 4s 9d (£9.60) each. She intended to be comfortable in retirement.

Meanwhile Eric continued to set himself up in the manner required for the owner/manager of a prestigious department store: in **1934** a made to measure worsted suit £4 14s 6d (£194.70), three (more) soft felt hats at 10s 4d (£21) each, an Artsilk sports shirt 5s 8d (£10.40), a sports shirt and tie 5s (£10.20) and three Poplin ties at 3s (£6.10) each. Also listed was a Li Lo 9s 11d (£20) and a box of cigars £1 5s (£51.20).

Then in **1935** his buying from the shop more than quadrupled to a total of £58 10s (£2,340). For himself were a more expensive Dexter raincoat £3 4s 9d (£130) and a Donegal overcoat £3 14s (£148), two more made to measure suits, grey worsted £4 16s (£192) and grey flannel £3 8s 6d (£138), a Harris tweed sports coat £2 5s (£90), another grey soft felt hat 10s (£20), three more ties, two Poplin and one Old Ludensian (Grammar School) 1s 9d (£2.20). Eric had also taken up golf: six clubs 4 guineas (£168), golf bag 8s 6d (£18) and half a dozen balls 4s (£8) with a further dozen 6s 6d (£13) the following month. He also bought a sleeping bag £1 2s 6d (£48), and was buying furniture: gent's oak wardrobe £8 10s (£340), dressing chest 4 guineas (£168) and a bookcase £3 5s (£130).

More furniture followed in **1936**, particularly in August and September, and it becomes clear that he was setting up a marital home. He was in fact demonstrating that Eve & Ranshaw could furnish a home (as they advertised). Major items were a Wilton carpet 8 guineas (£336), 12½ yards of staircarpet £3 8s 5d (£136), three-piece suite in moquette £14 17s 6d (£587), walnut bedroom suite £26 19s 6d (£1080), oak sideboard £11 17s 6d (£474), bedstead and dressing chest £4 10s (£180), dining table and four chairs £12 15s (£510), hall stand £3 17s 10d (£156), tallboy £2 5s (£90), Vito Monarch mattress and base £4 14s 8d (£188), bedstead £6 11s 6d (£263), bookcase £4 (£160), Jaspe lino £8 7s 10d (£297), Lloyd loom cupboard £1 11s 2d (£62) and a Bissell carpet sweeper £1 2s 6d (£45). All this did not prevent him buying another made to measure worsted suit £3 13s (£146), a summer jacket 8s 11d (£18), yet another soft felt hat, two ties, and a smaller box of cigars 16s 3d (£26.80). An unusual item was a black American broadtail hat 8s 11d (£18). It was Eric's most expensive year, total £162 19s 9d (£6,520), not to be exceeded, or come anywhere near it, for a decade.

The account for **1937** shows a new pattern of purchases with dresses and dressmaking materials for his wife, canvas and rug wool, and a child's cot, mattress and related items for their first daughter. Personal items included another American broadtail hat (brown), an Aquatite raincoat £2 3s (£81) and a tweed overcoat £3 15s (£104) plus two ties and an even smaller box of cigars 7s (£13.30). **1938** saw more children's items including a Bi bi baby blanket 12s 11d (£24), romper and crawler suits, a playpen 10s 6d (£19.40) with canvas surround 8s 4d (£15.50), a high chair 16s 2d (£29) and pushchair £1 16s (£66.60). There were household items including an oak trolley table £1 17s 4d (£68.50), Jaspe lino £6 6d (£222), sheepskin rug 19s 4d (£37), three Mirzapore rugs £3 19s 6d (£147.50) and an electric vacuum cleaner 5 guineas (£194). Also noted were a pair of Wellington boots 14s 7d (£26.50) and a hiker's tent 10s 8d (£19.40), and a different quality of cigars – 25 for 12s (£22.50) and 50 for 7s (£13).

The account for **1939** shows family clothing items including a Chilprufe tailored coat £1 1s 9d (£39), three shirts and a dozen collars £1 12s 3d (£59.50), a Country Life suit £4 14s 6d (£174.60), natural doe gloves 9s 4d (£16.60), a Marcasite tie pin 7s 6d (£13.70) and a green woollen dress £2 9s 11d (£92). Curtains and valances in Tootal casement cost £1 18s (£70), and there was a purchase of a gas mask bag 1s 9d in September. Total spend of £44 6s 3d (£1,639.40) was only about half of the previous year £82 3s 9d (£3,039.60), a sign of things to come in the war years.

Eric and his family's average annual spend in the shop during the war was £59 12s (£1,876). Blackout curtains for their home cost a mere 4s (£6.20), but it is interesting to compare the more expensive clothing against the baseline of a 9ft by 6ft Axminster carpet £2 5s (£74.30), a 10ft 10ins by 8ft 2ins Mirzapore carpet £4 15s 9d (£140), a blanket £1 11s 2d (£51) and lined gloves £1 9s (£47.80). The following examples range from **1940** to **1945**: check Country Life suit £6 16s 4d (£211), a Country Life coat £6 10s (£214.50), brown/blue floral frock £4 18s 1d (£152), fawn coat £4 2s (£135), black silk dress £3 9s (£107) (the same as a wing chair), check tweed coat £2 17s 6d (£88.40), navy two-piece £2 12s 6d (£86.60), raincoat £2 10s (£82.50), navy coat £2 6s 6d (£77.50), fuchsia/grey floral dress £2 5s 9d (£74.40), Harris tweed coat £2 5s (£69) and a Gor-ray skirt £1 6s (£52.30). The most expensive items were in **1945**: navy Elgara suit £13 16s 2d (£412), a floral dress £7 18s 8d (£246) and a pigskin bag £10 5s 4d (£317.80). Cigars were off the list, but Eric appears to have changed to cigarettes as in 1941 he bought himself a cigarette case for 9s 2d (£9.20).

1946 saw routine purchases including a Chilprufe cardigan 10s (£15.50) and a Chilprufe vest 9s 8d (£14), but no combs, and outfits for the daughters including a Grammar School blazer 19s 6d (£29.50). Eric treated himself to a golf jacket £3 16s (£110) and his wife to a dinner gown £10 7s (£320) and a grey costume £13 4s 3d (£409). And there was another Axminster carpet (12ft by 9ft) £14 17s 6d (£445). Total of all items for the year was £87 9s 3d (£2,711).

Then expenditure leapt to £238 4s 11d (£7,384) in **1947** and to £365 11s 1d (£10,600) in **1948**, largely due to two items – a dyed squirrel coat £71 2s (£2,204) in December 1947 and a three piece Airbourne suit £134 12s 3d (£3,903) in April 1948, and in October a silver fox cape £25 19s 3d (£752.50). There must have been some special occasion(s), and/or business was looking up after the war. The only out of the ordinary purchase in **1949** were a donkey coat £13 6d 7d (£386) and a donkey hat £4 2s 10d (£120), and new curtains for the bedroom and lounge £11 5s (£326).

Sources

Eve & Ranshaw Archives – Louth Museum

Censuses 1841 - 1901

Lincolnshire Directories 1792 - 1937

Lincoln, Rutland & Stamford Mercury

Louth & North Lincolnshire Advertiser

The Date Book for Lincoln and Neighbourhood, 1866

A Valuation of the Messuages, Tenements, Lands and Properties situated in the Parish of Louth 1823, 1838 and 1853

An account of the Origins, Proceedings and Intentions of the Society for the Promotion of Industry in the Southern Districts of the Parts of Lindsey in the County of Lincoln 1789

Aspin C: *The Woollen Industry,* Princes Risborough, 2006

Bartlett J N: *Carpeting the Millions: The Growth of Britain's Carpet Industry,* Edinburgh, 1977

Bennett I (ed): *Rugs and Carpets of the World,* London, 1977

Benson A & Warburton N: *Looms and Weaving,* Princes Risborough, 2002

Burnley J: *The History of Wool and Woolcombing,* London, 1880

Coggins D (ed): *People and Patterns: the carpet weaving industry in 19th century Barnard Castle,* Bowes Museum, 1996

Crake E E: *The Parish Registers of S.Giles, Scarthoe,* Lincoln, 1926

Franklin P: *The L'Oste Family of Lincolnshire,* Birmingham, 1994

Goulding R W: *Louth Old Corporation Records,* Louth, 1891

Goulding R W: *Louth Grammar School Old Boys 16th century – 1850,* Louth, 1925 - 1934

Green J: *Vicissitudes of a Soldier's Life 1800-1815,* Louth, 1827

Gurnham *R: A History of Louth,* Chichester, 2007

Hill Sir F: *Georgian Lincoln,* Cambridge, 1966

Perkins J A: *Sheep Farming in 18th and 19th century Lincolnshire,* Sleaford, 1977

Plummer A: *The Witney Blanket Industry,* London, 1934

Porter H: Lincoln Stuff Ball, *The Local Historian No 32 October 1941, pp1-7*

Robinson A W: What was it worth? *Lincolnshire Family History Society 1997, Vol 8, No 2, p.69*

Robinson D N: *The Book of Louth,* Buckingham, 1979

Robinson D N: *Eve & Ranshaw Ltd: The House of Fashion & Fabrics: Double Century 1781-1981,* Louth, 1981

Robinson D N: Louth Ingrain Flat Weave Carpets (Textile Society Museum Award 2006), *Text for the Study of Textile Art, Design and History,* Vol 34, 2006-07, pp72-73

Spring A: *Settlement to Suburb: A Landscape Survey of Scartho,* University of Nottingham, 2003

Steele M: *Lincolnshire Land Longwools & Legends,* Lingfield, 1996

Thompson M: *Woven in Kidderminster,* Kidderminster, 2000

Williams P: *Lincolnshire Stuff 1771-1810,* Louth, 1997

Young A: *General View of the Agriculture of Lincolnshire,* London, 1799

Zaczek I: *William Morris,* Bath 2001

Index

Illustrations in **bold** figures

The EVE Tree